Praise for *The Preventive State*

No one but Alan Dershowitz would seek to bring a common mode of thought to issues as diverse as bail, climate change, and terrorism. Agree or disagree, this book will broaden and sharpen the reader's thinking about the challenges facing our country and our world.

—Lawrence Summers,
Charles W. Eliot University Professor
and President Emeritus, Harvard University

Professor Alan Dershowitz has written an urgently important book about how to balance the desire to have governments prevent crises with the need to safeguard fundamental civil liberties. Dershowitz brilliantly describes how grave threats of many types have greatly increased, but so have preventative measures that are highly intrusive. Most importantly, he offers a framework for dealing with this vital issue in the years ahead.

—Erwin Chemerinsky,
Dean and Jesse H. Choper Distinguished Professor of Law,
University of California–Berkeley School of Law

In addition to his fame as a defense attorney and public explainer of the law, Alan Dershowitz is an erudite and analytic legal scholar who, during his distinguished career, has advanced our understanding of many foundational issues in jurisprudence. Here he elucidates the intricate issue of preventive law, while updating it to the unforeseen challenges of the twenty-first century.

—Steven Pinker, Johnstone Professor of Psychology,
Harvard University

The Preventive State is a masterful analysis of the conundrum of the government's growing (but still imperfect) ability to predict and prevent increasingly potent threats (such as serious crimes, dangerous speech, terrorism, AI, climate catastrophe, and the like). Both under-reaction and overreaction by the government can be deadly. Building on more than six decades of work and reflection, Dershowitz provides a brilliant roadmap for addressing the conundrum that maximizes both safety and liberty while recognizing that tradeoffs are inevitable.

—Jack L. Goldsmith, Learned Hand Professor of Law,
Harvard University

The concept of "ordered liberty" recognizes that security is an essential prerequisite for meaningful liberty; our freedom is undermined by government measures that inadequately protect our safety, as well as unduly intrusive measures. Therefore, even—indeed, especially—the most ardent civil libertarian has a stake in ensuring that public policy appropriately protects both liberty and security, including through preventive measures. This book serves as a compelling capstone to Alan Dershowitz's unparalleled analysis and experience, throughout his distinguished career as a professor and litigator. Building upon his unique record in confronting countless tragic choices between the inevitable false positives and false negatives resulting from inherently imperfect predictions, he constructs an essential framework for rationally resolving our increasingly urgent future challenges, which is sensibly tailored to a range of legal and factual situations. For example, he makes a powerful case that the First Amendment presumptively permits potentially dangerous speech rather than potentially dangerous censorship.

—Nadine Strossen, John Marshall Harlan II
Professor of Law Emerita, New York Law School

In *The Preventive State* Alan Dershowitz takes on perhaps the most vexing problem facing society and civil libertarians: When may fundamental liberties be lawfully overridden in the name of security? His analyses and suggested resolutions are nuanced, sensible, and, perhaps most importantly, constitutional. This book is a fitting capstone to a more than half-century career of litigating and writing about some of the most vexing cases in modern constitutional history, many of which were litigated by Dershowitz.

—Harvey A. Silverglate, coauthor of *The Shadow University: The Betrayal of
Liberty on America's Campuses*,
cofounder of The Foundation for Individual Rights
and Expression (FIRE)

Alan Dershowitz is a brilliant lawyer. You know that. What you don't know—but I have known since I was his student—is that he is a profound, mind-opening thinker about the law. Once you have read *The Preventive State*, a grand exploration of preventive capacities through an array of the law's facets that reconceives law itself, you will know it too.

—Richard D. Parker,
Paul Williams Professor of Criminal Justice, Harvard University

With clarity, wisdom, wit, and breadth of understanding, Alan Dershowitz argues that the legal system should be revamped to prevent—not just punish—wrongdoing. As humanity faces greater and greater risks—including from nuclear and biological terrorism—the need for a jurisprudence of prevention has never been more compelling. This book will serve as an indispensable guide to liberal democracies seeking to mitigate these risks.

—Jesse Fried,
William Nelson Cromwell Professor of Law, Harvard University

THE
PREVENTIVE
STATE

The Challenge of Preventing Serious Harms
while Preserving Essential Liberties

ALAN DERSHOWITZ

New York • London

Also by Alan Dershowitz

The Ten Big Anti-Israel Lies: And How to Refute Them with Truth

War Against the Jews: How to End Hamas Barbarism

Get Trump

War on Woke

Dershowitz on Killing

The Price of Principle

The Case for Vaccine Mandates

The Case for Color-Blind Equality in an Age of Identity Politics

*The Case Against the New Censorship: Protecting Free Speech from Big Tech,
    Progressives, and Universities*

Cancel Culture: The Latest Attack on Free Speech and Due Process

*The Case for Liberalism in an Age of Extremism: Or, Why I Left the Left But Can't
    Join the Right*

*Confirming Justice—or Injustice?: A Guide to Judging RBG's Successor Defending
the Constitution*

Guilty by Accusation: The Challenge of Proving Innocence in the Age of #MeToo

Defending Israel: The Story of My Relationship with My Most Challenging Client

The Case Against Impeaching Trump

*The Case Against BDS: Why Singling Out Israel for Boycott Is Anti-Semitic and
    Anti-Peace*

Trumped Up: How Criminalization of Political Differences Endangers Democracy

Electile Dysfunction: A Guide for Unaroused Voters

The Case Against the Iran Deal

Terror Tunnels: The Case for Israel's Just War Against Hamas

Abraham: The World's First (But Certainly Not Last) Jewish Lawyer

Taking the Stand: My Life in Law

The Trials of Zion

The Case for Moral Clarity: Israel, Hamas and Gaza

*The Case Against Israel's Enemies: Exposing Jimmy Carter and Others Who Stand
    in the Way of Peace*

*Is There a Right to Remain Silent? Coercive Interrogation and the Fifth
    Amendment After 9/11*

*Finding Jefferson: A Lost Letter, a Remarkable Discovery, and the First
    Amendment in the Age of Terrorism*

Blasphemy: How the Religious Right is Hijacking our Declaration of Independence

Pre-Emption: A Knife That Cuts Both Ways

Rights from Wrongs: A Secular Theory of the Origins of Rights

America on Trial: Inside the Legal Battles That Transformed our Nation

The Case for Peace: How the Arab-Israeli Conflict Can Be Resolved

The Case for Israel

America Declares Independence

Why Terrorism Works: Understanding the Threat, Responding to the Challenge

Shouting Fire: Civil Liberties in a Turbulent Age

Letters to a Young Lawyer

Supreme Injustice: How the High Court Hijacked Election 2000

Genesis of Justice: Ten Stories of Biblical Injustice that Led to the Ten Commandments and Modern Law

Just Revenge

Sexual McCarthyism: Clinton, Starr, and the Emerging Constitutional Crisis

The Vanishing American Jew: In Search of Jewish Identity for the Next Century

Reasonable Doubts: The Criminal Justice System and the O. J. Simpson Case

The Abuse Excuse: And Other Cop-Outs, Sob Stories, and Evasions of Responsibility

The Advocate's Devil

Contrary to Popular Opinion

Chutzpah

Taking Liberties: A Decade of Hard Cases, Bad Laws, and Bum Raps

Reversal of Fortune: Inside the Von Bülow Case

The Best Defense

Fair and Certain Punishment: Report of the Twentieth Century Fund Task Force on Criminal Sentencing

Courts of Terror: Soviet Criminal Justice and Jewish Emigration (coauthored with Telford Taylor)

Criminal Law: Theory and Process (with Joseph Goldstein and Richard Schwartz)

Psychoanalysis, Psychiatry, and Law (with Joseph Goldstein and Jay Katz)

© 2025 by Alan Dershowitz
Introduction © 2025 by Stephen Breyer

First American edition published in 2025 by Encounter Books,
an activity of Encounter for Culture and Education, Inc.,
a nonprofit, tax-exempt corporation.
Encounter Books website address: www.encounterbooks.com

Manufactured in the United States and printed on
acid-free paper. The paper used in this publication meets
the minimum requirements of ANSI/NISO Z39.48-1992
(R 1997) (*Permanence of Paper*).

FIRST AMERICAN EDITION

LIBRARY OF CONGRESS CATALOGING-IN-PUBLICATION DATA IS AVAILABLE

Library of Congress CIP data is available online under the following
ISBN 978-1-64177-440-6 and LCCN 2025932088.

This book is lovingly dedicated to my early mentors Chief Judge David Bazelon and Justice Arthur Goldberg, who taught me how to strike appropriate balances between liberty and security, precedent and pragmatism, theory and practice—as well as between the professional and the personal, work and family. They started me on my long path to this book.

CONTENTS

Foreword by Stephen Breyer   XI

_____

PART I

The Issue Defined and Placed in Its Historical Background

INTRODUCTION   Preventing Cataclysmic Threats   3

CHAPTER 1   A Brief History of Prediction and Prevention: 25
            From Reactive to Proactive

_____

PART II

The Preventive State in Action

CHAPTER 2   Preventing Presidential Assassinations: 41
            From Richard Lawrence's Attempt to Kill
            President Andrew Jackson to Recent Attempts
            to Kill Presidential Candidate Donald Trump

CHAPTER 3   Preventing Crime: Bail, Sentencing, and   57
            Preventive Detention

CHAPTER 4   Preventive Police Interventions: From   75
            Searches and "Stop and Frisks" to Shooting or
            Choking Suspects

CHAPTER 5   The Preventive State and Military Action   81

CHAPTER 6   Preventing Terrorism: Military Actions, Detention, 91
            Waterboarding, and Other Extreme Tactics

CHAPTER 7   Preventive Medical Intrusion   99

CHAPTER 8   Preventing a Global Environmental Catastrophe   109

CHAPTER 9   Preventing Dangerous and/or Offensive Speech   115

CHAPTER 10   Red Flag Laws and Gun Violence   129

CHAPTER 11   The Surveillance State   135

CHAPTER 12   The Private State   141

PART III

Constructing a Jurisprudential Framework

CHAPTER 13   The "Science" of Prediction   147

CHAPTER 14   The Need for a Jurisprudential Framework   157
             for the Preventive State

CHAPTER 15   The Procedural Component of a Jurisprudential   169
             Framework for the Preventive State

CHAPTER 16   A Suggested Jurisprudential Framework   175
             for Mistake Preferences: How Many False
             Positives for How Many False Negatives?

CONCLUSION   Predicting the Future of the Preventive State   185

Appendix: The Ancient Rabbinic Approach to Prevention   189

Acknowledgments   195

Notes   197

Index   215

FOREWORD

by Justice Stephen G. Breyer

Alan Dershowitz and I have been friends ever since we were both law clerks for Justice Arthur Goldberg, Alan a year before me. Alan has since become an eminent law professor, an experienced trial lawyer, and a much-admired author. Arthur Goldberg taught us in part the value of noticing new ways of looking at old problems and doing our best to use those new ways to devise practical methods that will help ameliorate those problems. That is what Alan Dershowitz has done in this book. And he has done it well.

The old problem is that facing any democratic society: How, without sacrificing too much or too many of the values that society seeks to protect (e.g., individual liberty) can society prevent the occurrence of events, behaviors, activities, that will harm components, say members of, the society?

Criminal law is an example. Oliver Wendell Holmes Jr. argued in his book *The Common Law* that "prevention" is the "Chief and only universal purpose of punishment." There can be no criminal case, he added, "in which the lawmaker makes certain conduct criminal without thereby showing a wish and purpose to prevent that conduct." Here Holmes was drawing on the words of the eighteenth-century English jurist William Blackstone, who said that "if we consider all human punishments in a large and extended view, we shall find them all rather calculated to prevent future crimes than to expiate the past."

For the most part, of course, criminal law punishes persons who have already committed crimes. The harm has not been prevented; it has already taken place. But when we consider the reasons for punishing the person for committing that harm, they seem aimed at preventing harms in the future. For example, the American Law Institute's Model Penal Code for sentencing lists general deterrence as a core purpose of punishment. General deterrence, of course, discourages others from acting as the punished person did. Specific deterrence incapacitates the punished person, thereby preventing him from committing a further crime, say, while he is imprisoned. And rehabilitation changes the imprisoned person's character so that he will not want to commit crimes in the future.

Although the reasons for an action coming within the scope of the criminal law may in part reflect efforts to prevent future harms, the law itself focuses primarily upon the past: What did the defendant do? And the law is filled with requirements (defense lawyers, trials, juries) that help to guarantee basic rights and that seek to prevent an innocent person from being punished.

But what about actions that the state (or sometimes private persons) take to prevent future harm by imposing requirements or unwanted conditions on persons who as yet have done nothing wrong? The activity to be prevented has not yet taken place and is usually not accompanied by legally forbidden activity that did take place. And crucially, unlike ordinary criminal punishments, these preventive punishments are often not accompanied by legal safeguards or basic constitutional protections.

That is the kind of state activity that Alan Dershowitz writes about. He argues that we can and should often see preventive measures as part of a larger whole; that we should study them; that we should look at coherent ways to achieve our preventive goals; and that we should consider the inclusion of proper safeguards related to human rights and to the Constitution.

I.

Citing examples ranging from speech regulation to preemptive warfare, Dershowitz argues that many of our efforts to prevent harms that have not yet occurred share three important features:

First, we require that those persons who may help to bring about harm suffer confinement or undertake activities that they do not wish to perform, or refrain from activities they wish to undertake. Indeed, these preventive measures will often deprive an individual of basic, sometimes protected, human rights. And they will do so before that individual has actually run away or committed another crime—the future activities that bail laws are designed to prevent.

Second, to decide to whom these undesired requirements will apply, we must make predictions. We wish to apply them to those who are likely to bring about the ends we wish to prevent but not to those who (if free from the requirements) would likely not bring about the ends we wish to prevent.

Third, in separating goats from sheep, we will inevitably make mistakes. Consider, for example, a person arrested for having committed a crime. Long before trial, a judge or magistrate will likely have to make a bail decision. That decision reflects an effort to prevent a harm that has not yet occurred: his running away or his committing another crime before trial. If the judge decides to order pretrial confinement, the accused person will not run away (too difficult), but he might not have run away anyway—even if he had been released. If that is true, the result is what Dershowitz calls a "false positive"; the event we are trying to prevent—running away—would never have occurred. But the price of our doing so is that we have confined a person unnecessarily. If we had perfect knowledge (which we do not have), we would have known there was no need to do so.

On the other hand, suppose the bail judge does not confine that person before trial. If the person does not flee, no harm is done. But if he does flee, the judge has brought about the very harm the bail law has sought to prevent. Moreover, the judge will likely know that that has happened, and he may be criticized publicly for having failed to confine the person. Dershowitz calls this kind of mistake—not imposing the kind of restraint designed to prevent the future harm, which then occurs—a "false negative." Whenever we decide to impose (or not to impose) a restraint in order to prevent a future harm, we almost always suffer from imperfect knowledge; and we will therefore make a certain number of "positive" and a certain number of "negative" errors.

Dershowitz then argues that many different otherwise unrelated situations share these characteristics. Because these types of preventive activity share so much, Dershowitz believes that we should study them as a single genus of cases. He argues for a jurisprudence that will allow us to systematically prevent harms while minimizing prevention-related deprivations upon individuals. And he provides tentative examples.

II.

Several areas of preventive action involve criminal law. As I discussed above, the criminal law's robust protections of the individual disappear as soon as we approach the law's need to prevent evils that that have not yet occurred.

Consider bail or confinement prior to trial. The system aims to prevent the accused from committing a crime while out on bail or from running away.

But how well do protections work? As I discussed, the psychological pressure on the judge leans toward confinement. No one will know if the judge detains a defendant unnecessarily, but the entire community will know if he releases a defendant who goes on to harm innocent people. Why not, asks Dershowitz, require the government to pay for electronic monitoring—a system that may not be too expensive, that will allow the accused to spend time preparing for trial while he is outside of confinement, and which might at least be used in less serious cases.

Or, what about lengthy sentences, say, fifteen, twenty, or thirty years imprisonment? These are often imposed by state judges with the expectation that the prisoner will be released on parole after a few years; and parole will depend upon whether a board believes the prisoner will commit new crimes. The system in part is designed to prevent future crimes; not simply to punish for past ones. But the parole board is subject to the same psychological pressure as the bail judge. And the procedural protections for the inmate before the parole board pale in comparison to those available to a defendant at trial. Should the inmate receive additional protections—particularly insofar as the purpose of continued detention is the prevention of future criminal behavior rather than further punishment for past bad acts?

Further, to what extent should we criminalize behavior, that, while not itself directly harmful, often leads to harm. When should we create an inchoate crime, such as an attempt, a conspiracy, or reckless endangerment?

III.

Dershowitz's analysis of the preventive state extends well beyond his initial focus on criminal law. He considers when a nation, believing an enemy is about to launch a terrible war, should unleash a preventive war to stop it. Here a false positive creates an unnecessary military conflict. Yet, as Dershowitz observes, a false negative could have existential consequences. What about assassinations? Are there (or should there be) legal limits on spying? What about terrorism? Is waterboarding ever justified?

Moving to a field truly remote from the criminal law: Consider required vaccinations designed to reduce the spread of disease, say COVID. How should courts respond to those who believe those vaccinations are less than fully effective and that the requirement violates their religious beliefs?

Another field, speech: What limits does the First Amendment impose upon government seeking to limit, say false speech and information (potentially causing hatred or other harms) disseminated via the Internet?

Environmental laws also resemble those in this category insofar as they impose taxes or forbid the use of certain products in order to prevent future disasters.

To return to crime: What about guns? After all, only a few persons who wish to possess guns will use them to engage in criminal activity. But that activity can cause the most serious harm.

The list could go on.

At the same time, satisfactory answers to questions that arise in these areas require information. In a forthcoming paper, Professor Crystal Yang and coauthors study judges making bail decisions with access to computer algorithms. Only 10 percent of judges managed to override the algorithm at the right times, reducing false positives and negatives. The paper concludes that outcomes are "most likely driven by how the judges use the private information that is unavailable to the algorithm." Some judges put information to good use; others added only "inconsistency and noise." A separate paper (also by Professor Yang and coauthors) finds that inexperienced bail judges rely heavily on racial stereotyping and make more errors as a result. As Dershowitz observes, making the right preventive decisions requires gathering information and using it the right way, all without violating the public's interest in privacy.

Dershowitz writes enough about the problems in these fields for us to see a relationship: We seek to prevent future harms. Imposing unwanted restrictions on some persons can help to do so. Efforts to impose restrictions will lead to both positive and negative errors. What restrictions should the law allow and under what circumstances?

IV.

Dershowitz now turns to the main argument of his book: We should develop a jurisprudence, studying what would amount to proper legal controls in these areas. And, to show that doing so would be helpful, he provides several first-draft answers.

A future jurisprudence may focus upon areas where common protective procedural requirements would help. Consider detention, for example. Should there not be common burden-of-proof requirements irrespective of the nature of the future harm that present confinement is intended to prevent? Compelled confinement, he points out, is a "serious intrusion on liberty" irrespective of the government's intent in imposing it. Thus its imposition should involve "a significant degree of procedural protection," involving a "high standard of proof, right to counsel, right to confront witnesses," and others. The longer the confinement at issue, the higher the burden of proof, ranging from "more probable than not," as in a civil case, to "beyond a reasonable doubt" as in a criminal case. Other procedural protections might also vary, depending upon the length of the confinement and the likelihood of mistakes being made.

Similarly, we might often insist upon an explicit effort to determine the likelihood of positive and negative errors before imposing a serious restriction. And, depending upon the nature of the restriction and the harm it seeks to prevent, we could insist upon a certain minimum ratio between them. In a criminal case, for example, we sometimes say we should prefer that ten guilty persons go free to the conviction of one innocent person. So we could insist, for example, that, where confinement is at issue, our process ensures that it is ten times more likely that not restricting will lead to the harm than that restricting would have proved unnecessary. We could vary this "more-likely-than/less-likely-than" ratio depending upon the severity of the restriction and the nature of the harm it seeks to avoid. Thus, a year's confinement, a few days' confinement, and an unwanted vaccination could be treated differently. By researching the likelihood of false negatives and positives, we could impose preventive measures in a more accurate, honest, and rigorous way.

V.

Drawing on his practical knowledge as well as his scholarly research, Alan Dershowitz has provided us with an argument for further thought and practical legal results. We should see many different government impositions as similar in that they impose restrictions now to avoid greater harms later. He highlights the similarities. And, critically, he advocates the development of a jurisprudence based on these similarities. He believes that by thinking about the risk of mistakes, we can better protect basic civil liberties while better and more rationally protecting ourselves from future harms. He provides initial examples of how this might be done.

Dershowitz makes his case. Both scholars and practitioners of the law should read this book. It may open their eyes, as it opened mine, to important practical similarities among instances where the law restricts the freedom of individuals in important ways to avert future harms. To think about these instances together, to help develop a rational jurisprudence where they are at issue, is a worthwhile task. I believe it will prove to be a valuable one. We shall thank Alan Dershowitz for writing this book.

Cambridge, September 10, 2024

PART I

THE ISSUE DEFINED AND PLACED IN ITS HISTORICAL BACKGROUND

INTRODUCTION

PREVENTING CATACLYSMIC THREATS

Rarely in the long history of our planet have we faced such dire threats to our survival: nuclear annihilation, out-of-control pandemics, international terrorism, famine, environmental disasters, abuses of artificial intelligence, racial and ethnic divisions, dangerous hate speech, challenges to the rule of law, attacks on basic liberties including speech and due process, health care policies (or lack thereof) that create disparate life expectancies based on race and nationality, rampant crime, police misconduct, mass shootings, and additional dangers, some known, others not yet cognizable.

The combination of these individual dangers—for example, terrorism, nuclear weaponization, and artificial intelligence—has increased the threats exponentially.

But never before in our history have we developed tools, individually and in combination, so capable of predicting and preventing many of these potential disasters. This capability is also growing exponentially with the increasing power of new technologies, including artificial intelligence and genetic engineering—which carry their own additional benefits and dangers.

It is the juxtaposition of these two phenomena—increasing dangers coupled with increasing capabilities by governments (often aided by private technology) to *prevent* them—that has given rise to the preventive state, and has created the impetus for this book.

The world has always faced the dangers of war, famine, disease, violence, racism, sexism, crime, and other evils. Indeed, as my colleague Steven Pinker has demonstrated in his brilliant book *The Better Angels of Our Nature*,[1] many of these scourges have diminished in frequency and intensity over the centuries. But today's threats tend to be more global, especially the nuclear (because of proliferation), terrorism (because of its internationalization, especially by Iran), pandemics (because of more widespread and quicker travel), environmental (because of the global spread of industrialization), and technological (because of the pervasiveness of the Internet and AI). Also, the preventive measures available to the state have dramatically improved, and continue to improve, though they are far from perfect, thus raising the likelihood of increasing governmental powers, intrusions on the liberties of its citizens, abusive misuses of these preventive measures, and inevitable false positives. Indeed, governments—both democratic and tyrannical—often use the legitimate need to prevent real dangers as a justification or excuse for repressive measures. (Recall the detention of Japanese Americans following Pearl Harbor, and the extralegal abuses following the 9/11 attacks.) To paraphrase Charles Dickens:[2] we surely live in the best of times and in the most dangerous of times.

This conundrum and the challenges it entails are the subjects of the present book. Whenever the state is empowered to take preventive steps based on predictions of harm, there are—at least conceptually—four possible outcomes:

1. The government can accurately predict a harm and act to prevent it; that counts as a *true positive*.
2. It can accurately predict that a harm will not occur and take no preventive action; that is a *true negative*.

If those were the only outcomes—if the state's ability to predict and prevent harms were perfect—there would be little reasonable basis for concern. Both of these outcomes would benefit society.

But the next two outcomes show why increasing the power of the state to take preventive actions based on imperfect predictions is a knife that cuts both ways. So here are the other two possible outcomes:

3. The state can predict that a harm will occur and take steps to prevent it, but no such harm would have occurred if nothing had been done; that is a *false positive*.
4. The state can predict that no harm will occur and take no action, but the preventable harm occurs; that is a *false negative*.

Both of these outcomes hurt society.

An early variation on these different predictions and outcomes was put forward by the seventeenth-century mathematician Blaise Pascal in his famous wager about believing in God: A true positive—believing in God and he exists—produces heaven. A false negative—disbelieving in God and he exists—produces hell. A false positive—believing in God and he doesn't exist—produces only wasted prayer. And a true negative—disbelieving in God and he doesn't exist—produces no harm. So a rational person should bet he exists.[3]

A contemporary everyday application of this decision process can be illustrated by the issue of predicting the weather: Will it rain or not? Here too there are four possible outcomes—assuming that the rain–no rain outcome is absolute. If the local weatherman predicts rain and it rains, this is a true positive. If he predicts no rain and it doesn't rain, that is a true negative. A weatherman whose predictions come true is someone you can count on in deciding whether to carry an umbrella. But if he predicts rain and there is no rain—false positive—then you will needlessly carry your umbrella. If he predicts no rain and it rains, you will needlessly get wet. No big deal in the context of rain–no rain, but a very big deal in other contexts.

The outcomes from this simple prediction can be diagrammed by the following four boxes:

PREDICTIONS	OUTCOME	
	Did rain	Did not rain
Will rain	**TP: True Positive**	**FP: False Positive**
Will not rain	**FN: False Negative**	**TN: True Negative**

The far more complex and weighty issue of efforts to prevent a feared act of mass terrorism, can also be conceptualized by the four boxes:

PREDICTIONS	OUTCOME	
	They bombed it	They didn't bomb it
A specific group will bomb a building in NY	**TP: True Positive**	**FP: False Positive**
They will not bomb the building	**FN: False Negative**	**TN: True Negative**

A false negative in this context is a really big deal. A false positive may also be a big deal depending on the actions taken to prevent the predicted outcome that did not occur.

This four-part breakdown obviously oversimplifies extraordinarily complex and multifaceted problems. Even the simple prediction by a weather forecaster will have calibrated outcomes: downpours, drizzle, sun-shower, and so on. But simplifications can often serve as a heuristic aid identifying the core policy choices.

The policy question will always come down to this: "How many false positives are we prepared to accept in order to avoid how many false negatives?" I have been asking that question, and others based on it, since I started thinking, writing, teaching, and litigating about the issue of prevention in the early 1960s.[4] I have tried to apply that conceptual approach to real-world decisions in a number of contexts: How many non-terrorists are we prepared to kill or detain (and for how long) in order to prevent how many serious terrorist attacks? This complex and serious cost-benefit issue must be addressed in the larger context of wars against terrorism, such as those waged by Israel against Hamas, and by the United States against ISIS, the Houthis, and other terrorist groups. These wars also illustrate the complex relationship among the goals of prevention, preemption, deterrence, retaliation, and other factors that enter into decisions to attack an enemy.[5]

Or to reverse the above policy question: How many false negatives (mass-casualty terrorist attacks) are we prepared to accept to avoid how many false positives, namely, over-detaining mistakenly suspected potential terrorists, or killing too many innocent civilians in a legitimate effort to neutralize terrorists? How many terrorist attacks are we prepared to accept in order to prevent the detention or killing of how many non-terrorists?[6] In a different, but related context: How many defendants who would not flee or commit crimes are we prepared to confine before trial (deny bail) in order to prevent how many flights or crimes (and of what type)? How many vaccine deaths are we prepared to accept in order to prevent how many COVID deaths? How many hate speeches are we prepared to censor in order to prevent how many hateful acts are incited by such speeches?

These questions can be asked in the more current and complex context of the two attempts to assassinate Donald Trump while he was running for president. As will be elaborated in chapter 2, the failure of the Secret Service to secure the building from which the shots were fired, or to delay Trump's appearance until all suspicious persons were questioned and/or removed, produced a near-fatal false negative with regard to the first attempt. There were similar failures with regard to the second attempt as well.

But if all buildings at all such events were cleared and secured and all suspicious persons questioned and removed, there would be many false positives, since actual assassination attempts are extremely rare and very few suspicious people in unsecured buildings become assassins. Because these types of false positives pale in comparison to even one false negative—a successful assassination—they should be routinely implemented, even if they result in inconvenience and delay.

If, on the other hand, the question is whether to shoot a suspected assassin before he could fire—as was reportedly possible in the first Trump situation—the cost of *both* a false positive (mistakenly killing an innocent kid who was merely climbing on a roof to get a better look at the speaker) and a false negative (mistakenly *not* shooting a guilty assassin before he could fire), would be extremely high. A shot was fired in the direction of the second attempter, and he fled.

A policy decision would have to be made as to the level of certainty required for such a preventive shooting. The level of certainty would determine the ratio of false positives to false negatives.

It is rare, but not unprecedented, to put choices of this kind in so quantitative a format.[7] One early precedent goes back to the book of Genesis, where Abraham bargained with God about the number of innocent residents of Sodom God should be willing to kill in order to punish the guilty and prevent their recidivism. After back-and-forth negotiations about numbers (fifty, forty, etc.) God agrees on less than ten, thus giving rise to the current quantification of the appropriate ratio of false positives to negatives in the context of convicting defendants of crimes: we have generally agreed on the somewhat arbitrary formula under which it is better for ten guilty defendants (including terrorists) to go free (to be false negatives) than for even one innocent defendant to be wrongfully convicted (to be a false positive). We accept that skewed ratio (at least in theory) because the consequences of a false conviction are so severe— executing or imprisoning an innocent person. But so are the consequences of ten false acquittals: the falsely acquitted can recidivate and commit numerous horrible new crimes. That is probably why many jurors, judges, and prosecutors pay only lip service to the theoretical ratio.[8]

A related example was Israel's decision in 2011, to release 1,027 prisoners in exchange for one kidnapped soldier.[9] One of the released prisoners, Yahya Sinwar, became the military leader of Hamas responsible for planning the massacres and kidnappings of October 7, 2023. Others of the released prisoners reportedly participated in the subsequent murders, rapes, and kidnappings of nearly 1,500 Israelis.[10]

Moreover, the explicit quantification of outcomes—measuring the benefits of the positives and negatives against the costs of false positives and false negatives—risks the loss of nuance. Outcomes are often matters of degree that are difficult to quantify with precision. It also risks discounting values that are by their nature unquantifiable, such as fear, trust, honesty, and principle.[11]

The types of harms that a government may seek to prevent vary considerably, from the macro to the micro, from global to individual, from remediable to irremediable, from those caused by humans to those caused by nature. They include natural disasters such as floods, earthquakes, even asteroid strikes;[12] combined natural and human-caused disasters, such as pandemics, famine, and environmental pollution; large-scale harms caused by humans such as wars, terrorism, biological attacks, and nuclear accidents; intermediate-scale human-caused harms, such as school shootings, terrorist attacks, building collapses; smaller-scale human-caused harms such as individual homicides, sexual assaults, and other crimes and torts.

There are some serious harms that endanger everyone, such as full-scale nuclear war, and their seriousness should not be subject to rational debate. Many however, are hotly disputed, such as climate threats, nuclear weapons proliferation, pandemics, gun crimes, and censorship. In our age of deep divisions about so many issues, a consensus about which harms warrant what degree of intervention cannot be taken for granted. In a democracy, there must be processes and procedures for resolving such disputes.

When I started writing and teaching about these issues in the 1960s, I often had to employ examples from science fiction to illustrate the legal and moral questions that would be raised if we could predict natural and human harms with a high, but less than perfect, degree of accuracy—that is, with a relatively high percentage of true positives and a relatively low percentage of false positives.

Here is how I began an article in 1973:

> A science fiction writer once created a machine called a sanity meter that automatically gauged a person's potential for dangerous conduct. The meter, installed in all public places, registered from zero to ten. A person scoring up to three was considered normal; one scoring between four and seven, while within the tolerance limit, was advised to undergo therapy; one scoring between eight and ten was required to register with the authorities as highly dangerous and to bring his rating below seven within a specific probation period; anyone failing this probationary requirement, or anyone passing the red line above ten, was required either to undergo immediate surgical alteration or to submit himself to "the academy"—a mysterious institution from which no one returned. The meter was not a diagnostic machine: it measured solely the intensity of an individual's potential for harm, not its underlying cause or amenability to treatment. Since the machine never erred, everyone in the society knew everyone else's danger rating and acted accordingly. Its widespread use finally succeeded in eliminating crime and other social evils.[13]

Today science fiction is quickly being replaced with science fact, as technology—including AI, PET scans, and genetic testing—is coming close to being able to discern some of the content of thought patterns in the brain and predispositions toward negative outcomes. We are not there yet, but it is not too soon to begin exploring the ramifications of such breakthroughs, were they to become reality. Breakthroughs in other areas should be anticipated as well.[14]

In this book, I will review the mixed history of efforts to prevent perceived harms and then discuss the most serious current harms and the efforts being made to prevent them. I will assess the benefits, both achieved and anticipated, from these efforts, as well as their costs, both incurred and likely. Finally, I will undertake the daunting task of trying to construct a jurisprudential framework or model whose ambitious goal is to maximize the positives of these developments while minimalizing their negatives. Because prediction will never be perfect—there will always be false positives and negatives—it is also necessary to devise processes and procedures for deciding the acceptable ratio of costs and benefits of each kind of inevitable error.

This book will necessarily be a work in progress, since both the anticipated harms to be prevented and the measures being devised to prevent them are quickly changing—but the broad outlines of the cost-benefit ratios should be based on enduring values and principles over time.

When it comes to prevention, there are few free lunches. Intrusions on liberty are generally required for effective prevention. Rarely can we emulate the folk wisdom that "a stitch in time saves nine." When we can, we should. Benjamin Franklin wisely cautioned that "Those who would give up essential Liberty, to purchase a little temporary Safety, deserve neither Liberty nor Safety."[15] But it may be reasonable to make temporary sacrifices of some nonessential liberties to achieve large benefits in preventing short- or long-term serious harms. It is always a matter of degree. And that is what democracy, the Constitution, and the rule of law are all about: providing procedures for deciding often controversial matters of degree and safeguarding against abuses of these procedures. Mathematics, science, and other empirical disciplines can provide essential information, but in a democracy the ultimate policy choices—often tragic choices among evils—must be made by its citizens.

As I will show, preventive measures have been part of governance since the beginnings of recorded history. The Bible prescribes harsh measures for dealing with recalcitrant children who are deemed likely to become difficult adults,[16] as well as more benign measures to prevent the spread of contagious diseases.[17] Early law sought to prevent harm to kings by disabling those who even "compass"—that is, imagine—the king's death. Exile was a preventive measure, as were surety bonds. History even provides examples of preventive murders of innocent children who, it was feared, would seek revenge on those who killed their parents—or as in the case of the execution of the entire Romanov family by Bolsheviks, to prevent the reestablishment of czarist rule. The list is long, ranging from the most brutal to the relatively benign.

History also provides examples of failures to act, when action might well have prevented catastrophic harms. Perhaps the most telling example is the failure of Great Britain and France to enforce the Versailles Treaty by preventing—through military action—the military buildup of Germany following the First World War. A military attack on Germany, when its war machine was still weak, might have prevented the Second World War, with its tens of millions of deaths. As I will show in chapter 5, Joseph Goebbels anticipated that such preventative intervention might occur and was surprised it did not. Here is what he wrote in his memoir:

> In 1933 a French premier ought to have said (and if I had been the French premier, I would have said it): "The new Reich Chancellor is the man who wrote *Mein Kampf*, which says this and that. This man cannot be tolerated in our vicinity. Either he disappears or we march!" But they didn't do it. They left us alone and let us slip through the risky zone, and we were able to sail around all dangerous reefs. *And when we were done, and well armed, better than they, then they started the war!*[18]

The rest is tragic history. Germany built up its armed forces without countermeasures by its intended enemies, and conquered most of Western Europe, killing tens of millions of people. Most of those deaths could almost certainly have been avoided had Great Britain and France engaged in preventive military action before Germany became "well armed" and capable of inflicting so much damage on the world.

But at the moment in history when Great Britain and France could have prevented the horrendous harm done by Nazi Germany, there was no way of knowing in advance—predicting—the extent of what Hitler would do.

Yes, he wrote *Mein Kampf*, but many would-be conquerors do not follow through on their threats. (Recall Khrushchev's threat to "bury" the United States, yet he backed away from a nuclear confrontation over Cuba.) There was no way of predicting, with any degree of certainty that Hitler would personally turn his belligerent rhetoric into military invasions of Poland and then the Soviet Union. It was, as it always is, a question of cost-benefit probabilities. This was a classic case of a false negative: implicitly predicting that Hitler would *not do* what he in fact *did*, and failing to take action in an effort to prevent it. If France and Great Britain had accurately predicted his actual harm correctly, they would almost certainly have taken preventive military action, even if the cost were high—because it would never have been nearly as high as it turned out to be in the absence of such action.

But history is blind to the predictive future. Had Great Britain and France decided to take preventive military action in the mid-1930s, and done so successfully, no one would ever know *what* was prevented. If a leader, say Churchill, had correctly predicted that Hitler would kill tens of millions of people unless he was stopped at that time by preventive military action, the leader would have been disbelieved, even mocked (as Clement Atlee was for taking military action against Egypt in 1956 and George W. Bush was for taking military action against Iraq's suspected nuclear arsenal in 2003). Had Great Britain and France engaged in preventive military action in the 1930s that resulted in say, the deaths of 10,000 German and 5,000 British and French soldiers and civilians, the leaders who undertook such a military adventure would have been condemned as warmongers, because no one would ever know how many deaths they prevented by the sacrifice of those 15,000 lives. Ignorance of the hypothetical future is often the reason for failure to act in the present. Had Great Britain and France acted, everyone would know about the 15,000 deaths their action caused, while no one would know about the tens of millions of lives their actions saved.

We now know about the tens of millions of deaths these leaders indirectly caused—or at least made possible—by not taking preventive military action, but we don't accuse them of actually causing these deaths, because inaction that indirectly leads to death is not generally blamed as much as action that directly and visibly produces a body count. That is the dilemma of invisible false negatives in failing to take preventive military action.

A preventive attack would not have been cost free, and it was not undertaken, because the British and French did not accurately predict and assess the cost of not acting. The result was a catastrophic false negative.[19]

History also provides examples of false positives. The U.S. attack on Iraq in 2003 was in response to the prediction that absent an attack, Saddam Hussein might deploy weapons of mass destruction including nuclear and biological warfare. That prediction was almost certainly wrong and resulted in false positive actions with numerous casualties and the strengthening of the far more dangerous Iran.[20] So too the attack on Pearl Harbor by Japan may well have been based on a questionable prediction by Japan that the U.S. Navy would soon attack the Japanese military. History is filled with both types of mistakes based on costly false predictions, or on accurate predictions not acted on.[21] I will provide examples of such errors in the chapters to come.

THE ABSENCE OF A JURISPRUDENCE OF PREVENTION

It is remarkable that in light of the high stakes, no systematic jurisprudence has ever been constructed to govern and constrain preventive measures. There have been efforts over the millennia to quantify reactive measures. There is no preventive equivalent to the effort at quantifying the costs and benefits of punitive, as distinguished from preventive, measures: no articulated policy that it is better to have x number of false negatives than even one false positive. That would be a daunting task, since the types and degrees of preventive measures, and the harms they seek to prevent, are so variable, as compared to punishments for crimes.

I ended a previous book, with the following challenge:

> We need to develop a jurisprudence for the emerging preventive state. This jurisprudence should contain both substantive and procedural rules governing *all* actions—"acts of state" as well as "acts of law"—taken by government officials to prevent harmful conduct, such as terrorism. Black holes in the law are anathema to democracy, accountability, human rights, and the rule of law. I urge citizens, legislators, judges, and scholars to take up this important agenda.[22]

No one to date has done so. It falls to me therefore to take the next steps toward what will be a long-term effort, hopefully by many, to develop such a jurisprudence. I will attempt in this book to outline a roadmap to a comprehensive jurisprudence of preventive intervention. The process of constructing such a jurisprudence is an ongoing one, based in large part on changing experiences. As the legal philosopher and historian Roscoe Pound put it: "Law is experience developed by reason and applied continually to further experience."[23] And as retired justice Stephen Breyer put it more recently: "It is experience, not a treatise, that is more likely to help a judge determine whether a decision that resolves a dispute should be written in a broad or narrow way."[24] He cautioned that, "human life itself is far more capacious, filled with far more incidents, subject to more vicissitudes, unexpected and unforeseen events and consequences, than human beings writing a set of laws could possibly cover."[25] He understands how daunting a task it is, therefore "to capture the infinite varieties of human experience withing the confines of any single set of laws."[26]

A similar point can be made concerning jurisprudence, which is simply the philosophical structure of law. Pound astutely observed that "in Anglo-American, more than in other systems, juristic theories come *after* lawyer and judge have dealt with concrete cases and have in some measure learned how to dispose of them."[27]

The justice for whom both Breyer and I clerked back in the early 1960s—Arthur Goldberg—taught us to look at law as "a practical enterprise" that requires looking both to past cases and future consequences as guides to our own roles as scholars, government officials, advocates, and (in Breyer's case) judges. Any enduring jurisprudence must learn respectfully, if critically, from history, while focusing pragmatically on the future.

As I will show in part 3, we are still at the preliminary stage of this process: lawyers and judges have been disposing—largely on an ad hoc basis—of preventive cases thrust upon them by recurring emergencies. The time has now come for the next phase: to begin the construction and articulation of "juristic theories"—of a systematic jurisprudence of harm prevention. This book is an effort to jump-start—but certainly not to finalize—this undertaking.

I have been writing and teaching about "the preventive state" (a phrase I coined during my teaching in the 1960s) over my entire career. My earliest law review article—"Why Do Criminal Attempts Fail?" written in 1960—analyzed "inchoate" crimes that cause no current harm, but pose future dangers.[28] My two clerkships, with Chief Judge David Bazelon and Justice Arthur Goldberg, included cases involving predicted harms and efforts to prevent them. My earliest classes dealt with issues of prevention—from the law of attempted crimes, to commitment of the mentally ill, to pretrial detention of dangerous defendants, to efforts to anticipate and prevent terrorism, to preemptive warfare. For decades, I taught courses and seminars on "The Prediction and Prevention of Harmful Conduct" and related subjects. I believe I was the first contemporary academic to devote so much of my writing and teaching to this project.[29] My writing focused on the most serious and concerning threats of the day. Even before the 9/11 airplane attacks on the World Trade Center and Pentagon I posed to my students "tragic choice" hypotheticals, which were not very far from the realities that were in our future, including a hijacked airliner headed toward the Empire State Building that could be shot down while still over the ocean. Then following 9/11, I constructed the following hypothetical problem based on the actual situation then confronting us:

> If reliable intelligence determined that a large-scale terrorist attack in your city were highly likely during the next few weeks, and it also pointed to a particular suspect, would you support the preventive detention of that suspect for a period of time—say, a month—until it could be determined whether he or she was, in fact, planning the attack.
>
> What type and level of interrogation would you authorize to elicit the information necessary to prevent the attack?
>
> If arrest were not feasible because the suspected terrorist was hiding in an enemy country, would you support his targeted assassination if that were the only way to stop the attack?
>
> What if the attack could be prevented only by a military strike against a terrorist base in a foreign country?
>
> What if a full-scale invasion were required?
>
> If the feared attack involved a weaponized virus, such as smallpox, whose deadly impact would be substantially reduced by massive inoculation, which would, however, kill 150 to 200 of those inoculated, would you support compulsory inoculation? If an article demonstrating how to manufacture and weaponize smallpox were about to be published, would you support the preventive censorship of that article?[30]

These are the kinds of tragic choices that every democratic society is now—or soon will be—facing with regard to many issues beyond terrorism. Yet we have not even begun to develop an agreed-upon jurisprudence, morality or even strategy governing such drastic preventive and preemptive actions by our government. Instead, we are simply taking such actions on an ad hoc basis as we face the ongoing threats in real time.

The twenty-first century has brought us the most devastating terrorist attacks, dangerous pandemics, increasing environmental dangers, the development of remarkable artificial intelligence tools capable of both predicting and causing harms, the proliferation of nuclear weapons to rogue regimes, and the threat of all-out nuclear war in Ukraine, the Middle East, and other places. These and other threats have changed preventive intervention from an interesting academic subject into a current front-burner issue, but without sufficient attention by academics, policymakers, or the general public.

Consider the decision whether to seek to prevent Iran from constructing a deliverable nuclear arsenal. A false positive response—a military attack on Iran's nuclear facilities that would never have produced such an arsenal—might needlessly kill many innocent Iranians. But a false negative—failure to attack that resulted in the nuclear bombing of Tel Aviv—would cause many more deaths. Or consider the excruciating difficult tragic choice of whether to torture a captured terrorist who is withholding information needed to prevent a mass-casualty bombing. Most democratic countries have or will engage in some degree of physical or psychological pressure to elicit such life-saving real-time intelligence. The United States, Israel, and other nations have already done so. But none has constructed a jurisprudential framework for making these choices.[31] Indeed, arguments have been offered against even suggesting a jurisprudence cabining the use of torture, lest it legitimate that barbaric practice.[32] But the reality is that torturing captured terrorists to obtain real-time intelligence deemed essential to prevent mass-casualty attacks will continue, with or without a limiting jurisprudence.

Or consider the issue of censoring or limiting dangerous speech. Social media has made freedom of expression both more dangerous and more widely accessible. Online bullying, false "medical" information, incitement, racism, anti-Semitism, sexism, doxing, and other current uses and misuses of the Internet have caused considerable harm to their victims. But the Internet has also opened up the marketplace of ideas to many who had no previous access. Like most technologies it is a knife that cuts both ways.

THE 9/11 ATTACK ACCELERATES
THE NEED FOR PREVENTIVE ACTIONS

It was the terrorist attack against the United States on September 11, 2001, that expedited and, in the minds of many, legitimated the ongoing shift from after-the-fact punishment to anticipatory preventive measures. Following the attack, the then attorney general John Ashcroft described the "number one priority" of the Justice Department as "prevention."[33] The Justice Department announced that the prevention of future crimes, especially terrorism, is now regarded as even "more important than prosecution" for past crimes. In his confirmation hearings for attorney general, Alberto Gonzales reiterated that the administration's "top priority is to prevent terror attacks."[34] The tactics that have been employed as part of this preventive approach include more extensive profiling, preventive detention, gathering of preventive intelligence through rough interrogation, expansive surveillance, targeting of potential terrorists for assassination, preemptive attacks on terrorist bases, and full-scale preventive war. Border control and the political controversy surrounding it is also designed—at least in part—to prevent terrorism.

Israel has been dealing with this plethora of preventive issues since its establishment in 1948 and the terrorist attacks that have persisted. The issue of preventive military action came to the fore following the Hamas massacres of October 7, 2023, the promise of its leaders to repeat it, and Israel's military response.[35]

Despite the more extensive employment of preventive actions, there has been no comparable effort to construct a relevant jurisprudence. Most of today's preventive actions are being undertaken without a firm basis in law, jurisprudence, or morality, though there are historical precedents—many questionable—such as the detention of Japanese Americans following Pearl Harbor,[36] the mass sterilization of so-called "imbeciles" in the 1920s and 1930s to prevent crimes and social problems,[37] and the forced vaccination to prevent the spread of smallpox.[38]

In our age of partisan division about everything, it is not surprising that the proper role of government in preventing harms would also differ along political and ideological lines. But these lines sometimes seem inconsistent. For example, many on the right favor substantial intrusions on liberty to prevent terrorism, while opposing vaccine and mask mandates to prevent the spread of COVID. Many on the left take the opposite view: favoring intrusive measures to prevent COVID, but not terrorism. The difference may lie, at least in part, on *whose* liberty would be intruded upon: for terrorism prevention, it would likely be people of Muslim or Arab background. For COVID, it would more likely be people of Christian and/or conservative background. On the issue of identification documents, the left generally favors them for vaccines, while the right condemns them as repressive "passports" (Your papers, please!!). For voting, however, the right favors identification cards, while the left regards them as barriers to voting, especially among citizens of color. Identity politics trumps consistency in our current world of partisan division.

Another currently divisive issue is the deportation of illegal immigrants and the related call for increased border security. A major justification for proposed mass deportations and border closings is preventive: preventing violent crime attributed to illegal aliens; preventing the importation of dangerous drugs; and preventing the misallocation of resources to non-citizens. These remedies necessarily entail over-prediction of the feared harms. Thus, many on the left oppose them.

The important point for this book, however, is that prevention as a *general matter* should not divide along partisan lines. Everyone favors some intrusions to prevent some harms, and everyone opposes other intrusions to prevent other harms. It depends, as all seems to depend in our partisan world, on whose ox is being gored. "Liberty for me, but not for thee." "Not in my back yard." As I will argue in chapter 15, a jurisprudence of prevention should not be based on identity politics or partisan advantage. It must set out neutral criteria that can be applied fairly to all—a daunting task anytime, but especially at this time, when neutral principles are anathema to partisans on both sides, who want the rules that favor them and them alone.

Any credible jurisprudence must satisfy the "veil of ignorance" criteria articulated by the philosopher John Rawls:[39] It must be theoretically acceptable by and applicable to people in a "nether world" who have no idea whether they will be rich or poor, male or female, Black or white, Muslim or Jewish, terrorists or victims of terrorism, contagious or vulnerable to catching a contagious illness, criminal or falsely accused, and so on—if and when the rules are applied to them. In simpler terms, it must pass the "shoe on the other foot" test. (More on this in chapters 14 and 15.)

PREVENTIVE INTERVENTION IN MEDICINE

Though this book is largely about legal and political interventions, the preventive state is also having an impact on medicine and health, even beyond current debates over vaccine and other mandates. The role of prediction and prevention in medicine even for noncontagious diseases like cancer and coronary illness is raising important public policy issues that go beyond legal intrusions and compulsions.

In a brilliant article in the *Wall Street Journal*, Dr. Siddhartha Mukherjee cautions us about a medical phenomenon that is analogous, at least in some respects, to the preventive state.[40] He calls it "cancerland," and invokes a "strange new term, '*previvor*,'" to designate a person who has "not yet experienced an illness she is predisposed to have."[41] This new vocabulary reflects an emerging reality in which technology and medicine, including artificial intelligence and genetic engineering, can predict and often prevent the occurrence of cancer well before the first symptoms become discernible:

> The first [technology] involves genetic surveillance—the attempt to quantify an individual's inherited predisposition for cancer.

The second is physiological surveillance, which seeks to detect chemical markers of incipient cancers in blood.[42]

These and other technological miracles hold out the hope of "life-saving therapies to people who might not otherwise have known of their cancers until much later." That's the good news. But Dr. Mukherjee also cautions of the cost of such early predictive measures:

> By pulling increasing numbers of people into the domain of surveillance and screening, they encourage people without current cancer, but with the prospect of future cancer, to become citizens or permanent residents of cancerland.[43]

He warns that settling into this domain "can be life-distorting," because "the shadow of future illness dilates and magnifies, so too to the shadows of anxiety and dread."[44]

There are obviously many benefits associated with these and other predictive-preventive medical technologies, but there are also costs. The first, which Dr. Mukherjee focuses on, is to the individual patient whose life may be altered by the new knowledge of his or her vulnerability. The second is to society in general and to the treasury in particular. Predictive-preventive technologies and medical interventions are expensive. The costs also involve numerous false positives—that is, predictions of future cancer that would not materialize even if no preventive measures were undertaken. But the benefit is the avoidance of false negatives—that is, the failure to predict case of cancer that might have been prevented or cured by earlier intervention. As with all predictive endeavors, the costs of false positives must be balanced against the costs of a false negative (or the benefits of a true positive in early treatment).

The question in any democracy is who should be making these balancing decisions and with what processes? Who should decide whether an alleged threat or danger is real? Or if it's sufficiently serious to warrant what degree of intrusion? Who should judge whether the prediction is accurate or whether the preventive measures will be and have been successful?

As to Dr. Muhkerjee's first cost—a possible life of anxiety as the price for more information that may help prevent or cure cancer—it would seem clear that the decisions should be made by each individual competent adult. Every person has different risk tolerances and different attitudes toward knowing about risks. Some people take existing genetic tests measuring propensities toward Alzheimer's. Others "don't want to know." That is their option. So should early testing for predisposition to cancer or other noncontagious but life-threatening illnesses. As George Bernard Shaw quipped: "Do not do unto others as you expect they should do unto you—their tastes may be different." Or as an old limerick put the choice: "My doctor has made a prognosis, / that intercourse fosters thrombosis, / but I'd rather expire fulfilling desire / then abstain and develop neurosis." These are choices that in a democracy must be left to competent individuals and based on credible information, since the costs and benefits of an erroneous decision will be borne primarily by the individual who makes them.

The second cost of massive preventive testing is borne by society in general in the form of governmental expenditures, prioritization of resources, and other traditional democratic choices. Decisions about these costs must be made collectively, so long as individuals retain the option of using their own resources to obtain testing. This raises, of course, the general issue of the unfairness of medical benefits—even those with mixed benefits and costs—being more easily obtainable by those who can afford them. This kind of disparity exists in a free-market democracy with regard to many benefits, such as housing, education, and medicine in general. This important social, economic, and political issue is beyond the scope of this book.

Beyond these two specific costs lies the specter of "Big Brother." Although that fear is generally associated with governmental intrusion and surveillance, the line between big government and big tech has been growing thinner and vaguer in recent times, especially with the advent of private-information-gathering giants such as Meta (formerly

Facebook), X (formerly Twitter), and Alphabet (formerly Google), the increasing cooperation between social media and government,[45] and the growth of AI. The collection of medical data, though regulated by laws such as HIPPA, also raises concerns, especially if it is expanded to cover "previvors" as well as those actually suffering from illnesses.

All in all, the "tragic choices" of evils or even of goods with some negative consequences—decisions that involve high costs on both sides—are similar in many predictive-preventive decisions, whether they involve big government, big tech, big AI, big medicine, big pharma, big education, big media, or any other large-scale institutions that affect the lives of people. There are, to be sure, real differences in kind and degree, depending on the nature and function of the institutions—especially in the power to compel. For Example, an Israeli ambulance service (Hatzalah) is using artificial intelligence to predict where and when accidents are most likely to occur. By pre-positioning ambulances in these locations, they have decreased response time. These and similar innovations help inform thoughtful consideration of options and may provide insights into any effort to construct a jurisprudence of prevention based on predictions of harm.

So, too, does history provide important insights and lessons. Human beings, as distinguished from other species, have the ability to record the past and present and thus to transmit to the future. This ability is considerably strengthened by improvements in AI and other technologies.

We (and the machines we create) are capable of learning not only from our own mistakes, but also from those of our predecessors. The recognition of past wrongs often gives rise to present rights, as I wrote in my book *Rights from Wrongs*.[46] With these considerations in mind, let us now turn to a brief history of past efforts to predict and prevent harms.

CHAPTER 1

A BRIEF HISTORY OF PREDICTION AND PREVENTION

From Reactive to Proactive

From the very beginning of human history, knowledge has been power, and knowledge about the future—the ability to predict events—has bestowed great power on those who claimed the ability to prophesy.

The Bible recounts Joseph's prediction, based on Pharaoh's dream, of "seven years of great plenty," followed by "seven years of famine." This successful prediction allowed the Egyptians to prevent the famine from "consum[ing] the land," by "gather[ing] up all the good of those good years" and "stor[ing]some of it for the bad years."[1] As a result of this predictive-preventive strategy, Egypt was saved, and Joseph became a powerful leader.

Joshua ordered the "Sun [to] stand still over Gibeon,"[2] thus allowing the Israelites to defeat their enemy in battle. Astronomers have speculated that Joshua had merely predicted "the annular solar eclipse of October 30, 1207, BCE," and that his knowledge allowed him to gain the military advantage.[3]

Prophets as well as charlatans throughout the ages have attempted to foresee harmful occurrence, such as flood, famine, pestilence, earthquake, volcanic eruption, tsunami, war, and death. An old joke has Hitler asking a fortune teller to advise him as to the day of his death. The prognosticator tells Hitler that he cannot determine the precise date, but he can tell him it will be on "a Jewish holiday." So Hitler takes special precautions on Rosh Hashana, Yom Kippur, and other Jewish holidays. The teller's assistant asks his boss how he can be so sure that Hitler will die on a Jewish holiday, to which the con man replies: "Whatever day Hitler dies on will *become* a Jewish holiday!"

Some religious "prophets" have predicted the "end of days" for all humankind, or for specific nations or groups. The Talmud cautions that true prophesying ended with the destruction of the Temple in Jerusalem, but this has not ended the human urge to peek into the future, both on the micro and macro levels.

Some historical predictions have been based on information-gathering techniques, such as spying, surveillance, and eavesdropping. The biblical Moses sent spies who reported of the difficulties the Israelites would face from enemy fortifications;[4] and Mordechai predicted an attempt to kill the king of Persia based on overhearing the plotters.[5]

On the micro level, the ability to predict ordinary crime—to determine who is likely to become a criminal—has also captured the imagination of humankind for centuries. From the Bible's "stubborn and rebellious son,"[6] identifiable by his gluttony and drunkenness; to nineteenth-century criminologist Cesare Lombroso's "born criminal and criminaloid,"[7] identifiable by the shape of his cranium; to Shelton and Eleanor Glueck's three-year-old delinquent,[8] identifiable by a composite score derived from familial relationships, "experts" have claimed the ability to spot "the mark of Cain"—the potential criminal before he or she has committed serious crimes. (Cain himself secured the mark *after* he killed Abel, in order to prevent others from harming him.)[9] Though the results have not generally met with scientific approval, it is still widely believed—by many police officers, judges, psychiatrists, lawyers, and members of the general public—that there are ways of distinguishing "criminal types" from the rest of us, even before they commit any crimes. A popular film, *Minority Report*, was premised on this widespread belief and fear.

When teaching about these issues, I would show the students an 1882 photograph of a well-dressed, handsome man. When I asked them to speculate about his occupation/status, the answers would range from Supreme Court justice, to accountant, to actor, to minister. No one guessed he was Charles Guiteau, the man who assassinated President Garfield. Guiteau had asked to have his formal picture taken just days before he was executed. Serial killers like Ted Bundy succeeded because they don't look like killers!

In the 1920s and 1930s eugenicists not only in Germany but in the United States, Great Britain, and other Western nations believed that they could prevent criminal behavior in specific individuals or groups through sterilization and other eugenic measures. Harvard University was at the center of such thinking, which was championed by its president A. Lawrence Lowell, who was a self-admitted "racialist," believing that there were inherent differences among the races in intelligence, work ethic, and morality.[10] Oliver Wendell Holmes, in his notorious decision upholding mandatory sterilization of "imbeciles," reflected the widespread thinking at Harvard. His opinion focused on the prevention of criminal behavior by the mentally deficient: "It is better for all the world, if instead of waiting to execute degenerate offspring for crime, or to let them starve for their imbecility, society can prevent those who are manifestly unfit from continuing their kind."[11] We now know that false positives—likely including Carrie Buck herself, the appellant in *Buck v. Bell*—probably outnumbered true positives, and that many who were sterilized would have produced healthy and productive children, and relatively few would have been "execute[d]...for their crimes" or starve. But Holmes insisted that "it is better for the world" if numerous false positives were sterilized than if some false negatives be allowed to produce children who might do harm, especially if the false positives were mentally challenged and thus unproductive, even if they would not produce children who would kill or starve.

Buck v. Bell will be remembered by history as among the handful of the worst Supreme Court decisions, though authored by one of the greatest jurists (Holmes) and joined by some of our most distinguished justices (Brandeis, Taft, and Stone). The accepted scientific "truths" of one age may turn out to be dangerous lies when subjected to the empirical testing of a subsequent age. Justice Brandeis himself cautioned that the greatest dangers to liberty lurk in the "insidious encroachment by men of zeal, well-meaning but without understanding."[12] This well describes his own misguided vote in *Buck v. Bell*.

Even before the Holocaust, the German government forcibly sterilized hundreds of thousands of men and women, nearly one percent of Germans of childbearing age, believing that "[I]t is better to sterilize too many rather than too few." (Better many false positives than even one false negative!) The legislation authorizing sterilization was called "The Law for the Prevention of Genetically Diseased Offspring." Nazi doctors invoked Justice Holmes's decision in justification of their "preventive" actions. Although this "science" became justly discredited following the Holocaust, as recently as the 1970s it was suggested that the presence of the XYY karyotype in a man might be associated with, and consequently predictive of, certain kinds of violent crime. In an article about this claimed association, I exposed the mathematical errors underlying this pseudoscience that Harvard and other respected researchers had promoted.[13]

The mapping of the human genome has stimulated contemporary genetic research into the predictability of violence and other harms. Racial, ethnic, religious, and other "profiling" is now thought by some to hold promise in the effort to identify potential criminals. It has also generated research into the predictability of diseases.

Historically, the widespread use of early intervention to preempt serious threats to the state has been associated with tyrannical regimes. Hitler, Stalin, Mao, Castro, and Putin excelled at killing their enemies before they could rise up against them. But preventive approaches have been championed by progressive forces as well. The detention of Japanese Americans to prevent espionage and sabotage was advocated by progressive California governor Earl Warren, implemented by progressive president Franklin Roosevelt, and upheld by liberal justices, including Hugo Black.[14] Most recently, aggressive efforts to prevent the spread of COVID—including state-imposed mandates—have been advocated by some progressives and opposed by many conservatives and some libertarians.[15]

All people in all eras have favored some preventive or precautionary measures while opposing others. The differences over which preventive measures are favored and which are opposed depend on many social, political, religious, and cultural factors. As I shall argue throughout this book, it is meaningless to declare support for, or opposition to, prevention or precaution as a general principle, because so much properly depends on the values at stake—on the content of the costs and benefits, the substance of what is being regulated, and the identity of those on whom the costs are imposed and the benefits realized.

One can of course sympathize with efforts to predict and prevent at least some harms before they occur, rather than wait until the victim lies dead. Indeed, Lewis Carroll put in the queen's mouth an argument for preventive confinement of predicted criminals that Alice found difficult to refute. The queen says:

> "[T]here's the King's Messenger. He's in prison now, being punished; and the trial doesn't even begin till next Wednesday; and of course the crime comes last of all."
>
> "Suppose he never commits the crime?" said Alice.
>
> "That would be all the better, wouldn't it? The Queen said....
>
> Alice felt there was no denying *that*. "Of course that would be all the better," she said: "but it wouldn't be all the better his being punished."
>
> "You're wrong…" said the Queen. "Were *you* ever punished?"
>
> "Only for faults," said Alice.
>
> "And you were all the better for it, I know!" the Queen said triumphantly.
>
> "Yes, but then I *had* done the things I was punished for," said Alice: "that makes all the difference."

> "But if you *hadn't* done them," the Queen said, "that would
> have been even better still; better, and better, and better!" Her
> voice went higher with each "better," till it got quite to a squeak.…
> Alice [thought]: "There's a mistake here somewhere—"[16]

There are numerous mistakes and perils to liberty implicit in this kind
of magical thinking, and they are not being sufficiently debated today.

For some civil libertarians, any form of detention or imprisonment
based on predictions of harm would be alien to our traditions. Lord
Justice Denning, one of the most prominent common law jurists of
the twentieth century, purported to summarize the irreconcilability
of preventive punishment with democratic principles: "It would be
contrary to all principle for a man to be punished, not for what he has
already done, but for what he may hereafter do."[17] It may be contrary
to all *principle*, but it is certainly not contrary to all *practice* or history.
Preventive measures have been practiced throughout history, despite
theoretical concerns about their justification.

In the appendix I describe how Jewish Rabbinic law has struggled
with the tensions between the formal law of the Torah and the pragmatic "needs of the time," especially in the context of preventing
threats to the community by dangerous individuals who cannot be
constrained by the formal rules. Other cultures and societies have
expressed similar conflicts and have sought to develop mechanisms
for resolving such conflicts.

The thorny issue of preventive intervention was mentioned, but
not developed, by many jurisprudential giants, especially in the last
centuries. Oliver Wendell Holmes Jr., in a celebrated passage from *The
Common Law*, argued that "prevention" is the "chief and only universal
purpose of punishment" and that "probably most English-speaking
lawyers would accept the preventive theory without hesitation."[18] He
observed that "There can be no case in which the law-maker makes
certain conduct criminal without thereby showing a wish and purpose
to prevent that conduct."[19] William Blackstone, the eighteenth-century
British jurist who had considerable influence on the development of

American law, observed in a chapter entitled "Of the Means of Preventing Offences," that "if we consider all human punishments in a large and extended view, we shall find them all rather calculated to prevent future crimes, than to expiate the past."[20]

Other legal authorities have argued in equally categorical terms that prevention has no proper role in the Anglo-American system of criminal justice. Francis Wharton, in his influential nineteenth-century *A Treatise on the Criminal Law of the United States*, dismissed "prevention" as a "proper theoretical justification" for criminal punishment: "If the[prevention] theory be correct, and be logically pursued, then punishment should proceed and not follow crime. The state must explore for guilty tendencies, and make a trial consist of the psychological investigation of such tendencies. This contradicts one of the fundamental maxims of English common law, by which not a tendency to crime, but simply crime itself, can be made the subject of a criminal issue."[21]

The past debates, superficial as they have been, over the proper role, if any, of prevention in criminal punishment have not been limited to Anglo-American legal writers. The Marchese di Beccaria, one of the founders of modern-day criminology, in his classic eighteenth-century *Essay on Crimes and Punishment* put forth an essentially preventive justification for the criminal sanction: "It is better to prevent crimes than to punish them. This is the fundamental principle of good legislation.... [T]he intent of punishment is not ... to undo a crime already committed.... [It is] no other than to prevent the criminal from doing further injury to society, and to prevent others from committing the like offence."[22]

Immanuel Kant, the eighteenth-century German philosopher, in his *Metaphysical Elements of Justice*, took issue with Beccaria. For Kant, it was intolerable to impose punishment for any future-looking purpose: "Judicial punishment can never be used merely as a means to promote some other good for the criminal himself or for civil society, but instead it must in all cases be imposed on him on the ground that he has committed a crime."[23]

To illustrate the categorical nature of his insistence on retribution for past crimes, rather than prevention of future harms, Kant constructed the following hypothetical scenario:

> Even if a civil society resolved to dissolve itself with the consent of all its members—as might be supposed in the case of a people inhibiting an island resolving to separate and scatter themselves throughout the whole world—the last murderer lying in prison ought to be executed before the resolution was carried out. This ought to be done in order that everyone may realize the desert of his deeds, and that blood-guiltiness may not remain upon the people; for otherwise they might all be regarded as participators in the murder as a public violation of justice.[24]

These extreme views—prevention or "retribution" as the "only" legitimate purposes of punishment, or as absolutely illegitimate—have been expressed by philosophers over time. They both lack nuance, as a matter of history, morality, or justice. I am aware of no systematic attempt to construct a coherent philosophy of preventive intervention.

Some of the disagreement over the proper role of prevention in a system of criminal justice results from a failure to define precisely what was being considered. "Prevention" obviously meant something very different to Holmes, for example, from what it did to Wharton. Holmes was not advocating routine "psychological investigation" for "guilty tendencies" or a system of justice under which "punishment should proceed and not follow crime." (Although he did support preventive sterilization of the "mentally degenerate.") What Holmes meant by "preventive" was simply a forward-looking approach designed to reduce the frequency of harmful events in the future: "A wish and purpose to prevent that conduct."

Blackstone also defined "preventive" in a general way: "[A]ll punishments inflicted by temporal laws may be classed under three heads; such as tend to the amendment of the offender himself, or to deprive him of any power to do future mischief, or to deter others by his example: all of which conduce to one and the same end, of preventing future crimes."[25]

When prevention is defined as broadly as Holmes and Blackstone defined it, most authorities, though not Kant, would agree that curtailing future crimes is one permissible function of any legal system.[26]

In recent years, there has been more emphasis on explicitly preventive interventions designed to avoid cataclysmic harms. This shift from responding to past events to preventing future harms is one of the most significant but largely unnoticed trends in the world today. It challenges our traditional reliance on a model of human behavior that presupposes a rational person capable of being deterred by the threat of punishment. The classic theory of deterrence postulates a calculating evildoer who can evaluate the cost-benefits of proposed actions and will act—and forbear from acting—on the basis of these rational calculations. It also presupposes society's ability (and willingness) to withstand the harms we seek to deter and to use the visible punishment of those harms as threats capable of deterring future dangers. These assumptions are now being widely questioned (at least in practice) as the threat of weapons of mass destruction in the hands of suicide terrorists who welcome martyrdom becomes more realistic and as our ability to deter such harms by classic rational cost-benefit threats and promises becomes less realistic.

The decision whether to intervene based on predictions of harm, writ large, may involve war and peace. Writ small, it may involve the decision whether to incarcerate preventively, as in pretrial denial or bail, an individual who is thought to pose a high degree of likelihood that he will kill, rape, assault, or engage in an act of terrorism between arrest and trial. At an intermediate level, it may involve the decision to quarantine dozens, or hundreds, of people, some of whom may be carrying a transmittable virus like COVID, smallpox, or avian flu. At yet another level, it may raise the question of whether to impose prior restraint on a magazine, newspaper, television network, or Internet provider planning to publish information or incitement that may pose an imminent danger to the safety of our troops, our spies, or potential victims of aggression. Since the introduction of the Internet, which, unlike responsible media outlets, has no "publisher" who can be held accountable after the fact, there has been more consideration of before-the-fact censorship, difficult as that may be.

At every level, preventive decisions must be based on uncertain predictions, which will rarely be anywhere close to 100 percent accurate. We must be prepared to accept some false positives (predictions of harms that would not have occurred) in order to prevent some predicted harms from causing irreparable damage (true positives). The policy decisions that must be made involve the acceptable ratios of false to true positives and negatives in differing contexts.

Over the millennia we have constructed a carefully balanced jurisprudence or moral philosophy of after-the-fact reaction to harms, especially crimes. We have come to accept a widely agreed upon calculus: better ten guilty go free than even one innocent be wrongly convicted. Ten is not a number fixed by morality. The accepted number could be five or fifteen—some have even suggested one hundred. It is a reflection of the widely accepted—at least in theory by democracies—of the preference for false acquittals over false convictions. Should a similar moral calculus govern preventive decisions? If so, how should it be articulated? It is better for ten possibly preventable terrorist attacks to occur than for one possibly innocent suspect to be preventively detained. Should the answer depend on the nature of the predicted harm? The conditions and duration of detention? The past record of the detainee? The substantive criteria employed in the preventive decision? The ratio of true positives to false positives and false negatives? These are the sorts of questions we shall have to confront as we shift toward more preventive approaches—whether it be to terrorism, the spread of contagious diseases, preventive warfare, or simple criminal behavior. History provides some guides and cautions, but not definitive answers. We will need to struggle to construct our best (or least worst) answers based on experience, democratic values, civil liberties, and rule of law.

In the early 1970s I wrote a series of law review articles setting out a detailed history of preventive actions under Anglo-American common law. They focused on micro decisions involving the preventive confinement of dangerous mentally ill individuals who were not subject to after-the-fact conviction for crimes already committed. A review of this history led me to several tentative conclusions that may be relevant to all preventive decisions, both micro and macro. Among these conclusions were the following:

> One conclusion derived from this overview is that the preventive confinement of dangerous persons who cannot be convicted of past criminality but who are thought likely to cause serious injury in the future has always been practiced, to some degree, by every society and history regardless of the jurisprudential rhetoric it has employed. Moreover, it is likely that some forms of preventive confinement will continue to be practiced by every society.
>
> Another conclusion is that much of what has passed for "preventive confinement" has really been mechanisms for detaining persons who are thought to have committed past crimes but who, for one reason or another, cannot be convicted. Thus, the original jurisdiction of the justices of the peace, though preventive, often require a "finding" (but a far less rigorous finding) of past criminality.[27]
>
> A third conclusion suggested by the historical material is that, all other factors being equal, the necessity for and emergence of informal preventive mechanisms will increase as it becomes more difficult to secure convictions against persons thought to be guilty of past serious crime. Thus, if two countries are experiencing similar crime problems in a similar sociopolitical context, and if one of those countries enacts a series of legal protections that has the effect of freeing more guilty persons (that it may also have the effect of freeing more innocent persons is irrelevant to this hypothesis), it should follow that this country will perceive a greater need for informal "preventive" devices and will develop them.

Another conclusion, related to the previous one, is that mechanisms of social control, more specifically of confinement and isolation, frequently operate on a balloon principle: if you squeeze the air out of one end, the other will become more inflated. Thus, it is a fairly constant phenomenon in most societies that dangerous and bothersome people will be isolated by one means or another: if banishment is available, imprisonment may be employed less frequently; if there is no law of criminal attempts, then peace bonds may be used against those who attempt, but fail, to do harm; If insane asylums become available, then vagrancy and poor laws will be used less frequently against the insane. But this balloon phenomenon does not operate in isolation from other social dynamics. For example, it is well recognized that available spaces and custodial institutions will generally be filled, even if the actual need for confinement has decreased. This model is useful, at least, as a caveat—when a particular mechanism of confinement is rendered useless (or less useful), one should at least search to see whether the slack has been picked up, in whole or in part, by other mechanisms.

Another important conclusion, perhaps the most important for purposes of this study, is that although preventive confinement has always been and will always be practiced, no jurisprudence of preventive intervention has ever emerged. It may sound surprising, even arrogant, to say this, but it appears to be true. No philosopher, legal writer, or political theorist has ever, to this writer's knowledge, attempted to construct a systemic theory of when it is appropriate for the state to confine preventively. This is so for a number of reasons. The mechanisms of prevention have been, for the most part, informal; accordingly, they have not required articulate defense or justification. Moreover, there are many scholars who simply deny that preventive intervention, especially preventive confinement, really exist. Or if they acknowledge the existence of these mechanisms, they deny their legitimacy, thus obviating the need for a theory or jurisprudence.

Finally, it is extremely difficult to construct a theory of preventive confinement that neatly fits into existing theories of criminal law and democracy.[28]

The upshot of this history is that there has always existed a widespread series of practices involving significant restraints on human liberty without an articulated jurisprudence circumscribing and limiting its application. Numerous people are confined to prevent predicted harms without any systematic effort to decide what kinds of harms warrant preventive confinement; or what degree of likelihood should be required; or what duration of preventive confinement should be permitted; or what relationship should exist between the harm, the likelihood, or the duration. This is not to say that there currently exists a completely satisfactory jurisprudence or theory justifying the imposition of punishment for past acts. But at least many of the right questions have been asked, and some interesting answers have been attempted. Even Blackstone's primitive formulation "that it is better that ten guilty persons escape, than that one innocent suffer"[29] tells us something important about how to devise rules of evidence and procedure. There is no comparable aphorism for preventive confinement: is it better for X number of "false positives" to be erroneously confined (and for how long?) than for Y number of preventable harms (and of what kind?) to occur? What relationship between X and Y does justice require? We have not even begun to ask these kinds of questions in a systematic fashion, or to develop modes of analytic analysis for answering them.

In the chapters to come I will try to develop modes of analysis that are consistent with democratic values, the rules of law and the needs of society.

PART 2

THE PREVENTIVE STATE
IN ACTION

CHAPTER 2

PREVENTING PRESIDENTIAL ASSASSINATIONS

From Richard Lawrence's Attempt to Kill President Andrew Jackson to the Recent Attempts to Kill Presidential Candidate Donald Trump

Since 1835, there have been numerous attempts to assassinate presidents, former presidents, presidential candidates, and other public officials. Four presidents—Lincoln, Garfield, McKinley, and Kennedy—have been killed. Presidential candidate Robert Kennedy was also killed. Ronald Reagan and Donald Trump were wounded. Several others—including both Roosevelts, Harry Truman, and Gerald Ford—were subjected to failed attempts or plots.[1]

Over the past nearly two hundred years, preventive measures of varying sophistication have been put in place to protect presidents and candidates. The emphasis, especially recently, has been on prevention and planning, rather than deterrence and reaction, although the latter play a role as well. The protectees are closely guarded, and efforts are made to secure areas from which threats may emanate. These are not always successful, as evidenced by the assassinations that succeed—or the ones that failed because of luck, like Trump's. The job of protecting presidents and others was originally allocated to the Treasury Department, which assigned the Secret Service that role, along with other responsibilities, such as investigating counterfeiting. Now the Secret Service is under the jurisdiction of the Department of Homeland Security, but it still investigates counterfeiting.

In our early history, fewer proactive measures were taken, resulting in the preventable murders of Lincoln, Garfield, and McKinley. This was true as well of the first attempted presidential assassination in 1835. So let us begin by examining in some detail the earliest case, which has implications for the thesis of this book.

Richard Lawrence, the first person to make an armed assault upon a president of the United States, tried to kill Andrew Jackson in 1835. Approaching the president with two well-loaded pistols, he fired the first from a distance of about thirteen feet and the second from point-blank range. The percussion caps of both pistols exploded but neither succeeded in igniting the powder. The pistols, which were both in excellent working order and properly loaded, were fired successfully in hundreds of tests conducted after the attempted assassination. It was never determined why they had misfired at the critical moment, though some observers attributed the fortuity to unusual dampness in the weather.[2]

Having been observed by dozens of prominent witnesses and "arrested in the very act," Lawrence was immediately "brought before the chief judge at his chambers." He was accused of "an assault upon the president of the United States...with intent to murder him"—a common law charge that was "not a penitentiary offense, there having been no actual battery."[3] The maximum penalty that could have been imposed under the indictment was a "fine and imprisonment"; and although the precise range of punishments that could have been imposed for this "misdemeanor"[4] was not clear, it was probably in the area of a year in jail and a fine of less than $1,000.[5]

It may sound strange to the modern ear that an attempt to kill the president—prevented solely by the chance misfiring of two properly loaded pistols—should be treated so lightly by the law. In part, this reflects the early result focus of the formal system of criminal law, both in this country and in England. Felonies—with the exception of treason-type crimes—were defined, for the most part, in terms of the harm actually caused, rather than the risk created. Thus, since there had been "no actual battery" upon the president—he literally had not been touched—the crime committed was an inchoate one. Though the law of "attempts" had its origins many centuries prior to Lawrence's crime, it was still not well developed in the United States. There was an attempt statute in the District of Columbia,[6] but apparently few, if any, cases had been brought under it at the time of the Jackson episode. Nor could there have been a statutory indictment for assault with intent to kill, for the applicable statute punished "assault *and* battery with intent to kill" (two to eight years), and there had been no battery upon Jackson (emphasis added).

Thus, the prosecution was relegated to bringing a "common law" indictment against Lawrence for assault with intent to kill.[7] There is even some question whether this common law indictment would have been sustained by the Supreme Court, since in 1812 a unanimous court had held that the circuit courts of the United States could not "exercise a common law jurisdiction in criminal cases."[8] The applicability of this landmark decision to the District of Columbia was not certain at the time of the *Lawrence* indictment, but there must have been some doubts about the legality of a common law charge.

It is against this background that certain important aspects of the *Lawrence* case can be understood. The first judicial decision involved bail. It may sound strange that bail would even be considered for a thwarted presidential assassination, but since the crime with which Lawrence was charged was not a capital one, it was thought that bail had to be set. Even the prosecutor—Francis Scott Key (a part-time poet who was the United States attorney)—acknowledged this, and limited his argument to raising the bail amount from the $1,000 proposed by the chief judge to $1,500. The report of the case indicates that Mr. Key at first acquiesced in the judge's proposal:

[B]ut having conversed with some of the president's friends who stood around him, he suggested the idea that it was not impossible that others might be concerned, who might be disposed to bail him, and let him escape to make another attempt on the life of the president, and therefore thought that the larger sum should be named.[9]

The judge responded that:

[T]here was no evidence before him to induce a suspicion that any other person was concerned in the act; That the constitution forbade him to require excessive bail; And that to require larger bail than the prisoner could give would be to require excessive bail, and to deny bail in a case clearly bailable by law.[10]

This statement by the respected chief judge Cranch of the District of Columbia Circuit Court has relevance to the current debate over the constitutionality of pretrial detention. If the words stood alone, outside the context in which they were delivered and apart from the actions that accompanied them, they would make a powerful case against the constitutionality of such detention in noncapital cases. After all, it was acknowledged by all concerned that the judge could not refuse to set bail, even if there had been evidence of a continuing conspiracy to kill the president. He could, in such a situation, raise the bail; but there were limits even to that. Had the offense been a capital one, bail could have been denied—even if there was no continuing danger. This strongly suggests that the underlying reason why bail was denied in capital cases was not because capital offenses, as a class, were thought to be the most dangerous, but rather because, as a class, they provided the greatest incentive for flight from the jurisdiction to avoid the ultimate penalty.[11]

The words of the chief judge also seem to suggest that he believed pretrial release could not be denied on economic grounds: that the maximum bail that could properly be set was the highest sum that the defendant was capable of raising. If this were in fact the original historical understanding, then it would pose considerable questions about current bail practices and judicial pronouncements. The chief judge went on, however, to say—and more significantly, to do—various things that diminish the significance of his quoted statement. First, he decided to set bail at $1,500, reasoning as follows:

> This sum, if the ability of the prisoner only were to be considered is, probably, too large; but if the atrocity of the offence alone were considered, might seem too small, but taking both into consideration, and that the punishment can only be fine and imprisonment, it seemed to him to be as high as he ought to require.[12]

Although the judges asserted that "the prisoner had some reputable friends who might be disposed to bail him," Lawrence was not, in fact able to find bail to that amount and was "committed for trial, by warrant of the Chief Judge."

Thus, despite the judge's statement of the law that "to require larger bail than the prisoner could give would be to require excessive bail," the net result of the case was that the prisoner was denied pretrial release because of his inability to raise the bail money.

It is interesting to speculate whether a man who almost succeeded in killing the president would actually have been set free—released to the street—if he had been able to raise the bail money. There are some suggestions in the case that Lawrence might not have obtained his freedom even if he had posted the $1,500. These suggestions appear in that portion of the opinion devoted to the habeas corpus petition brought on the prisoner's behalf. That petition alleged that Lawrence was insane and requested that: "he may be discharged from imprisonment 'for the cause for which he is now confined,' and that your honor do them in the premises what belongs to humanity and the unfortunate Richard Lawrence, and also to secure the public peace by proper restraint." In other words, the petition did not seek outright release for the prisoner; instead, it requested the court to confine him not as a suspected criminal awaiting trial, but as a dangerously insane person. The place of confinement would not be different, since in those days the dangerously insane in the District of Columbia were confined in the same jail as indicted criminals. (There was no insane asylum in the district until 1852; between 1841 and 1852 the dangerously insane from the district were accommodated in the Maryland hospital in Baltimore, and before then they were left in jail.) Counsel for the prisoner intimated, however, that the court could "meliorate his condition, or change his custody."

Despite the prosecutor's agreement that the writ should issue, the court denied the petition on grounds that again showed the intimate relationship between the various mechanisms of preventive confinement:

> I would remark, here, that if the prisoner is a dangerous maniac, the only manner in which I could secure the public peace (or rather secure the public safety) would be, to remand him to the prison where he now is. His imprisonment then would be interminable; he would have no day in court; no means to compel a trial; no right to apply for a discharge for want of trial, and no right to bail. He could not be bound to keep the peace. If sureties should be bound for his keeping the peace, it is doubtful whether they could ever be liable upon their recognizances, whatever acts he might do; as I apprehend, a madman cannot be guilty of a technical breach of the peace. I have said that I could only remand him to the prison where he now is.[13]

The court then contrasted the situation in the district with that existing in Great Britain where the court had discretion to determine the "custody" of a person acquitted by reason of insanity or found incompetent to stand trial. The British situation, which resulted from the statute enacted following Hatfield's acquittal by reason of insanity of attempting to kill King George III at the Drury Lane theater in 1800,[14] had changed the common law. Since there had been no statutory change in the district, the court felt constrained to follow the common law, which precluded a transfer of custody or an amelioration of the prisoner's condition.

The court's reasoning, and its citation of the English experience, once again illustrates the close connection between the various preventive techniques available at common law and by early statutes. Here we have a paradigm case of an allegedly insane man who has caused no actual harm (other than, perhaps, psychological, which was not well protected at common law), but who might well have been quite dangerous.

The first problem was what to do with him in the interim between his arrest and the final disposition of the case. There were a number of possibilities: (1) the court could refuse to set bail; (2) bail could be set in an amount higher than he could raise; (3) he could be required to post a peace bond; or (4) he could be confined as dangerously mentally ill. Pragmatically, the basic choice is twofold: confinement or release.[15] In this kind of case, despite the rhetoric of liberty, it is extremely unlikely that any defendant would have actually been released pending final disposition of the case.

The next problem was how to dispose of the case on the merits. Again, there were a number of possibilities: (1) the defendant could be convicted of an inchoate crime, such as assault with attempt to kill, attempted murder, or—as Hatfield was in England—treason; (2) he could be found incompetent to stand trial and remain in confinement awaiting the restoration of his competency; or (3) he could be acquitted by reason of insanity and confined as criminally insane.[16]

Pragmatically, the first alternative is the one least well designed to protect the community (at least at the time of the *Lawrence* case). Punishment for inchoate crimes was of relatively short duration. And it was not deemed treason to attempt to kill an American president. If convicted of an attempt or assault, Lawrence would have had to be released within a few years, at most. Moreover, there may have been doubts whether, on the facts of the case, a conviction would have been sustained on appeal.

The second alternative—incompetency to stand trial—is well designed for low visibility decision-making. It requires no trial, and therefore no public disclosure of the government's evidence. It might well have been employed if the government's case were weak or embarrassing. In the *Lawrence* situation, however, there was every reason for the government to put its case on to prove that the attempted assassination was the work of a solitary deranged individual.[17] Historically, many attempts to kill political leaders have been attributed to insanity, rather than political grievances, even absent a history of mental illness.

The third alternative—acquittal by reasons of insanity followed by confinement as mentally ill—has been widely employed in attempted political assassinations. (This is by no means to imply that all of these defendants have not, in fact, been mentally ill. It is to suggest that other defendants, who have been *as* seriously deranged, have probably been convicted, when their crimes were not of a political nature.) Acquittal by reason of insanity followed by indefinite confinement is ideally suited for an attempted assassination. The government can prove the facts (especially that the crime was the act of a madman). It can obtain a jury verdict that "closes" the case, and it can secure the defendant's safe confinement for an indefinite time.

It is not surprising, therefore, that the prosecution in the *Lawrence* case did not vigorously contest the plea of not guilty by reason of insanity.

Robert Donovan, who chronicled the trial of Lawrence in a series appearing in the *New Yorker*, takes the common but naive view that the prosecution, in not contesting the insanity "defense," was necessarily acting with "magnanimity, humaneness and liberality." Donovan observes that a relentless prosecution was possible considering the political climate of the trial. It seems that Key (the prosecutor) could have waged "a very strong prosecution along the lines that Lawrence knew right from wrong."[18] But Donovan fails to understand that a "strong" prosecution that resulted in a misdemeanor conviction was less to be desired by the government than a "weak" prosecution that culminated in lifetime confinement. Accordingly, Key acquiesced in a very broad instruction on insanity—one reminiscent of the modern *Durham* rule.[19] It took the jury five minutes to conclude that Lawrence had "been under the influence of insanity at the time he committed the act."[20]

The judge then concluded from the evidence that it would be extremely dangerous to permit him to be at large while under this mental delusion and remanded him to jail.[21] In 1855, after twenty years in jail, Lawrence became one of the first inmates confined in the new Government Hospital (now Saint Elizabeths) where he died in 1861. Had he been convicted of the crime for which he was charged, he might have lived the last twenty years of his life at liberty—or he might have tried to kill another president!

The *Lawrence* case illustrated the close connection between the various techniques of preventive confinement, especially the manner by which lacunae in the substantive criminal law are filled by other—less formal—preventive devices. A man arguably insane commits an act manifesting extreme dangerousness, but subjecting him to only minor criminal punishment. The technique of high bail is employed to confine him until trial; and the technique of insanity acquitted commitment is employed to confine him thereafter. The rhetoric of liberty is loudly proclaimed, but the reality of preventive confinement is silently enforced.

The nonlethal failure to protect President Jackson was followed by the lethal failures to protect presidents Lincoln, Garfield, and McKinley. Lincoln had been shot at before his murder at Ford's Theatre. A bullet had pierced his stovepipe hat. He was the commander-in-chief of an army at war, and numerous threats on his life had been made. Yet when he went to Ford's Theatre, he was accompanied by one guard who reportedly went to a saloon during the intermission, leaving the president unprotected when John Wilkes Booth opened the door to his box and shot him.

Just sixteen years later, President Garfield went to a train station—ironically accompanied by Robert Todd Lincoln, the assassinated president's son, who was then secretary of war—without any guards. He was shot at point-blank range by an aggrieved job seeker, who had previously visited the White House and had made his grievances known.

Then, just twenty years later, President McKinley was shot by an anarchist who advocated assassination as an appropriate response to perceived tyranny. Although McKinley was surrounded by both federal and local guards, Leon Czolgosz was able to shake his hand and then shoot him with a pistol concealed in a handkerchief. Following this assassination, the Secret Service was assigned to protect presidents.

It is fair to say that the first four presidential assassination attempts could have been prevented by careful planning and proactive steps. Following these early failures, protection improved somewhat. Nevertheless, there were several near misses during the first half of the twentieth century—including attempts on the lives of both Roosevelts and President Truman. Then came the successful assassination of John F. Kennedy, with the continuing controversy surrounding the circumstances. (Woody Allen said he was waiting for the "non-fiction version of the Warren Commission report.") Robert Kennedy's assassination was less controversial, although his son has questioned the official narrative. As a candidate, Robert Kennedy was not protected by the Secret Service. Following the two planned assassinations against Donald Trump, presidential candidates are accorded maximum protection.

The two near misses against Trump resulted in the nearly universal condemnation of the Secret Service for its ineptitude in not preventing twenty-year-old Thomas Crooks, armed with his father's rifle and a range finder, from reaching a roof within easy sight line and range of the large, stationary target. The agents who immediately ran to protect Trump after the shooting deserve praise, but those whose job it was to prevent any shooting must be criticized.

It is not as if this attack could not have been anticipated and planned for. It is quite similar to the shooting of then president John F. Kennedy from the sixth floor of the Texas School Book Depository in Dallas. The major difference is that Lee Harvey Oswald shot at a difficult moving target, whereas Crooks shot at an easier stationary target. In both cases, there was a failure to secure an obviously dangerous location. One would think that the Secret Service would have learned from their failure in Dallas. They obviously did not.

The second foiled plot by Ryan Wesley Routh should have been even easier to prevent, because the perpetrator was hiding in the bushes near Trump's golf course for hours before an alert agent spotted his gun sticking through a fence.

There must be changes in the protective procedures employed by the Secret Service, especially at large outdoor rallies. Everyone admitted to the venue is vetted for weapons, but apparently there is insufficient protection against potential snipers shooting from outside the actual venue. This failing must be remedied.

For large events like the ones at which Trump was targeted, the Secret Service should designate one senior agent who has the sole authority to green light the appearance of the protectee. This agent should check every risk factor, such as suspicious persons, unsecured buildings, and crowd warnings. At the Trump events, some of these concerns fell through the cracks—different agencies were responsible for different aspects, and there was a lack of coordination. Placing one person in charge of assuring that all bases have been covered, would help protect against the breakdown of communication that led to the near misses in Pennsylvania and Florida.[22]

The Secret Service should be devoted exclusively to preventing and responding to attacks on its protectees. It must get out of the unrelated business of investigating currency counterfeiting and other crimes. Perhaps it should be joined with other protective agencies, such as the State Department Diplomatic Services and the United States Marshal Services, with each having separate responsibilities, but sharing intelligence and other information.

The Secret Service should have five basic responsibilities: (1) short- and medium-term intelligence operations designed to predict and prevent in advance any threats; (2) securing of all venues at which protectees may appear; (3) identifying and preventing immediate threats by suspicious persons at or near the venues; (4) halting the event and the appearance of the protectee if there is any perceived threat; and (5) immediately responding to attacks by protecting the target from further attacks and neutralizing the attacker or attackers.

The first of these responsibilities—predicting and preventing future attacks—is the most difficult (and the most relevant to this book). It will necessarily require many false positives to prevent even one false negative, because attempted assassinations are such rare events over time. Many individuals and groups threaten—either explicitly or implicitly—presidents and other protectees, but very few actually act on these threats. All such threats should obviously be investigated, but not all suspects should be detained. It is a crime to threaten the president—an inchoate crime designed to reduce threats of future harms. But few potential assassins openly threaten and thus violate the statute. Some say and do things that increase the likelihood that they will actually try to attack. But even among those, only a small fraction will cross the line into action. It is the difficult—perhaps nearly impossible—job of the Secret Service to distinguish between true and false positives, while reducing false negatives to zero. It is unlikely that Crooks or Routh could have been identified *before* the days in question based on their words and deeds—without also identifying many individuals with similar predictive profiles who would never pose a real threat.

When I began to research the issues associated with predicting and preventing violence, including assassinations, I came across a category of detainees known as "White House Cases." These cases involved individuals who sought entry to the government buildings, especially the White House, in order to talk to officials. If they appeared to be mentally ill or "disturbed," they were referred to the Secret Service, which then sought their commitment to locked wards of mental hospitals. I studied one case that seemed to typify this category.

Bong Yol Yang, an American of Korean origin, appeared at the White House gate asking to see the president about people who were following him and "revealing his subconscious thoughts." He also wondered whether his talents as an artist could be put to some use by the government. The gate officer called the Secret Service, which then had him committed to a mental hospital. Yang demanded a jury trial, at which a psychiatrist testified that he was mentally ill—a paranoid schizophrenic—and that although there was no "evidence of his ever attacking anyone so far," there was always a possibility that "if his frustrations…became great enough, he may potentially attack someone." On the basis of this diagnosis and prediction, the judge permitted a jury to commit Yang to a mental hospital until he was no longer mentally ill and likely to cause injury.

This was almost certainly an example of a false positive, who was confined in an effort to avoid even the slightest possibility that if released he would become a false negative—that is, an actual assassin whose deadly act was falsely not predicted and thus not prevented. The calculus for "White House Cases" was that it is better that one hundred or more non-assassins be erroneously detained than even one potential assassin be erroneously released.

The issue of false positives and false negatives also arose in the moments preceding the wounding of Donald Trump. According to reports, a Secret Service sniper aimed at Crooks and could have killed him before he fired at Trump, rather than immediately after. But what if Crooks had turned out to be an innocent twenty-year-old who was in the wrong place at the wrong time. His death would have been a terrible false positive. So the sniper erred on the side of not shooting, with the result that it was a near-lethal false negative.

All of this could easily have been prevented if the Secret Service had secured the building, even with its slanted roof, before the shooter got near it. A false positive in unnecessarily securing a building that would *not* have been used to shoot is no big deal. A false negative in *not* securing a building that was then used to shoot is an enormous deal. So better one hundred buildings that would not be used be unnecessarily secured than even one building that would be used be falsely *not* secured.

Another example of how the desire to avoid a trivial false positive resulted in a disastrous false negative was the decision—or nondecision—by the Secret Service not to delay Trump's appearance on stage until all doubts concerning the person deemed "suspicious" were resolved. There were several people who were deemed suspicious before the Trump shooting, as there apparently are at many events. Each such person should be investigated as soon as practical. Had Trump's appearance been delayed or even canceled and the suspicious person had turned out to be harmless, that would have been a false positive that caused inconvenience. But failure to delay caused a near-fatal false negative.

Trump has said that "nobody mentioned" the presence of a suspicious person. "Nobody said there was a problem." He went on: "And I could have waited fifteen—they could have said, 'let's wait for fifteen minutes, two minutes, five minutes, something.'"

This raises a related and complex issue. Under current law and practice, the protectee has the power to overrule the Secret Service and make the ultimate decision whether to delay or cancel an event deemed dangerous by Secret Service agents. And history shows that protectees have ignored the expert opinions of the Secret Service in several instances, placing themselves in danger.[23] It must be recognized that when a protectee's life is endangered by a possible assassin, more is at stake than the life of the protectee. The entire nation—indeed the entire world—is affected by a successful assassination, especially of a president or presidential candidate.

Perhaps the law ought to be changed to reflect this reality. The Secret Service should have more power to delay or even cancel events that in its view pose too great a danger to the nation. This will not be easy to implement in practice, but it could have an impact on the acceptance by the protectee of the more expert opinions of the Secret Service.

To summarize, the preventive intelligence aspect of the Secret Service's role should favor many false positives—investigative leads that turn up empty—over even one false negative as in not pursuing a lead that could have prevented an assassination. The same is true of securing venues, questioning subjects, delaying the appearance of protectees, and surrounding a protectee. Detaining a suspect for more than a brief period should require some degree of probable or at least plausible cause. Shooting a suspected assassin requires a far different calculation, because it pits life against life.

These are the kinds of judgments that must be made by all preventive law enforcement agencies. The Secret Service has a mixed history in regard to this critical mission. To be sure, we do not know how many potential assassinations were prevented by the Secret Service. Neither do they. It is certainly possible that some of those arrested or detained might have gone on to try to kill a protectee. We know about attempts that were thwarted, as was the attempted shooting of President Ford by Squeaky Fromme, or the attempt on the life of President Truman by a Puerto Rican liberation group. But potential assassins who were deterred, or even those who were prevented by early interventions, are difficult to identify and quantify. The utter failure of the Secret Service to prevent or thwart the shooting of Donald Trump should be evident to all. The resignation of the then director was an important first step in the implementation of significant changes in approach to predicting, preventing, and responding to threats to protectees. These changes should reflect the costs of different types of errors—false positives versus false negatives in differing, but always crucial, contexts.

CHAPTER 3

PREVENTING CRIME

Bail, Sentencing, and Preventive Detention

Writ large, the preventive state may engage in preemptive military attacks, mandatory vaccinations, climate control, and other measures designed to reduce the likelihood of cataclysmic, mass-casualty threats. Writ small, it may employ preventive measures to reduce the incidence of singular (small or multiple) crimes by allegedly dangerous individuals.

This chapter deals with the latter and focuses on five decision points in the criminal process:

1. Preventive crimes: punishing, as crimes, behavior that has caused no past harm but that is thought to be dangerous and predictive of future harm. These are called "inchoate" crimes and include "attempts," "conspiracies," "reckless conduct," and other crimes that do not require the prosecution to prove actual "harm" as an element.
2. Bail: the decision whether to confine or release a defendant accused of crime between the time of arrest and his trial.
3. Sentencing: the decision whether and to what extent to factor assessments of future dangerousness, in addition to past and present culpability for the crimes of which the defendant stands convicted.

4. Post-sentence confinement: the decision whether to continue the confinement of alleged predators after they have completed service of their sentence, based on predictions of future criminality or other harm (3 and 4 may overlap since sentencing decisions may include mechanisms for extending confinement beyond the original sentence).

5. Some governments have the power, under certain circumstances, to confine allegedly dangerous individuals even before they are arrested or indicted for any past crimes.

CRIMES THAT HAVE CAUSED NO PAST HARM BUT MAY BE PREDICTIVE OF FUTURE HARM

Most crimes cause harms, such as death, bodily injury, or financial loss. Generally, the criminal justice system starts with the harm and works backward. Someone has been killed, raped, or robbed, and law enforcement officials seek to find out who caused the harm. "Who killed Cock Robin?" is the paradigmatic question. For traditional crimes four elements must be proved.

First, the defendant engaged in a prohibited act or omitted to take a required action. For example, he filed a false tax return (a prohibited act), or he failed to file any return (a required act that he omitted). This is called the "act" or "omission" element.

The second element is intent or some other mental factor such as recklessness. This is called "mens rea" or "the mental element."

The third element is "causation." The act or omission must have caused the harm. This is called the "causation" element.

The fourth element is the harm itself—death, injury, being defrauded. This is called the "harm" or "result" element. Some crimes do not require any specific harm. A perpetrator is arrested after he shoots and misses his intended victim. Even if the victim never becomes aware of the attempt on his life, the shooter is guilty of attempted murder. In a more common example, a driver is stopped going twenty miles above the speed limit, or he is drunk, or he doesn't have a license. He has caused no harm, but he is guilty of engaging in dangerous behavior, which, if not deterred by punishment, may eventually cause future harm—by him or by others.

In this genre of inchoate crime, the government need not prove causation or harm. It is enough to prove act (or omission) and intent (or another mental element). The act and intent requirements may be established by proof of something as vague as an "agreement" do something unlawful.

Blackstone may have been correct when he opined—as quoted above—that "If we consider all human punishment in our large and extended view we shall find them all rather calculated to prevent future conduct, than to expiate the past."[1] He was referring to the deterrent function of criminal punishment—namely, punishing those who have committed past crimes, most of which caused past harms, in order to send a message to those who might contemplate causing future harms. But he would have to acknowledge the difference between punishments that *both* expiate for past harm *and* prevent future harms, and punishments that *only* prevent future harms. The latter are necessarily more speculative. Both involve probabilistic judgments. Expiation for past harms involves a trial requiring proof beyond a reasonable doubt—sometimes defined as 90 percent certainty. Preventing future harms by identifying and punishing future harm-doers generally involves legislative judgments that need not satisfy such a high standard of proof, for example, that drivers who speed or drink will eventually cause an accident.

An example of a crime that was based on a questionable legislative predictive judgment is the old obscenity laws that punished the mere possession of pornography on the assumption that people who view such material are likely to engage in harmful sexual assaults. I own an old poster that shows an adult viewing "French" pictures and being stimulated to go out and rape. Even if it were true that a significant number of rapists had viewed porn, it is also true that the vast, vast, vast majority of adults who view pornography do not rape or cause any harm. The number of false positives (adults who view porn, and are legislatively predicted to rape, but do not rape) far exceeds the number of true positives (adults who view porn and then rape). It is questionable therefore to characterize the relationship between the act (viewing pornography) and the harm (rape) as "causation."

There are some crimes in which the ratio may well favor true positives over false ones. Driving crimes include both: a defendant who repeatedly drives recklessly while drunk is highly likely to cause future harm if not stopped, though some managed to avoid actually hurting anyone. A heroin or cocaine addict who lacks the funds necessary to satisfy his addiction is likely to steal, rob, or cheat to obtain those funds. But even these highly predictive crimes are subject to false positives.

There are some crimes that combine reactive and preventive rationales. Conspiracy is preventive in so far as it punishes agreeing, planning, and other acts that have not yet resulted in harms. But it also enhances the punishment for harms already completed if committed by more than one defendant.

There is a proper role for some preventive crimes, but they should be restricted to legislative judgment that have a valid empirical basis.[2]

BAIL

Every society that mandates a fair trial for accused defendants must face the conundrum of how to deal with defendants who are arrested for serious crimes during the inevitable hiatus between arrest and judgment. That "meantime" can last anywhere from weeks to months and even to years, but it will always be present, since a fair trial requires preparation.

The conundrum results from the difference between what the law presumes and what reality informs legal decisions. Our legal system presumes all defendants to be innocent during the "meantime" between arrest and judgment. But every prosecutor, judge, and defense attorney knows the reality: that most arrested and charged defendants are in fact guilty of some crime, and will be found so after a trial, or as the result of a plea to a lesser offense. A high correlation between arrests and convictions is a hallmark of democracies governed by the rule of law.[3] So, presumption and reality come into conflict when a judge decides whether to order the pretrial release or confinement of a given defendant. He must afford the defendant a presumption of innocence, while recognizing the high likelihood of guilt. There is no perfect solution to this problem in any society that believes both in the presumption of innocence and the need to give every defendant sufficient time to prepare for trial after they are arrested. (Overcharging more serious crimes is a common prosecutorial tactic designed to encourage plea bargaining.)

There is also the issue of predicted flight—escaping to avoid trial and expected conviction. The elements that go into decisions regarding flight are similar in many respects to those regarding future crimes, though the stakes may be different. Both require the prediction of future conduct—crimes or flight—based largely on the past conduct of the defendant. Both risk false positives: confining defendants who would not, if free, commit crimes or flee before trial. Both also risk false negatives: crimes or flight committed by defendants who are allowed to remain free pending trial.

The Constitution does not provide much guidance. The Eighth Amendment prohibits "excessive bail," but it does not explicitly grant a right to be bailed—only a right to non-excessive bail, *if* bail is granted. And at the time of the Framers, many serious crimes—there were numerous capital crimes—were non-bailable.[4] The Framers contemplated what amount of monetary bail would be the norm in noncapital cases—requiring a defendant to put up enough money or property to deter flight or crime (or to motivate private bail bondsmen to capture escaped defendants).

Today, there is widespread opposition to the concept of monetary bail in most cases. Liberals believe that too many non-dangerous indigents are confined because they can't raise bail (false positives). And they are right. Conservatives believe that too many dangerous non-indigents are released, because they can raise bail (false negatives). And they, too, are right. The ability to make monetary bail is, at best, an inexact predictor of violence or flight. Accordingly, some have suggested the abolition of monetary bail (for most cases) and the substitution of an explicit system of non-monetary "preventive detention" of defendants who are predicted to do harm or flee in the "meantime" between arrest and trial. As a matter of logic, explicit preventive detention would seem preferable to monetary bail. But as Oliver Wendell Holmes Jr. reminds us, "The life of the law has not been logic, it has been experience."[5] And our experience with predicting short-term harms, such as violence or fleeing, has demonstrated that false positives and negatives are inherent in any such enterprise.

More than half a century ago, I warned that "predictions of the kind relied upon by the proponents of preventive detention are likely to be unreliable."

> Predictions of human conduct are difficult to make, for man is a complex entity and the world he inhabits is full or unexpected occurrences. Predictions of rare human events are even more difficult. And predictions of rare events occurring within a short span of time are the most difficult of all. Acts of violence by persons released while awaiting trial are relatively rare events (though more frequent among certain categories of suspects—such as drug addicts), and the relevant timespan is short. Accordingly, the kind of predictions under consideration begin with heavy odds against their accuracy. A predictor is likely to be able to spot a large number of persons who would actually commit acts of violence only if he is also willing to imprison a very much larger number of defendants who would not, in fact, engage in violence if released.[6]

This raises an obvious reality that is often overlooked in evaluating the accuracy of predictions. In order for the evaluation to be fair, there must be information about both sides: we must know not only how many crimes that would have been committed by defendants out on bail were prevented (true positives) but also how many defendants were erroneously imprisoned (false positives). Either of these data points alone tells you very little. It is no trick to spot a very high percentage of defendants who would commit acts of violence while awaiting trial: you simply predict that all or most all will do so. Of course, the number of erroneous confinements would be extraordinarily high, but most or all the crimes would have been prevented. Conversely, it is easy to avoid erroneous confinement if that is your only aim: simply predict that few or none of the defendants will engage in violence pending trial. In that case, you would prevent very few, if any, of the potential crimes, but the number of erroneous confinements would be minimal or nonexistent.

The difficult task is to select a category that includes the largest number of defendants who would actually commit violent crimes and the smallest possible number who would not. If it were possible to select a category that included all those, and only those, who would commit such crimes, there would be little problem. (See the science fiction machine described on page 10. But since this is impossible in real life, a choice must be made. We must decide how many defendants we should be willing to confine erroneously in order to prevent how many acts of violence. This will, in turn, depend on the nature of the violence to be prevented and the duration of the contemplated confinement: we should be willing to tolerate fewer erroneous confinements to prevent predicted purse snatching than predicted murder, and fewer again if the trial is a year off than if it can be completed within two months of the arrest.

Unfortunately, our ability to predict these short-term harms has not improved significantly over the past half century. Nor has the conundrum of the "meantime" gotten easier. There is a growing consensus against monetary bail, but no consensus on how to deal with defendants who are *legally* presumed innocent, but *empirically* likely to be found guilty, and who are thought to pose a danger of violence or flight between arrest and judgment. We have not developed a jurisprudence to guide this difficult choice. Instead, we have left it to individual judges to make ad hoc decisions based on largely unreviewable discretion.

Some defenders of the current system argue that since most defendants who are confined pending trial will be found guilty and sentenced to imprisonment, and since time served during pretrial confinements counts against the time that will be served under the eventual sentence, this is really not a deprivation of liberty; it is simply front-loading the imprisonment so that part of it is served before conviction. It is likely that some judges who deny pretrial release to defendants they believe guilty think that way. But some defendants who are thought to be guilty by judges are subsequently acquitted or receive no or little prison time, so there is a loss of liberty for them. It is probably true that most judges are fairly accurate in predicting which defendants are likely to be convicted—more accurate than in predicting which defendants will commit crimes or flee in "the meantime."[7] But we will never know for sure, because the decision to confine may well produce many undisclosed false positives. These mistakes remain invisible because confined defendants who would not have fled or committed crimes have no opportunity to show that they have been erroneously confined.

There are, however, technological developments that could, if more widely employed, help reduce at least some of the false positives and negatives. Electronic monitoring of defendants is being used in some places on some defendants who would otherwise be confined. Arm or leg bracelets transmit signals that alert law enforcement if a defendant leaves his permissible locations or if he tries to remove it. In some cases, armed guards secure house arrest. But these alternatives to incarceration are expensive, which gives rise to another conundrum: if the defendant is required to pay the cost of monitoring, it will be reserved for the wealthy, or at least the non-indigent. It is unfair to have differential treatment based on economic status—though this is inherent in monetary bail as well.[8]

Today many judges refuse to allow defendants who can afford to pay for monitoring to do so, on the ground that would discriminate against those who could not afford to pay for monitoring. This approach to "equal justice," produces "equal injustice," and denies those who can afford monitoring the right to be free pending trial because some can't afford it. It brings everyone down to what the poor can afford. Inequality is pervasive throughout the criminal justice system: the wealthy can afford better lawyers, investigators, jury consultants, daily transcripts, and other expensive legal assistance that raise the likelihood of acquittal or a more favorable plea bargain. Under the "logic" of denying monitoring to those who can afford it because others can't, should wealthy defendants in general be brought down to the level of the poorest defendants so as to avoid inequality? Or should non-wealthy defendants be brough up to the level of the wealthiest? That utopian solution would be as impossible in the area of criminal justice as in health care, education, housing, and other aspects of life where money matters. But it would be reasonable to take steps in the direction of making monitoring more accessible to the poor rather than less accessible to the wealthy.[9]

Electronic monitoring technology is not that expensive—far less than individual guards. If the law were to require the government to pay for electronic monitoring, and if no defendant could be confined unless such monitoring were insufficient to protect against flight or violence, at least some of the conundrum could be avoided. It would not be a perfect solution. There would still be some defendants who are so violent or so likely to flee that electronic monitoring, even coupled with home confinement, would not be enough. But many, perhaps most, of those confined today, would be eligible for modified release if all defendants, even those who couldn't afford it, were provided, at government expense, the option of electronic monitoring or home confinement.

There might be some wealthy defendants, with access to private planes or other expensive means of escape, who would not be eligible for release based on electronic monitoring alone, but who might be eligible based on twenty-four-hour armed guards surrounding the house. I have had such cases and persuaded the judge to allow my client to pay the high cost of such surveillance. I would not expect the government to pay that kind of money. But neither would I advocate denial of pretrial release to such a defendant solely on the ground that other defendants could not afford it.

Whichever way one comes out on the difficult question of whether the wealthy should be denied the right to pretrial freedom with expensive guards because the poor cannot afford to pay for such guards, that issue involves only a small number of individuals. If the government were legally obliged to pay the relatively small amount needed for electronic monitoring—as distinguished from the large amount needed for twenty-four-hour surveillance by guards—the major conflict between the presumption of innocence and the reality of crime and escape would be ameliorated. The vast majority of defendants who are today held in abysmal pretrial conditions would be allowed to remain free with governmentally paid electronic monitoring of the conditions of their release. This might well result in a decrease in the number of defendants willing to plead guilty in exchange for a reduced sentence, since the pretrial detention of such defendants—often in horrendous conditions—gives prosecutors considerable leverage in eliciting guilty pleas. The cost to the taxpayer would be relatively small, compared to the benefits to the presumed innocent defendants who are now confined because they can't pay bail or the cost of monitoring.

Requiring the government to pay the cost of electronic monitoring could significantly reduce the number of false positives (confined defendants who would not do violence or escape if freed under monitoring) without significantly increasing the number of false negatives (monitored defendants who do violence or escape). This would be a worthwhile and reasonable tradeoff and should be done.

SENTENCING

The jurisprudential debate about the role of prevention in the criminal justice system has often focused on its role in criminal sentencing. In actual practice, as distinguished from philosophical theory, neither extreme view of prevention has been adopted. Criminal sentencing reflects a composite rationale incorporating several distinct, but overlapping, goals: incapacitation of dangerous defendants; specific deterrence of the particular defendant; general deterrence of potential criminals; rehabilitation of the defendant; retribution against the defendant for the crime he committed; restitution to the victim of the crime; and other, less easy to catalogue or define, elements.[10]

The inclusion of past-looking factors such as retribution does not negate the important role played by prevention in criminal sentencing, especially if we define prevention more broadly than simply constraining the capacity of a particular defendant from recidivating.

Defined broadly, few would join Kant in denying any legitimate role to prevention in criminal sentencing. The question is how much of a role should be given to prevention of future crimes and how much to retribution for past crimes. Obviously, in some cases there is a direct correlation between the two: career armed robbers or serial rapists are both future dangers and also deserving of serious retribution for what they have done. They will likely receive a significant sentence without the need to parse the precise weight given to the future and the past.

But there will be some criminals for whom it will matter whether the future or past are most important. I have litigated several such cases involving situational crimes (often family) that the prosecution acknowledged are not likely to recur, but that call for retribution for what has occurred. In such cases the defendant is culpable but not dangerous. There are even death penalty cases that fit into that category. I sought a commutation of the execution of a man named Brandon Bernard who while a teenager participated in a brutal double murder, but by his mid-thirties had become totally rehabilitated and was doing much good for fellow prisoners.[11] The president acknowledged his rehabilitation and that he posed no future danger. But he concluded that the past crime was so horrendous that it deserved no compassion. So he denied the commutation and the man was executed. This outcome would have pleased Kant and other retributivists who favor the death penalty, but not those who seek to balance the various aims of criminal punishment.

In the death penalty context, some states do require a balance between the past and future. They require both that the past crime be especially heinous, and that the defendant be especially dangerous. In Texas, a particular psychiatrist—colloquially known as "Dr. Death"—could be counted on to predict that defendants subject to possible execution fit into that latter category, despite the reality that the alternative to execution was life imprisonment without possibility of parole.[12]

Predicting dangerousness over a defendant's lifetime—future criminality—is not quite as daunting as predicting it for the short period between arrest and judgment, but it is daunting nonetheless. Another difference is that in the pretrial bail context, the decision regarding future dangerousness, must generally be explicit. The judge must find it and declare it. In the sentencing context, on the other hand, it needn't be explicit. It can be rolled into a general conclusion combining all the permissible aims of sentencing, without separating out the individual weight attributed to each. It is, therefore, less subject to scrutiny on judicial review or in academic evaluations. But implicit predictions of future criminality do play a role in much sentencing, though a less visible one than in pretrial decisions.[13] Predictions play an even more prominent role in decisions to release prisoners on parole, before the expiration of their formal sentence. They also play a dispositive role regarding the preventive detention of convicts who have completed service of the sentence they received for their past crime or crimes but who are deemed to be a continuing danger. It is to this issue that we now turn.

POST-SENTENCE PREVENTIVE DETENTION

Several states have enacted post-sentence preventive detention laws for alleged sexual predators or other special categories of convicted offenders. Under these laws, that vary from jurisdiction to jurisdiction,

the government asserts the power to keep certain allegedly dangerous criminals with high rates of recidivism in confinement after they
have completed serving their sentence for their past crime or crimes,
explicitly in order to prevent them from committing future crimes.[14]
(They also have to register as sex offenders, another less intrusive preventive mechanism.) In other states, this form of explicit post-sentence
prevention detention is unnecessary because the original sentence for
past crimes incorporates an implicit power to detain. Long sentences,
such as life imprisonment or indeterminate sentences, such as twenty
years to life, often include eligibility for parole after a portion of the
sentence has been served.[15] This sort of sentence, purportedly for past
crimes, empowers the parole authorities to engage in implicit preventive
detention to prevent future crimes. Since parole authorities generally
have enormous discretion and are rarely subject to meaningful review,
this implicit form of preventive detention may be even more troubling
from a civil liberties perspective than the explicit form that exists in
some states. In the explicit form, the burden is on the state to prove
that the inmate would continue to be dangerous after release. It must
prove a positive, though not necessarily beyond a reasonable doubt.
In the implicit form—long sentence, subject to parole—the burden
is on the inmate to prove a negative: that he will not be dangerous if
released. Moreover, the former is generally subject to more testing
review than the latter.

There is, of course, an inevitable relationship between punishment
for past crimes and detention based on predictions of future crimes.
The past generally is the best predictor of the future, so decision-
makers will base their predictions of future criminality largely on
convictions for past crimes.[16]

The problems regarding sentencing go well beyond the difficulty
of predicting future violence and determining what weight, if any, to
give it. Sentencing today is plagued by unfairness. The primary cause
is what is called "the trial penalty"—additional years given to defendants who invoke their constitutional right to go to trial and make
the prosecution prove its case beyond a reasonable doubt to a jury.

Supporters of this unfairness argue that it is a "reward" for waiving trial, rather than a "punishment" for invoking a constitutional right. This is sophistry. What if a Republican operative were to offer to pay money to any Democratic voters who waived their rights to vote and stayed home? He would be charged with bribery. Why is giving a defendant a lower sentence for waiving his right to trial constitutionally different from giving a higher sentence for invoking that right? It is not as if there is one "right" sentence—say, ten years for armed robbery—and the defendant gets five if he waives and fifteen if he invokes his right. That, too, would be wrong. But today there is no abstract "right" sentence. Those who invoke the right to trial simply get higher sentences than those who waive. That is why approximately 90 percent of defendants engage in plea bargaining, rather than risking trial, conviction, and the "penalty"—or "non-benefit."

Encouraging (or coercing) pleas rather than trials is the way the system keeps functioning: if 90 percent of defendants demanded their right to trial, the system would collapse of its own weight. The best proof of this truism is that when a legal aid agency in New York City wanted to protest poor conditions, they didn't strike, they simply pleaded all their defendants not guilty! That brought the system to a grinding halt.[17]

So, until something is done about the trial penalty, our sentencing system will remain unfair and broken. The nature of the crime itself will continue to play a role in sentencing. So will the nature of the criminal and his alleged propensity to recidivate. But an overlarge role will continue to be played by a factor that bears little or no relationship to the legitimate goals of punishment, namely, the defendant's willingness to waive his constitutional right to trial.[18]

Let us get back now to the explicit preventive detention of criminals who are alleged to remain dangerous after they have served their sentence. Although the numbers of inmates currently confined on this basis is relatively small, because of the sentencing reasons stated above, the issue is an important one. This is pure preventive detention: confining someone not based on what they have done—he has already served his sentence for that, if he was previously convicted—but solely on the basis of a prediction of what he might do in the future. It is not quite as bad as testing every citizen for criminal tendencies and confining those who "fail" even if they never did anything wrong, but it raises profound issues, even if it is limited to criminals who have served their time for past crimes.

The logical extension—or at least the slippery slope—of continuing the detention of allegedly dangerous criminals who have completed their sentences for past crimes, is to apply this predictive mechanism to criminals who have already been freed and are living at liberty, but who pose a continuing risk of sex crimes, terrorism, or other serious harms. This is not generally authorized today in the United States,[19] but it is a short step from continuing the confinement of those still in prison who have completed their original criminal sentence. Another somewhat longer step would be to eliminate the requirement of a conviction for a past crime altogether and employ genetic factors (XYY chromosomes),[20] psychiatric history, affiliation with violent groups, testing, Internet posting, a strong motive, or other allegedly predictive factors. This step would bring us closer to the science fiction machine described on page 10.

The "slope" from preventive detention after completion of the sentence is indeed slippery especially absent rigorous jurisprudential limits to this well-intentioned *Brave New World*[21] or *Minority Report.*[22]

JUDICIAL PRONOUNCEMENTS

Some judges, legal historians, and other experts have argued that any form of preventive detention is incompatible with the Anglo-American rule of law and the Constitution. The late Justice Robert Jackson put it this way: "The jailing of persons by the courts because of anticipated but as yet uncommitted crimes [cannot be reconciled with] traditional American law."[23] He cautioned that "imprisonment to protect society from predicted unconsummated offenses [is] unprecedented in this country [and] fraught with danger of excess."[24]

As I showed in chapter 1, academics have expressed the absolutist view that it is categorically wrong to punish anyone *not for what he has already done, but for what he may hereafter do.* This may be true as a matter of judicial philosophy, but a review of history demonstrates that it is somewhat overstated.

The catalogue of preventive detention measures that have been employed over time runs long and deep. Every society has incapacitated—through detention or other means—people believed to be dangerous before they have committed any crimes. During wartime, many nations, including our own, Great Britain, Israel, Canada, Australia, and other democracies, have preventively detained wide categories of people based on the prediction that they might engage in terrorism, sabotage, espionage, or other disloyal acts. These preventive decisions have not, for the most part, been based on what these people *did*, but rather on who they *are*: enemy aliens; ethnically or religiously related to enemies; politically sympathetic to enemies; immigrants from countries that are now enemies; and other groups suspected of disloyalty or dual loyalty. For some, of course, the prediction of future harm is predicated, at least in part, on evidence of past harm, though the evidentiary standards for establishing past misconduct are generally lower than for proving crimes.

The detention of far more than 100,000 Americans of Japanese descent in camps following Japan's attack on Pearl Harbor is perhaps the most notorious and best-known example of mass detention based on racial stereotypes and erroneous predictions.[25] Other democracies have also detained people suspected of disloyalty during wartime or other emergencies on the basis of predictions of future harm. "Martial law," such as that declared for Hawaii after Pearl Harbor, provided a justification for decisions to detain allegedly disloyal or dangerous citizens and aliens.

Nor has preventive detention been limited to national emergencies. Throughout history, the mentally ill have been detained based on a combination of factors, including the prediction that if allowed to be free, they might cause harm to themselves or others. They have also been sterilized, lobotomized, shocked, and drugged, based on a combination of diagnoses, a prognosis, and prediction.

In sum, therefore, the predictive state continues a long history of trying to anticipate and prevent retail crime by individuals or groups by making often questionable predictions based on factors including race, ethnicity, loyalty, political affiliation, mental status, prior history, immigration status, and other characteristics and acts. Millions of people have been detained on the basis of predictions that if they were allowed to remain free, they would or might commit future crimes or other dangerous acts. And they have been detained for tens of millions of person-years without a clear jurisprudential basis.

When I began my research on preventive detention back in the mid-1960s, more Americans were being confined on the basis of predicted future harms than for convictions of past crimes. The largest proportion of these preventively detained inmates were in mental institutions and in jails based on a denial of bail.[26] Since that time, many institutionalized mental patients have been released, and many of them have been convicted of crimes. But there are still far too many individuals who are currently confined based on questionable predictions and vague laws.

This is an unacceptable deprivation of freedom and civil liberties in any democracy under the rule of law. If the preventive state is to continue in its commendable goal of reducing crime by predicting and confining future criminals, it must be cabined by a jurisprudence that fairly balances security and liberty.

CHAPTER 4

PREVENTIVE POLICE INTERVENTIONS

From Searches and "Stop and Frisks" to
Shooting or Choking Suspects

Police and other law enforcement officials play both preventive and reactive roles in relationship to criminal conduct. They seek to prevent future crimes by patrolling the streets, engaging in "stop and frisks," investigating threats, employing undercover agents, monitoring suspicious communications, using video and high-tech intelligence gathering, and by employing other tactics, some more questionable than others.

At the same time, and by somewhat similar mechanisms, they seek to solve crimes that have already been committed. The lines between preventive and reactive measures are not always clear. There are often elements of both at the same time.

Consider the controversial and contentious issue of the use of deadly force to apprehend and subdue a suspected criminal. Police actions in these cases are designed to bring to justice individuals suspected of committing past crimes, but also to prevent them from escaping and committing possible future crimes. This is especially so in light of high rates of recidivism for many types of crimes and criminals. Arresting and convicting a suspected criminal for past crimes may prevent—or at least delay—him from committing future crimes.

Recall the transformative events surrounding the arrest, restraint, and death of George Floyd. The alleged crime for which he was arrested was relatively minor—passing a counterfeit $20 bill—but he did have a record of more serious crimes. Upon his arrest, Floyd engaged in conduct that could be described as uncooperative and somewhat resistant. The arresting officers were never in real danger, beyond the risk of a kick. Nor could he have escaped. Officer Derek Chauvin administered what is called "maximal restraint technique" and placed his knee on Floyd's shoulder or neck for a considerable period of time. The cause of his subsequent death was the subject of legal, scientific, and media dispute, but a jury concluded that Chauvin was guilty of murder. They found all the elements of murder: act, intent, causation, result. The mental element was disputed, as was causation, but the jury found them beyond a reasonable doubt.

There can be little doubt that the police overreacted to the immediate danger actually presented to them and employed excessive force under the circumstances. The difficult questions are how much force and of what kind would be appropriate under circumstances such as those presented by the Floyd case. Certainly not lethal force. But what constitutes lethal force is disputed. The maximal restraint technique (MRT) is always potentially lethal—as are many police techniques for apprehending and subduing a subject—though in the vast majority of cases it causes only minimal damage. But even a slight risk of death or serious injury does not seem warranted to subdue an uncooperative, even resistant, suspect in a $20 counterfeiting case. But once the suspect has been arrested and is resisting, it does not much matter what the originally suspected crime was. What matters most are the immediate dangers to the police and the longer-term dangers to the public if the suspect is allowed to escape.

The Supreme Court provided some general guidance on these issues in 1985 in a fleeing-felon case.[1] It subjected the difficult decision by police officials whether to shoot a fleeing felon to a rough cost-benefit analysis, and in doing so stated a preference for one type of error over another. In *Tennessee v. Garner*, a policeman shot and killed an unarmed suspect fleeing from arrest for a suspected home burglary. The young man was climbing a link fence and would probably have escaped had he not been shot. The majority found the shooting to be unconstitutional under the Fourth Amendment that prohibits unreasonable "seizures" (in addition to unreasonable searches). The court had previously articulated a "balancing test" as the "key principle" in evaluating the reasonableness of searches or seizures: "We must balance the nature and quality of the intrusion on the individual's Fourth Amendment interests, against the importance of the governmental interests alleged to justify the intrusion."[2]

The justices then struck that balance against the use of lethal force to prevent the escape of an unarmed fleeing felon who posed no immediate danger to the policemen who were chasing him. "It is not better that all felony suspects die than that they escape."[3] In articulating this rule, they expressed a constitutional preference in the context of that case for a false negative (failing to shoot an escaping felon) over a false positive (killing a suspect who posed no immediate danger, but whose escape would thwart justice and might pose a future danger).

They did not quantify this balance, by saying, for example, that it is better for ten suspects to escape than for one to be killed, but some such unquantified preference was implicit in the decision.

> The use of deadly force to prevent the escape of all felony suspects, whatever the circumstances, is constitutionally unreasonable. It is not better that all felony suspects die than that they escape. Where the suspect poses no immediate threat to the officer and no threat to others, the harm resulting from failing to apprehend him does not justify the use of deadly force to do so. It is no doubt unfortunate when a suspect [who] was in sight escapes, but the fact that the police arrive a little late or are a little slower afoot does not always justify killing the suspect. A police officer may not seize an unarmed, nondangerous suspect by shooting him dead. The Tennessee statue is unconstitutional insofar as it authorizes the use of deadly force against such fleeing suspects.[4]

The Court articulated a different preference for situations where the suspect poses dangers to the police or public:

> Where the officer has probable cause to believe that the suspect poses a threat of serious physical harm, either to the officer or to others, it is not constitutionally unreasonable to prevent escape by using deadly force. Thus, if the suspect threatens the officer with a weapon or there is probable cause to believe that he has committed a crime involving the infliction or threatened infliction of serious physical harm, deadly force may be used if necessary to prevent escape, and if, where feasible, some warning has been given.[5]

Again, the Court provided no quantified guidance as to the degrees of danger that would make it "reasonable" to shoot. Instead, it used general terms such as "serious," "probable cause," and "reasonable" to convey the constitutional preferences with regard to different types of errors. But it clearly expressed the constitutional preference for false negatives over false positives in situations where the fleeing felon poses no danger other than escape.

This type of cost-benefit balancing, either with or without explicit quantification, should be required of all intrusive police decisions, whether preventive or reactive. The relevant factors will differ depending on the nature, seriousness, duration, and other characteristics of the intrusion. But the need to balance liberty against security and to assign relevant values to each will be similar.

Contrast the use of deadly force by police with the far less intrusive police tactic of "stop and frisk." In 1968, the Supreme Court established the constitutional criteria—in effect the ratio of false positives to true positives—for a brief "seizure" and less intrusive "search," such as a pat-down. It ruled that the more demanding "probable cause" is not required for this lesser intrusion into the privacy and bodily integrity of the suspect:

our evaluation of the proper balance that has to be struck in this type of case leads us to conclude that there must be a narrowly drawn authority to permit a reasonable search for weapons for the protection of the police officer, where he has reason to believe that he is dealing with an armed and dangerous individual, regardless of whether he has probable cause to arrest the individual for a crime. The officer need not be absolutely certain that the individual is armed; the issue is whether a reasonably prudent man in the circumstances, would be warranted in the belief that his safety or that of others was in danger. And in determining whether the officer acted reasonably in such circumstances, due weight must be given not to his inchoate and unparticularized suspicion or "hunch," but to the specific reasonable inferences which he is entitled to draw from the facts in light of his experience.[6]

In subsequent cases, the High Court applied this type of sliding scale analysis to a variety of governmental intrusions, ranging from aerial photography,[7] to seizing garbage,[8] to GPS technology,[9] to sound images of the interior of dwellings.[10]

The justices did not always get it right, at least in my view. But they generally accepted the principle that the false positive to true positive ratio should reflect an appropriate balance between liberty and security. The precise nature of that ratio will depend on the circumstances, and absent a more quantitative jurisprudence, will generally be a matter of judicical discretion subject to appropriate review. This recognition of the need to strike a constitutionally appropriate balance is a good first step toward constructing a jurisprudential framework for analyzing preventive police interventions.

A recent phenomenon involving deliberately induced false positives demonstrates the difficulty of creating rules that can control all situations. It is called "swatting." The police receive a call falsely reporting that a violent crime is in progress at a given address. The crime can be an armed home invasion, an act of domestic violence, a terrorist attack, a hostage situation, or anything else requiring immediate police response. My wife and I were recently victimized by swatting. We were awakened in the middle of the night by loud banging on our door and shouts to "Open the door immediately or we will break it down." When we opened the door, we were greeted by six policemen with drawn guns. We were told to show our hands and remain outside while they searched the apartment.

The police intrusion was, of course, a false positive and so intended by the caller, but the police did the right thing because they could not know it was a false positive, and if they did not respond, it could have turned out to be a catastrophic false negative—a real criminal and potentially lethal act. So they correctly took the risk of creating a disturbing false positive rather than taking the risk of a far more dangerous false negative.

This exceptional situation—a deliberately induced false positive—should not discourage the development of a jurisprudence that governs most typical situations in which false positives are the unintended consequences of a process designed to produce more true than false positives.

CHAPTER 5

THE PREVENTIVE STATE AND MILITARY ACTION

Preventive warfare is as ancient as warfare itself. Nations predicting or fearing an attack from enemies have often decided to strike first. There are numerous examples throughout history of preventive military action. Edward Gibbon, in *The Decline and Fall of the Roman Empire*, described a particularly brutal example:

> On the appointed day, the unarmed crowd of the Gothic youth was carefully collected in the square or Forum; the streets and avenues were occupied by the Roman troops, and the roofs of the houses were covered with archers and slingers. At the same hour, in all the cities of the East, the signal was given of indiscriminate slaughter; and the provinces of Asia were delivered, by the cruel prudence of Julius from a domestic enemy who, in a few months, might have carried fire and sword from the Hellespont to the Euphrates.[1]

Machiavelli approved of Julius's preventive measures designed to "foresee [crises] and to make every effort to prevent them." He analogized military threats to medical ones:

For if you see them coming well in advance, then you can easily take the appropriate action to remedy them, but if you wait
until they are right on top of you, then the prescription will no
longer take effect, because the disease is too far advanced. In
this matter it is as doctors say of consumption: In the beginning
the disease is easy to cure, difficult to diagnose; but, after a
while, if it has not been diagnosed and treated early, it becomes
easy to diagnose and hard to cure. So, too, in politics, for if you
foresee problems while they are off (which only a prudent man
is able to do) they can easily be dealt with; but when because
you have failed to see them coming, you allow them to grow
to the point that anyone can recognize them, then it is too late
to do anything.[2]

There was precedent for Julius's preventive slaughter. The Bible
recounts several instances of biblical heroes taking preventive actions
based on the precept that "if someone comes to kill you, rise up and
kill him first."[3] These include the Jews of Persia who feared being killed
by the king's evil advisor Haman. In order to prevent this predicted
genocide, the Jews acted preemptively and "struck down all their
enemies with the sword, killing and destroying them."[4]

Today's Persia, now called Iran, poses a contemporary threat
of genocide against the nation-state of the Jewish people, Israel. If
Iran were to develop a nuclear arsenal and the capacity of deploying it against Israel, which the mullahs have called a "one-bomb
state" capable of being destroyed forever by one successful nuclear
attack, it could kill millions of Jews and Arabs. So, the issue very
much in the forefront is whether Israel and/or the United States
should engage in preventive military action to destroy, or at least
set back, Iran's nuclear arsenal program (as it did with Iraq and
Syria in the past).[5]

Military and quasi-military preventive actions can take several
forms, ranging from sabotage, to targeted assassinations, to an all-
out air and ground attack on nuclear facilities. Israel and the United

States have long been involved in ongoing preventive steps short of an all-out attack on Iran. The United States, over Israel's objection, is also involved in diplomacy, designed to constrain and delay Iran's development of a nuclear arsenal. If all this fails, and if it becomes likely that Iran is about to cross the threshold into making a deliverable nuclear weapon, the pressure on Israel to act, with or without the assistance and/or approval of the United States, will increase considerably. As I wrote back in 2015:

> No democracy can afford to wait until such a threat against its civilian population is imminent. Both Israel and the United States should have the right under international law to protect their civilians and soldiers from a threatened nuclear holocaust, and that right must include—if that is the only realistic option— preemptive military action of the sort taken by Israel against the Iraqi nuclear reactor at Osirak in 1981, especially if such action can again be taken without an unreasonable number of civilian casualties.[6]

Even if the number of likely casualties on both sides is high, there may be a cost-benefit case for preventive military action, because the cost of not taking such action may be far greater.

As detailed on pages 12–13, a prime example of the cost of the false negative of not taking preventive military action is provided by not-so-distant history. In the mid-1930s, after Hitler came to power and began building a military machine in violation of the Versailles Treaty, Britain and France—which were strong militarily but war weary—could have taken preventive military action against a still weak, but war hungry, Germany. Joseph Goebbels was surprised that "they didn't do it"—until it was too late.[7] Tens of millions of innocent people died as a result of this false negative failure to act.

There is also the dilemma of false positives, perhaps best illustrated by the United States and British attacking Iraq in 2003, based on erroneous information that led to a false prediction that Iraq was about to develop weapons of mass destruction capable of being used against the United States and its allies.

Then there is the concern that authorizing preventive military action will provide aggressors with an excuse for waging war. Both Germany and Japan claimed they were acting preventively when Germany invaded Poland and Japan attacked America's Pacific fleet at Pearl Harbor. Although they probably would not have done anything different absent the transparently false excuse of prevention, their actions demonstrate that nearly all aggressive military attacks can be "justified" by the benign language of "prevention."

Then there is the difference between a "preemptive" and "preventive" military action. The former suggests predicting and preventing an imminent attack, as Israel claimed in 1967 when it destroyed the Egyptian and Syrian air forces before they could take off and attack Israel. That claim has been disputed by those who argue that the Egyptians and Syrians were bluffing and would not have attacked. But Israel had a dual justification for its military action against Egypt, which had blocked the Strait of Tiran from Israeli shipping. That constituted a casus belli—an act of war—that justifies a reactive military response.

There will often be mixed justifications for a preemptive attack.[8] Were Israel to attack Iran's nuclear facilities today, it would have a reactive as well as preventive justification, since Iran fired hundreds of rockets and drones at Israeli targets in 2024.

In 1973, Israel failed to take preemptive action that might have reduced the large number of Israeli casualties that Egypt inflicted when it attacked on Yom Kippur. Israeli intelligence had information about the planned Egyptian attack, but it was warned by the United States not to wage a preemptive war because it had done so only six years earlier, and this time Egypt had not committed any actions that would justify a reactive attack. So, there was no mixed justification, as there had been in 1967. Israel's failure to take preemptive military action proved to be a serious false negative.

Preventive or preemptive warfare poses the usual dangers implicit in any actions based on uncertain prediction. There is the danger of false positives, as in the mistaken United States attack on Iraq. And there is the danger of false negative, as in the mistaken failure of Great Britain and France to attack German's growing capacity for aggressive warfare, and in Israel's failure to preemptively attack Egypt in 1973. Israel also failed to prevent the Hamas attack of 2023, but that was the result of an intelligence failure, not a decision to refrain.

Then there are the uncertain actions and inactions that historians judge differently. How would a preventive attack on Iran's nuclear program be judged by history? Whichever decision is taken (or not taken) will be more under conditions of probability not certainty. That is the nature of preventive warfare.

There may also be mixed justifications for a purely preventive attack, such as the bombing of Iran's nuclear facilities, if that were to take place. The primary motive for such an attack would be preventive—that is, to forestall Iran's future development of a nuclear arsenal, months ahead. But Iran has also engaged in acts that constitute a casus belli against Israel, both directly and indirectly, through its surrogates Hezbollah in Lebanon, Hamas in Gaza, and the Houthis in Yemen. Israel would be justified in reactively attacking Iran for these and other attacks, but its justification is enhanced by its legitimate need to prevent Iran from securing and deploying—as it promised (and also denied) it would do—a nuclear arsenal. This is especially the case, since Iran may be correct in describing Israel as "a one-bomb state." It is also relevant that Israel would not retaliate for the nuclear destruction of Tel Aviv by destroying Teheran. So prevention, rather than deterrence, may be its only realistic option. Former Israeli prime minister Menachem Begin announced after he authorized the preventive destruction of Iraq's nuclear program that even if Tel Aviv had been destroyed by an Iraq nuclear bomb, he would not authorize the retaliatory bombing of Baghdad: "That is not our morality...the children of Baghdad are not our enemy."[9] Israel also has a dual justification for attacking Hamas in the aftermath of the October 7 massacres, which Hamas has sworn to repeat. Israel has the right to retaliate and to prevent reoccurrence.

Israel has been accused of killing too many innocent civilians in its legitimate efforts to neutralize as many guilty terrorists as possible. In the terms employed by this work: too many false positives (civilians) in relation to too few true positives (combatants). This issue demonstrates the difficulty of placing so complex an issue into a simple true-versus-false positives and negatives analytic framework. It is accurate to say that every civilian killed (or wounded) is a false positive, and that every terrorist killed is a true positive. Further, every terrorist *not* neutralized for fear of killing innocent civilians is a false negative. The problem, among others, is that in a war against terrorism, the status of being an innocent civilian—which I call "civilianality"—is very much a matter of degree. To illustrate this reality, I have devised a nuanced concept I call "the continuum of civilianality," about which I have asked the following question:

> The news is filled with reports of civilian casualties, comparative civilian body count, and criticism of Israel for causing the deaths, injuries and "collective punishment" of civilians. But just who is a "civilian" in the age of terrorism, when militants don't wear uniforms, don't belong to regular armies, and easily blend into civilian populations?[10]

My answer is that we need a new vocabulary to reflect the realities of modern warfare. A new term should be introduced into the reporting and analyzing of current events in Gaza and elsewhere: "the continuum of civilianality" (or the continuum of culpability). Though cumbersome, this concept aptly captures the reality and nuance of warfare today and provides a fairer way to characterize those who are killed, wounded, and punished.

There is a vast difference—both moral and legal—between a two-year-old who is killed by an enemy rocket and a thirty-year-old civilian who has allowed his house to be used to store Katyusha rockets or to hide hostages. Both are technically civilians, but the former is far more innocent than the latter. There is also a difference between a civilian who merely favors or even votes for a terrorist group and one who provides financial or other material support for terrorism.

Finally, there is a difference between civilians who are held hostage against their will by terrorists who use them as involuntary human shields, and civilians who voluntarily place themselves in harm's way in order to protect terrorists from enemy fire. The late military head of Hamas in Gaza, Yahya Sinwar, once said that civilians who have been killed are "necessary sacrifices" that "infuse life onto the veins of this nation."[11] It was part of his strategy to weaken Israel's international standing by causing the IDF to kill civilians. Nonetheless, there are differences among totally innocent civilians, totally complicit "civilians" and civilians in different places along the continuum of culpability.

These differences and others are conflated within the increasingly meaningless word *civilian*—a word that carried great significance when uniformed armies fought other uniformed armies on battlefields far from civilian population centers. Today this same word tends to equate in the public mind the truly innocent with guilty accessories to terrorism.

The domestic law of crime in virtually every nation reflects this continuum of culpability. For example, in the infamous Fall River rape case (fictionalized in the film *The Accused*), there were several categories of morally and legally complicit individuals: those who actually raped the woman; those who held her down; those who blocked her escape route; those who cheered and encouraged the rapist; and those who could have called the police but did not.

No rational person would suggest that any of these people were entirely free of moral guilt, although reasonable people might disagree about the legal guilt of those in the last two categories. Their accountability for such a group rape is surely a matter of degree, as is the accountability for terrorism of those who work with the terrorists.

It will, of course, we difficult for international law—and for the media—to draw the lines of subtle distinction routinely drawn by domestic criminal law. This is because domestic law operates on a retail basis—one person and one case at a time. International law and media reporting about terrorism tend to operate on more of a wholesale basis—with body counts, civilian neighborhoods, and claims of collective punishment.

But the recognition that "civilianality" is often a matter of degree, rather than a bright line, should still inform the assessment of casualty figures in wars involving terrorists, paramilitary groups, and others who fight without uniforms—or help those who fight with uniforms.

Turning specifically to the fighting between Israel and Hamas, the line between Israeli soldiers and civilians is relatively clear. Hamas rockets target and hit Israeli restaurants, apartment buildings, and schools. They are sometimes loaded with antipersonnel ball bearings designed specifically to maximize civilian casualties. The massacres of October 7 clearly targeted mostly civilians, many at a peace concert.

Hamas terrorists on the other hand, are difficult to distinguish from those "civilians" who recruit, finance, harbor, and facilitate their terrorism. Nor can women and children always be counted as civilians, as some news, medical, and human rights organizations claim. Terrorists increasingly use women and teenagers to play important roles in their attacks. Hamas counts anyone under eighteen—even a seventeen-year-old mass murderer and rapist—as "a child." They also count all adult females simply as "women," who the media is falsely led to presume are all "civilians."

If this "continuum" were to be adopted, it would be informative to learn how many of the alleged "civilian casualties" fall closer to the line of complicity and how many fall closer to the line of innocence. Every civilian death is a tragedy, but some are more tragic than others.

Because civilianality is on a continuum, so too are false positives in the context of killing or wounding adults claimed to be civilians, rather than combatants (also on a continuum).

To operate within the analytical framework suggested in this book, a percentage of civilianality (or "combatantality") could be assigned. For example, a full-time Hamas terrorist would be counted as 0 percent on this scale of civilianality, (or 100 percent on this scale of combatantality) whereas a five-year-old child would be at 100 percent. Different percentages could be assigned to "civilians" who allowed their homes to be used to store or fire rockets, volunteered as human shields, or contributed money or goods to the terrorists. A different number could be assigned to those who participated in the kidnapping or holding of hostages, or who revealed information about the Israeli targets while working in Israel before the attack. The fact that any such person was a woman or a teenager would not affect their status—only their individual actions would.

When these considerations are factored in, the ratios change dramatically. Assuming that the Hamas-controlled Gaza Health Services is accurate in the total number of Gazans that have been killed in the fighting, that number deliberately fails to distinguish between combatants and "civilians," even by Hamas' warped definitions. Instead, Hamas claims that most of those reported to have been killed are women and children, without disclosing how many of these are female or teenage terrorists. Nor do they distinguish between Gazans killed by misfired terrorist rockets and those fired by Israel.[12]

So we really have no reliable information on how many totally innocent 100 percent civilians—young children, the very old, and others who have nothing to do with Hamas—have actually been killed. We do have some idea, based on Israeli data, of the number of combatants who have been killed, including commanders. According to the IDF, that number is only slightly less than half the total number of Gazans killed, suggesting a ratio of between one or two civilians killed to every combatant killed.[13]

It is possible therefore, based on nuanced evaluations of the actual status of all of these killed in Gaza, that the number of totally innocent civilians and combatants may be roughly equal.[14] Even if one accepts the Hamas figures and rejects the Israeli ones, the ratios of civilians (properly defined) to combatants (properly defined) is unlikely to exceed two to one, or at most three to one—that is, two or three civilians killed for every combatant killed.[15] If this is the case, the IDF would have achieved among the lowest ratios of false to true positives ever in an urban terrorist war in which the terrorists deliberately hide among civilians.[16]

Preventive or preemptive warfare poses the usual dangers implicit in any actions based on uncertain predictions, but the stakes are generally much higher. Whatever military or quasi-military decisions are taken (or not taken) will be more under conditions of probability than certainty. That is almost always the nature of preventive warfare, especially urban warfare involving "civilian" human shields. It is also true of preventive or preemptive military actions waged by conventional armed forces against other conventional armed forces.

CHAPTER 6

PREVENTING TERRORISM

*Military Actions, Detention, Waterboarding,
and Other Extreme Tactics*

Terrorism is, of course, both a genre of crime and also of warfare. It often involves attacks causing mass casualties such as those inflicted against the United States on 9/11 and Israel on Oct 7, 2023. The 9/11 attack was a criminal act of war committed by non-state actors against a state and its citizens. The Oct 7 attack was committed by Hamas, a political and military terrorist group that controlled the Gaza Strip. The responses were a series of military actions by the United States and Israel that were both reactive and proactive: they were designed both to punish past crimes and to prevent future ones. The primary expressed goal was to prevent a recurrence by Al Qaeda, Hamas, Hezbollah, and similar groups that operated in certain states. But some actions—such as the killing of Osama Bin Laden who no longer presented a realistic future threat—was likely primarily reactive and punitive.

In addition to military action in Afghanistan, Gaza, and other places, there was extensive law enforcement activity that resulted in the detention of suspected past and future terrorists. There were also mixed military–law enforcement activities that resulted in detention and extreme tactics such as waterboarding, threatening, and other measures that were sought to be justified as necessary to obtain information that could prevent future attacks, especially imminent ones. The FBI, CIA, military and private entities, as well as the Israeli Shin Bet and Mossad, participated in these activities, both abroad and at home. British, French, and other intelligence services also played a supporting role.

As with so many other future-looking preventive measures, they were directed against people who were suspected of involvement in past acts of terrorism. But suspicion that is thought to justify preventive actions may not rise to a level of certainty necessary to prove criminal culpability, so mere suspicion is often used as a basis for preventive detention, extreme interrogation, and other preventive measures designed to obtain information deemed useful in the ongoing war against terrorism. This necessarily produces considerable numbers of false positives.

There are two basic objections to detention and what some call torture, while others call it "extreme measures" directed at suspected terrorists. The first is moral and legal: it is simply wrong and illegal to detain individuals on the basis of mere suspicion that doesn't rise to the level of provable crime; and it is far more unjustified to subject these people to what would be "cruel and unusual" punishment—waterboarding and other forms of physical and psychological pressures—if applied to American criminals serving prison sentences.[1] The second objection is empirical: critics claim that these extreme measures—whatever they are called—are ineffective: they simply don't work because anyone will tell you anything they think you want to hear, whether true or false, to stop the pain.

The first objection is subject to resolution by the courts and legislators. The second, which may influence the first, is largely a matter of degree. The reality is that some torture sometimes produces some useful preventive intelligence from some detainees. The legal and moral question, therefore, is whether securing that information justifies those measures.

If torture never produced any future-looking actionable intelligence, there would be no justification for ever employing it simply as retaliation for past terrorist acts.[2] If, on the other hand, an hour of medically supervised, nonlethal excruciating pain—in other writings[3] I have used the example of a sterilized needle being shoved under the fingernails—would demonstrably produce real-time intelligence that could prevent a 9/11 or October 7–type attack or a nuclear explosion in a populated area, the case for allowing the preventive use of such torture would strengthen. This would be so for some utilitarian moralists (like Jeremy Bentham) and some pragmatic jurists (like Oliver Wendell Holmes). For absolutists (like Immanuel Kant) the evidence would not matter, but for many it would. So, what does the evidence show?

The evidence is mixed, depending in part on the precise question. If the question is the zero-sum one: does any type of torture ever produce any actionable intelligence that may save lives, the answer is beyond dispute. The evidence clearly shows some such examples. The *Washington Post* has recounted a case from 1995 in which Philippine authorities tortured a terrorist into disclosing information that may have foiled plots to assassinate the pope and to crash eleven commercial airliners carrying approximately four thousand passengers into the Pacific Ocean, as well as a plan to fly a private Cessna filled with explosives into CIA headquarters. For sixty-seven days, intelligence agents beat the suspect "with a chair and a long piece of wood [breaking most of his ribs], forced water into his mouth and crushed lighted cigarettes into his private parts"—a procedure that the Philippine intelligence service calls "tactical interrogation." After successfully employing this procedure they turned him over to American authorities, along with the lifesaving information they had beaten out of him. Other such "successes" have been documented as well.[4]

History shows that brave members of the French Resistance disclosed the locations of dear friends under Nazi torture, that the French in Algeria used torture effectively, as did Great Britain. The United States Court of Appeals for the Eleventh Circuit justified the use of "rack and pinion techniques" to successfully uncover the whereabouts of kidnapped victims.[5]

If the question is a comparative one: does torture work *better* than other information-gathering methods, then the answer is less certain. Indeed, the evidence can never definitively prove or disprove the comparative advantages and disadvantages of torture. This absence of proof, taken together with the powerful moral arguments against torture, make a compelling case against its use—except perhaps in the most compelling but least likely situations, such as the ticking nuclear bomb.

Professor Marcy Strauss posed the following hypothetical situation:

> The police in New York have, in custody, a suspect known to be a terrorist. He is adjudged perfectly lucid and rational. He admits to planting a nuclear weapon in the heart of the city and informs the police that the bomb will go off within five hours. Other evidence obtained by the police make the threat totally credible. There is no possibility of evacuation and no possibility of finding the bomb, except by the most amazing stroke of luck, during this time. Would I really argue that the state must refrain from torture in this case?"[6]

For those who would quickly say no, she adds the following sequel:

> The state tortures this suspect—physically mutilating him until he is near death, all to no avail. He is a fanatic and no amount of pain inflicted upon him will cause him to thwart his mission. So, the police turn to the only option they have available. They bring into the interrogation room, the suspect's beloved four-year-old son. And they start to torture the child. As they strip the child naked, the suspect says nothing. They strike the child. The suspect reacts; he is obviously tormented by the treatment of his child. The police apply electrodes to the child's genitals. After the child is shocked several times, the suspect caves in and tells the police the location of the bomb. This scenario would clearly fit the "ticking bomb" exception. Arguments that the "ends

justify the means," or defense of others could easily justify such an action. Yet a nation that intentionally and brutally harms an innocent child has clearly lost its moral bearings. The United States should not become such a nation.[7]

Professor Strauss fails to provide us with the false negative implications of her hypothetical. The torturers do not want to lose their moral bearings by torturing the four-year-old child, and so the nuclear weapon explodes, killing a million innocent civilians, including the terrorist's four-year-old child along with thousands of other children. Does that outcome restore the moral bearing of the nation? Would any leader actually make the decision to sacrifice a million of its civilians on Strauss' altar of morality?

Dostoyevsky's character Ivan might well disagree about the "moral bearing" of a leader who chose to prevent a mass casualty bombing. He asks Alyosha:

> "Imagine that you are creating a fabric of human destiny with the object of making men happy in the end, giving them peace at last, but that it was essential and inevitable to torture to death only one tiny creature—that by beating its breast with its fist, for instance—and to found that edifice on its unavenged tears, would you consent to be the architect on those conditions? Tell me the truth."[8]

So might Bentham, who offered the following utilitarian justification for torturing a guilty torturer to prevent the further torture of innocent victims:

> Suppose an occasion were to arise, in which a suspicion is entertained, as strong as that which would be received as a sufficient ground for arrest and commitment as for felony—a suspicion that at this very time a considerable number of individuals are actually suffering, by illegal violence inflictions equal in intensity

to those which if inflicted by the hand of justice, would univer-
sally be spoken of under the name of torture. For the purpose
of rescuing from torture these hundred innocents, should any
scruple be made of applying equal or superior torture, to extract
the requisite information from the mouth of one criminal, who
having it in his power to make known the place where at this
time the enormity was practising or about to be practised, should
refuse to do so? To say nothing of wisdom, could any pretence
be made so much as to the praise of blind and vulgar humanity, by the man who to save one criminal, should determine to
abandon 100 innocent persons to the same fate?[9]

The decision whether to torture one guilty person in an effort
to prevent the deaths of multiple innocent people is a classic tragic
choice about which reasonable people can and do disagree. There is
no uncontroversial and absolutely correct answer.

In an effort to restrict the use of torture only to the most extreme
and unlikely situation, and limiting the type of torture to nonlethal
intrusions that only cause temporary pain, I proposed the requirement
of a "torture warrant," to be granted only by the Chief Justice of the
United States, based on specific and very narrow criteria. This proposal
generated considerable controversy and criticism, which included
false claims that I advocated the routine use of torture, have given
"thumbs up to torture," and can be characterized as "Torquemada
Dershowitz,"[10] a reference to the notorious torturer of the Inquisition.
This forced me to reiterate my position unambiguously:

I am generally against torture as a *normative* matter, and I would
like to see its use minimized. I believe that at least moderate forms
of non-lethal torture are in *fact* being used by the United States
and some of its allies today. I think that if we ever confronted an
actual case of imminent mass terrorism that could be prevented
by the infliction of torture we would use torture, (even lethal
torture), and the public would favor its use. That is my empirical
conclusion. It is either true or false, and time will probably tell.

I then present my *conditional normative* position.

I pose the issue as follows: If torture is in fact being used and/or would in fact be used in an actual ticking bomb mass terrorism case, would it be *normatively* better or worse to have such torture regulated by some kind of warrant, with accountability, record-keeping, standards, and limitations. This is an important debate, and a *different one* from the old, abstract Benthamite debate over whether torture can ever be justified. It is not so much about the substantive issue of torture, as it is over accountability, visibility, and candor in a democracy that is confronting a choice of evils."[11]

I hope we will never be forced to confront this terrible choice of evils, but if we do, Democratic accountability requires us to confront it transparently. In the aftermath of 9/11, the CIA apparently believed that we might be facing an equally serious threat. According to the *New York Times*,[12] it waterboarded Khalid Sheikh Mohammed in the "mistaken belief…that a nuclear attack in the United States was imminent" and that he had information that could prevent it. Mohammed "wanted to keep talking about" 9/11, but the interrogators thought he was trying to distract them "from another looming crime," so they "slam[med] him into a wall" and waterboarded him 183 times. They were not as interested in securing a confession of past crimes, including 9/11, as in obtaining real-time "actionable intelligence" in order to prevent a future mega-crime. There was no democratic accountability for this unlawful interrogation because it took place at "a secret, overseas CIA prison." Had the torture warrant proposal been implemented, there would have been accountability both before and after the application of extreme measures.

Accountability should be required of all terrible choices of evil thrust upon us by the evil of terrorism.

Consider the tactic of targeted assassination, widely employed by the United States,[13] Israel,[14] and other democracies. The virtue of this tactic is precisely that it is targeted, rather than random or collective, with the goal of minimizing "collateral damage" to innocents. The vice is that the target is selected by functionaries—military and/or political—without articulated criteria. Critics call it "extrajudicial" killing, ignoring the reality that all lethal military attacks are extrajudicial. This has led some civil libertarians to propose a warrant requirement similar to what I had proposed for torture. This "assassination warrant" would require the preapproval of a judge, whenever possible. Ironically, some of the same people and groups that were adamantly opposed to torture warrants strongly support assassination warrants. They argue that torture is always wrong, whereas assassinations can sometimes be justified. But for those of us who believe that death is worse than nonlethal pain, their categorical objection is not compelling.

Other preventive measures include spying, both on the ground and from the air, cyber intercepts and attacks, electronic tracking of cell phones, as well as infiltration of terrorist cells and organizations.

It is the nature of these measures that the precise results are often not known or acknowledged by either side. Secrecy is often the key to success. And even when the results are apparent, credit is not always publicly taken—at least not in real time. Accordingly, it is difficult for scholars and critics to assess the pros and cons of various preventive measures. One point should be clear: when it comes to fighting terrorism—as with all intrusive preventive measures—there are no free lunches or perfect solutions. The costs must always be weighed against the benefits. And in democracies, the key questions are: Who gets to do the weighing? Who gets to make the life-and-death decisions?[15] And who gets to know about them, whether before or after the fact?

CHAPTER 7

PREVENTIVE MEDICAL INTRUSION

Preventive medicine is generally noncontroversial and a "win-win" for good health and liberty. Most people seek to prevent illnesses and do not require compulsions to undergo safe, preventative procedures or medications.

Some religious groups eschew all medical interventions. Compulsion—especially when it involves children—is occasionally required. I recall a case, when I was a law clerk, when an adult Jehovah's Witness was about to die without a blood transfusion, which she refused on religious grounds. The judge compelled her to have it, saying that since she refused it, he—the judge—compelling it did not cause her to violate her religious beliefs. It would be he, the judge, who would go to hell, not her! She lived, but refused to thank him, for fear that doing so would suggest her acquiescence. (I have no idea whether he went to hell!)

Generally, judges will refuse to compel competent adults to receive preventive or curative medical interventions for noncontagious illnesses, and will allow them to die, but they will compel parents to allow such intervention for their children.[1]

I recall another case early in the history of kidney transplantation, in which a hospital refused to transplant a kidney from one healthy twin to the other twin whose kidneys were failing. Despite the desire of the parents and the two underage twins for the donation, the surgeon refused to remove the kidney from the healthy child, because although it would save the life of the recipient, it would not be medically beneficial to the donor. The law required a medical benefit to the underage subject of the medical procedure, and removal of a healthy kidney provided no such benefit to *that* twin. The court authorized the operation on the ground that it would be psychologically beneficial to the donor to know that he prevented the death of his sibling.[2]

These complex cases are, of course, the exception to the simple desire by the vast majority of people to receive safe preventive medical interventions. The practical problems connected to such health-protective and illness-prevention measures relate primarily to their limited availability, especially to those who may need them most—the poorest and least well educated. Most of those who are aware of, and can afford, preventive benefits are eager to obtain them, if not always sufficiently motivated.

There are, of course, some potential risks and downsides to all medical interventions, including preventive ones, as exemplified by concerns exposed by Dr. Siddhartha Mukherjee, as quoted on pages 22–23. But for the most part, it is uncontroversial that the advantages of scientifically validated preventive measures outweigh any disadvantages. The major controversies arise in the context of compelled medical intrusions, such as vaccinations to prevent the spread and often lethal consequences of COVID or other communicable diseases.

COVID and its variants moved the issue of preventive medical intervention—compelled vaccinations, masking, and other intrusions into bodily autonomy and integrity—to the forefront of legal and moral debate. Until recently, only a small number of ideological opponents of all vaccines—anti-vaxxers—objected to the routine inoculations against smallpox, polio, measles, and other contagious and dangerous diseases. Virtually all children receive them, and they have succeeded in virtually wiping out many of these plagues of the past. But COVID appeared in the midst of a highly politicized era, when many issues divided our nation along partisan, ideological, racial, religious, and other lines. And the usual preventive public health decisions and actions became part of that divide. The number and intensity of anti-vaxxers—those who believe that vaccines are dangerous and ineffective—increased.

In the course of the debate, a related group has become more vocal: those who are not necessarily opposed to vaccinations themselves on medical or scientific grounds—indeed, many of them have voluntarily been vaccinated. But they are strongly opposed to *compelled* vaccinations for anyone. Their opposition is political, constitutional, ideological, and religious. Obviously, these two categories of objection to vaccine mandates overlap in practice. Many of those who are against compelled vaccinations also are skeptical of the safety and efficacy of the vaccines. Some argue that their personal skepticism is not enough to stop them from resolving doubts in favor of being vaccinated themselves, but it is enough to stop the government from compelling others to be vaccinated against their wishes.[3]

In theory, there seems to be general agreement with the influential principle stated by John Stuart Mill: "That the only purpose for which power can be rightfully exercised over any member of a civilized community, against his will, is to prevent harm to *others*. His *own good*, physical or moral, is not a sufficient warrant."[4] In other words, no competent adult should be compelled to do anything—take a vaccination or medicine or undergo other procedures—if the only result of not taking a preventative measure would harm him alone. Noncontagious illnesses such as cancer, diabetes, heart attack, or stroke fit into this category. But compulsion may be warranted if the result of non-compulsion is to increase the likelihood that others will be infected with a potentially lethal or serious contagious illness. I have summarized this libertarian position in the context of cigarette smoking with the following quip: everyone has the absolute right to inhale but not to exhale! The resulting disagreement is largely empirical and a matter of degree: Does compelling Mr. X to be vaccinated against his will, "prevent harm to" Ms. Y or only to Mr. X himself?

And is the prevented harm to Ms. Y sufficiently great to warrant the compelled intrusion into the bodily anatomy of Mr. X?

Different varieties of COVID highlight the difficulty of answering these questions to the satisfaction of everyone, even those who may essentially agree with Mill. Among the most important variables are lethality, contagion, and the efficacy of the vaccine in reducing each. The evidence suggested that the initial iterations of COVID were apparently more lethal but perhaps less contagious than the Omicron variation (and some that have followed).[5] The available vaccines were less effective in preventing contagion from Omicron, but more (or at least equally) effective in preventing deaths and hospitalizations.[6] These conclusions are not static and vary with changing medical realities. What is constant is the debate over state compulsion in the context of preventing pandemics and other medical catastrophes.

An outbreak of measles in 2024 in Florida raised an interesting variation of the traditional arguments relating to compulsory vaccination. The measles vaccine was so effective—97 percent—that it virtually wiped out that highly contagious disease. So some parents refused to have their children vaccinated on the self-serving premise that since their children were not likely to catch it, why expose them even to the infinitesimal risks associated with vaccination. The result was a small outbreak. It was argued therefore by public health officials that the only fair approach was to compel vaccination for all children, so that those whose parents did not want them to be vaccinated would not be allowed to share the benefits of universal vaccination without also sharing the risks.[7]

The case for compulsion, at least in some contexts, was set out early in our history by General George Washington as he wrote to Dr. William Shippen:

> Finding the smallpox to be spreading much and fearing that no precaution can prevent it from running thro' the whole of our army, I have determined that the Troops shall be inoculated. This Expedient may be attended with some inconveniences and

some disadvantages, but yet I trust, in its consequences, will have the happiest effects. Necessity not only authorizes but seems to require the measure, for should the disorder infect the Army in the natural way and rage with its virulence we should have more to dread from it than from the Sword of the Enemy.[8]

I own a letter from Washington following up on this directive and demanding that "inoculation may not be delayed a moment longer," because it is "an object of great importance" to securing victory over the British.

Compulsion in the military is often the rule and does not serve as a precedent for compelling civilians. The president of the United States is the commander in chief of the military, but not of the citizenry, which has no commander, except the rule of law.

In 1905, the Supreme Court upheld the constitutionality of the following Massachusetts law that compelled ordinary citizens to be vaccinated:

Whereas, smallpox has been prevalent to some extent in the city of Cambridge, and still continues to increase; and whereas, it is necessary for the speedy extermination of the disease that all persons not protected by vaccination should be vaccinated; and whereas, in the opinion of the board, the public health and safety required the vaccination or revaccination of all the inhabitants of Cambridge; be it ordered, that all the inhabitants of the city who have not been successfully vaccinated since March 1st, 1897, be vaccinated or revaccinated.[9]

Henning Jacobson, a resident of Cambridge, said he had experienced a bad reaction from a vaccination "when a child," so he refused to comply and was charged by "a criminal complaint." He was found guilty and sentenced to "pay a fine of $5 and the court ordered that he stand committed until the fine was paid." He appealed his conviction to the highest court in Massachusetts, which affirmed it.

Jacobson then sought review by the United States Supreme Court on due process grounds. Justice John Marshall Harlan rejected Jacobson's argument:

> The authority of the state to enact this statute is to be referred to what is commonly called the police power,—a power which the state did not surrender when becoming a member of the union under the Constitution. Although this court has refrained from any attempt to define the limits of that power, yet it has distinctly recognized the authority of a state to enact quarantine laws and "health laws of every description."[10]

Harlan then acknowledged that:

> No rule prescribed by a state, nor any regulation adopted by a local government agency acting under the sanction of false legislation, shall contravene the Constitution of the United States, nor infringe any right granted or secured by that instrument.[11]

Justice Harlan then applied these generalities to Jacobson's specific appeal:

> Upon the principle of self-defense, of paramount necessity, a community has the right to protect itself against an epidemic of disease which threatens the safety of its members.[12]

The court then addressed an objection that may sound familiar to current ears: that some doctors "attach little or no value to vaccination as a means of preventing the spread of smallpox, or who think that vaccination causes other diseases." Justice Harlan's answer also has relevance to today's debate:

> we must assume that when the statute in question has passed, the legislature of Massachusetts was not unaware of these opposing

theories, and was compelled, of necessity, to choose between them.[13]

Finally the court appended a caveat to its broad decision:

Extreme cases can be readily suggested. Ordinarily such cases are not safe guides in the administration of the law. It is easy, for instance, to suppose the case of an adult who is embraced by the mere words of the act, but yet to subject whom to vaccination in a particular condition of his health or body would be cruel and inhuman in the last degree. We are not to be understood as holding that the statute was intended to be applied to such a case, or, if it was so intended that the judiciary would not be competent to interfere and protect the health and life of the individual concerned.[14]

But the court distinguished such an "extreme" situation from claims that a vaccination may be "distressing, inconvenient, or objectionable to some."[15] In such cases, it is "the duty of the constituted authorities primarily to keep in view the welfare, comfort and safety of the many and not permit the interests of the many to be subordinated to the wishes or convenience of the few."[16]

The court thus upheld the Cambridge compulsory regulation as constitutional.

A quarter century later, the Supreme Court cited the Jacobson case in support of the worst and most dangerous "preventative" medical intervention decision in American history. The High Court, in an opinion authored by Justice Oliver Wendell Holmes and joined by Justice Louis Brandeis and six other justices, cited Jacobson in support of mandatory sterilization of "epileptics and feeble minded" persons. Here is the Court's dangerously overboard reasoning:

We have seen more than once that the public welfare may call upon the best citizens for their lives. It would be strange if it could not call upon those who already sapped the strength of the state for those lesser sacrifices, often not felt to be such by those concerned, in order to prevent our being swamped with incompetence. It is better for all the world, if instead of waiting to execute degenerate offspring for crime, or let them starve for their imbecility, society can prevent those who are manifestly unfit from continuing their kind. The principle that since sustains compulsory vaccination is broad enough to cover cutting the Fallopian tubes. Jacobson vs. Massachusetts, 197 U.S. 1, 25 S.Ct. 358, 49 L. Ed. 643, 3 Ann. Cas. 765. Three generations of imbeciles are enough."[17]

This imbecilic decision lasted less than "three generations" until it was overruled in 1942.[18] It turned out that Carrie Buck, who was forcefully sterilized, had been misdiagnosed and was neither "feeble minded nor an imbecile." She was only one of what almost certainly were many—far too many—false positives. Of course we can never know how many false negatives—unsterilized people whose children would have killed or been starved—might have resulted from the opposite decision, but it is likely that it would be far fewer than the thousands that were sterilized. The only "imbeciles" involved in the Buck case were the brilliant judges who argued illogically that a precedent involving contagious diseases that were easily diagnosed was fully applicable to a noncontagious condition that was easily misdiagnosed.

This dangerous precedent was cited by Nazi doctors in the 1930s and then by defendants at the Nuremberg trials in defense of their decisions to kill the feeble-minded.[19]

The unjustified extension of the "principle that sustains compulsory vaccination" to the very different and far more intrusive "cutting of the Fallopian tubes," should give every civil libertarian—indeed every decent person—pause. So should the uncritical acceptance of the science of the day by the Supreme Court. It is difficult to imagine a more absurd argument than equating a single compelled injection to a permanent deprivation of the right to reproductive freedom. Yet, eight justices accepted this argument over only one dissent. Eugenics—the preventive improvement of humankind by regulating reproduction as in animal breeding—was all the rage at Harvard and other universities in the 1920s. This misapplication of biologic Darwinism to social Darwinism clearly influenced Holmes, Brandeis, and other justices and policymakers.[20] It reminds us that we must be skeptical of scientists (and judges), and the abuse of science, while encouraging scientific experimentation, innovation, and validation.

The current scientific consensus would seem to support the commonsense conclusion that universal or near universal vaccination may help to slow down the spread of COVID, even if vaccinated individuals can still be contagious. The precise mechanisms through which this occurs may not yet be fully known with scientific certainty, but governments have the power to err on the side of safety benefits, when the cost of such safety is nothing more intrusive than an injection, as distinguished from the cutting of Fallopian tubes. But just because a rightly decided case was used as a precedent for a wrongly decided case does not by itself disqualify the original precedent, though it suggests caution in expanding it. Many "good" precedents have been used to bolster "bad" cases.

Buck v. Bell was wrong on the science, wrong on the morality, and wrong on the law. It should give us pause in compelling any intrusion into bodily integrity. But pausing is different than not acting to try to prevent the spread of a highly contagious and dangerous disease. We often have no alternative but to act, even in the absence of complete scientific certainty and unanimity of opinion.

The case for mandatory vaccinations against COVID or other potentially lethal contagious diseases, as a last resort, with reasonable exemptions, is a hard one. But a solid constitutional and philosophical case can be made for it, if it becomes necessary to prevent catastrophic consequences, which I surely hope it never does.

Hard cases sometimes do make bad law, but the courts cannot avoid making decisions in hard cases, including those pitting the safety of the many against the liberty of the few. All we can ask is that they make wise decisions based on the best available science, and that they remain open to reconsider their decisions as the science changes.

Prevention of serious medical harms justifies many costs, but the virtues of prevention can be seductive and can blind advocates to hidden costs, especially in liberty and basic rights. Striking the appropriate balance is one of the most challenging responsibilities of decision-makers in a democracy governed by the rule of law. A viable jurisprudential framework will assist in weighing the comparative costs of inevitable errors. There was no moral, legal, or scientific basis for tolerating the enormous number of false positives sterilized on the basis of eugenics claims. There is far more justification for accepting a small number of false positives to prevent the large number of false negatives that would result from the failure to inoculate against preventable, contagious illnesses.

History will judge whether the proper balance is being struck in the present and future, as it has judged—often negatively—with regard to the past. New rights are often based on lessons learned from past wrongs.[21] A viable jurisprudence should be based on these lessons and what they teach us about current conflicts.

CHAPTER 8

PREVENTING A GLOBAL ENVIRONMENTAL CATASTROPHE

In the film *Don't Look Up*,[1] the planet Earth is faced with an extinction threat in the form of a comet that could wipe out all human life. (Think Superman and the destroyed planet Krypton.) The film is intended as a metaphor for global weather changes and the failure of many leaders to "look up" and see the danger, so that they can take preventive action. It is in the nature of political leaders in democracies to focus on today's issues, tomorrow's elections, but not on the preventable dangers their successors may face, especially in the distant future—and in politics anything beyond the next election is the distant future.

It is not surprising, therefore, that although the problem of global weather changes has been evident to scientists for decades, it has only recently been prioritized by political leaders. Like so many other issues, it too has become subject to divisive partisan disputes. Democrats have focused more on the dangers of global weather changes, whereas Republicans, with some exceptions, have emphasized the dangers of taking steps that reduce energy supplies, increase short-term employment, and other alleged consequences of prioritizing the prevention of longer-term environmental damage.

There are some on the right who deny altogether the dangers of climate change, claiming that they are inevitable and natural, rather than humanly induced and preventable. And there are some on the left who deny the dangers of cutting back on energy needs and of reduced employment, claiming that we can take steps that prevent environmental damage without compromising other values. But most reasonable people agree that there must be some trade-offs, at least in the short term, and that preventive steps must be taken now, before the effects of climate change become irreversible.

There is, however, considerable disagreement about matters of degree and prioritization of concerns. What seems clear is that some steps can be taken now that can have some impact on the environment in general and climate control in particular, and that these steps will not be entirely cost free in terms of their short-term impact on energy, jobs, and other factors. As with other efforts to prevent bad outcomes, the questions in a democracy involve priorities, costs, and benefits—and, most important, who gets to decide these important policy issues that may impact future voters more than current ones.

Preventing environmental harm is different than preventing other harms, in that the preventive actions generally do not involve immediately depriving individuals of specific rights, such as liberty or choice. So both the costs and benefits of preventive actions seem somewhat less immediate and intrusive.

Protecting the environment requires macro as well as micro decisions. These decisions, such as banning or limiting fuels or other chemicals that contribute to environmental damage, do impact some individuals and businesses more than others, but the rules are general in nature, as distinguished from decisions to confine or target dangerous individuals or deny them access to guns. In this respect they are closer to decisions to engage in preventive wars or to fluoridate entire water-supply systems in an effort to prevent or reduce future dental problems.

Some such decisions can be made by individuals, such as using electric cars, solar panels, and carbon neutrality. Most require governmental action.

In an important respect, however, these decisions all involve cost-benefit analysis and a weighing of true and false positives and negatives. The most salient difference is the time horizon. Most preventive interventions are designed to have an immediate impact on violence, health, and safety. Those involving the environment tend to be longer term in their benefits but shorter term in some of their costs (e.g., lost jobs, more expensive energy costs). Accordingly, they are often less palatable to politicians who tend to focus on today and tomorrow, rather than on decades to come. Put another way, the benefits of preventive environmental measures that will accrue to our grandchildren are undervalued, while the costs to the current generation—to us—are overvalued in weighing false negatives (failing to take measures that might prevent damage) against false positives (taking measures that might not). This is especially so today, because protecting the environment has become a divisive political issue in which partisan versions of the "truth" often prevail over more objective scientific evidence.

The evidence of climate change and other environmental hazards seems obvious. Less obvious and more controversial are the immediate steps that should be taken by governments to prevent or slow down these dangerous changes. In a democracy, these decisions should be made by the political branches of government, informed by objective science. But when partisan and generational biases distort this process, the likelihood of balanced decisions diminishes.

Advocates of aggressive preventive environmental interventions have proposed what they call "the precautionary principle in environmental science."[2] The principle is defined as follows: "when an activity raises threat of harm to human health or environment, precautionary measures should be taken even if some cause and effect relationships are not fully established scientifically." It contains four central components: "taking preventive action in the face of uncertainty; shifting the burden of proof to the proponents of the threatening activity; exploring a wide range of alternatives to possibly harmful actions; and increasing public participation in decision making."

The original term for the principle was *Vorsorgeprinzip*, which in German means "foresight principle," which, according to its advocates, emphasizes "anticipatory action—a positive, active idea" rather than mere precautions. Translated into the language of this book, it means that governments should err on the side of avoiding any false negatives based on inaction, even at the risk of many false positives, i.e., taking actions that turn out to be useless or even negative.

A more technical terminology for the two types of errors that can occur when preventive action is contemplated based on uncertain prediction is "type 1 and type 2 errors." Advocates of environmental action argue that employing this formulation in "setting type 1 and type 2 error rates" may be biased against preventive intervention:

> Errors due to sampling variability are routinely quantified. However, standard practice has led to a conservatism that perhaps hinders precautionary action. When a scientific investigation is designed to test a hypothesis, there are two kinds of errors that one seeks to minimize. A Type I error is the mistake of concluding that a phenomenon or association exists when in truth it does not. (Technically, the Type I error is rejecting the null hypothesis when it is really true. The paraphrasing above, while valiantly railed against by statistic teachers everywhere, is the way it is thought of in everyday practice.) By convention, Type I (or alpha) errors are guarded against by setting that error rate low, usually at 5%. In other words, the finding must be so strong that there is less than a 5% probability that this result would have been seen by change alone in a world in which no such phenomenon actually exists. In this case the result is called statistically significant (with the clear implication that one is supposed to believe it). The Type II error, failing to detect something that actually does exist, is, by convention, often set at 20% (although practical limitations of sample size often result in a substantially higher or lower Type II error). Twenty percent of the time, a real phenomenon will be missed because the data were not strong enough to convincingly

demonstrate its existence. There is an implicit bias here: the test is set up to be more cautious about falsely detecting something than about failing to detect something.[3]

The above reasoning makes sense when falsely failing to detect and prevent a particular "something" poses greater risks than falsely detecting and trying to prevent that something. But it is dangerous to extend this reasoning to other areas, where false positives should be deemed to be more harmful than false negatives. For example, in the contexts of criminal prosecutions or censorship of free speech (see chapter 9) the opposite reasoning may be warranted. In other contexts, such as gun control and "red flag" laws (chapter 10), a different calculus may be appropriate. There is no one right calculus that fits every situation, as we shall see in the coming chapters. But thinking about the comparative costs and benefits of any actions or inactions is crucial. Constructing a jurisprudential framework for evaluating such decisions is essential to democratic decision-making. But such a framework must explicitly acknowledge the differing values that should be assigned to inevitable type 1 and type 2 errors, depending on the costs of such errors and the anticipated benefits of actions that are being considered. One size does not fit all, and the numbers assigned to errors should be tailor-fitted to these costs and benefits. This is precisely the role of a general jurisprudence of preventive intervention.

CHAPTER 9

PREVENTING DANGEROUS AND/OR OFFENSIVE SPEECH

As long as some humans have been able to speak or write, other humans have tried to prevent them from doing so if their spoken or written words were deemed dangerous, offensive, or in any way undesirable. Censorship is as old as speech, and as enduring. Nearly every society has established mechanisms for controlling and preventing communications. Many governments today have variations on our First Amendment—theoretical protections for free speech against government interference. But these parchment preachments have generally given way to the realities of governmental censorship. "Free speech for me but not for thee," "for my party but not yours," "for my ideology but not yours," "for my truth but not your falsity," "for my religion, not your heresy." These self-serving limitations have been more often the rule in practice than the attitude reflected in the famous quote attributed to Voltaire: "I disapprove of what you say, but I will defend to the death your right to say it."[1] Throughout history, and continuing to this day, most governments have said that if they "disapprove of what you say," they will "defend" their power to censor it—sometimes "to the death" of the disapproved speaker. Today's Russia, under Putin, has continued this double standard, the violation of which can be punished "to the death." Other tyrannical regimes follow suit. Freedom of speech has been and remains the exception throughout the world. Censorship is the rule.

Our own experience as a nation illustrates the distinction between theoretical protection and practical curtailment of speech. In 1791, the United States adopted the First Amendment, which explicitly directed "Congress" to "make no law...abridging the freedom of speech, or of the press."[2] Yet in 1798—just seven years later—Congress enacted, and President John Adams signed, the Alien and Sedition laws, which fundamentally abridged these rights, and imprisoned speakers and writers who dared to "write, print, utter or publish...any false, scandalous and malicious writing or writings against the government of the United States, or either house of the Congress of the United States, or the president of the United States, with intent to defame...or to bring them, or either of them, into contempt or disrepute; or to excite against them, or either or any of them, the hatred of the good people of the United States, or to stir up sedition within the United States, or to excite any unlawful combinations therein, for opposing or resisting any law."[3]

Thomas Jefferson strongly opposed these restrictions on free speech, while George Washington and Alexander Hamilton, though critical of some aspects, generally supported them as necessary war measures during the naval conflict with France.

The statute included explicitly preventive elements: "to stir up sedition," to "excite against them" or to "excite any unlawful combinations...for opposing or resisting any law" or to "encourage" any "hostile designs of any foreign nation." Similar statutes were enacted by several states.

Punishing speech already spoken is designed, at least in part, to deter speech not yet spoken. But sometimes deterrence against future speech by punishing past speech is not enough. Most governments—including our own—deem some potential speech so dangerous that they will seek to prevent it before it is uttered or printed. They seek to accomplish this through prior restraint—such as injunctions—as they tried to do with regard to the Pentagon Papers. I was one of the lawyers who litigated successfully against this effort. That case represented an exaggerated fear of harm, but some such fears are realistic.

Imagine an American publisher announcing that he intended to publish the medical records of all recipients of Medicare or Medicaid. Or all the confidential communications between clients and their lawyers, as well as between parishioners and clergy. Should the government be empowered to prevent the dissemination of such speech? Would such prior censorship constitute "abridging the freedom of speech and of the press" in violation of the text of the First Amendment that demands that Congress (which has been expanded to mean government) "shall make no [such] law"? What would be the correct civil liberties answer to that question? Are there any reasonable First Amendment absolutists who would allow the publication of such speech? Or must every reasonable libertarian acknowledge that there must be some exceptions to what appears to be the absolute prohibition against "abridging the freedom of speech and of the press"? What if abridgement is necessary to protect other constitutional rights, such as to a fair trial? (Gag orders against defendants are another form of prior restraint.)

Some may quibble about the meaning of the wording of the amendment: "Abridging" means "reducing," not totally "banning." "The freedom of speech and of the press," refers to established rules at the time, which did contain exceptions (e.g., libel, slander, obscenity, national security, trade secrets, privileged communications, and others). But regardless of these quibbles, it is clear that the prior censorship of an article that advocated the end of all censorship—and to emphasize its political message insisted on publishing the above "secrets"—would constitute a technical abridgment of the above rights. The honest question is whether such an abridgement would be justified as a matter of law, morality, and democratic values?

The honest answer would depend largely on the specific facts. History has provided many examples of efforts to abridge, indeed to prevent, core speech: the Pentagon Papers case of 1971, the anti-Communist statutes of the late 1940s and early 1950s, and the Alien and Sedition Laws of 1798 being only three. History has also shown that many claims of national security and other pressing needs for secrecy have too often been exaggerated and used as a justification for preventing partisan, ideological, and personal embarrassment, and exposure.

The effort to prevent publication of the Pentagon Papers turned out to be a relatively easy case, because much of the content was stale, already published or not dangerous to national security. It was, however, damaging to the reputations and legacies of some officials. But imagine a radical publisher announcing that he intended to publish the names of every CIA spy, undercover agent, double agent, and information source currently operating in foreign countries. Or the codes that enable the launching of nuclear missiles, or the home address of Supreme Court justices and their families. Should the government be empowered to prevent the dissemination of such national security secrets? History provides few actual examples of intended publications that could justifiably be subject to prior censorship in order to prevent post-publication harm that warranted pre-publication censorship. But this doesn't necessarily mean that there are not—at least in theory—legitimate claims for prior censorship. There most certainly are some such situations—but they are extremely rare.

The prosecution of Julian Assange, who I helped represent, presents a contemporary case about which reasonable people disagree. Gag orders on criminal defendants, like Donald Trump, constitute another controversial issue.

One principle underlying our First Amendment is the so-called marketplace of ideas. Jefferson relied on that theory in a letter he wrote on the twenty-fifth anniversary of the Declaration of Independence. (I own the original of that letter.[4]) In that important response to a minister who suggested censorship of speeches advocating violence, he wrote: "[W]e have nothing to fear from the demoralizing reasoning of some, if others are left free to demonstrate their errors, and especially the law stands ready to punish the first criminal act produced by false reasoning. These are safer correctives than the conscience of a judge."[5] This presupposes an opportunity to respond to false ideas with truthful ones. (It also assumes that truth will prevail over falsehood.) But some genres of speech do not allow for timely response. There is no marketplace of ideas when it comes to the disclosure of legitimate secrets, such as those discussed above. Once out of the bag, there is no complete remedy for these "speeches."

Yet, at least some such unanswerable and harmful disclosures are protected by the First Amendment, and are not subject to prior restraint or censorship under existing law.

Free speech is not free of all costs. It can be dangerous, hurtful, and reprehensible. (I know because I have defended the rights of Nazis, communists, pornographers, and others to engage in such speech.[6]) But is it generally better than the alternative. Sigmund Freud observed that civilization began on the day someone hurled an insult instead of a spear. Insults hurt, but not as much as spears. Nazi speech hurts, but not as much as pervasive censorship—at least in the United States today. Campus rhetoric against Jews and Israel makes life difficult for Zionist students especially since they are often victims of a double standard. The never-ending question all democratic societies face is how to balance the dangers and hurt of some speech against the dangers and hurt of censorship. This complex question becomes even more daunting when the issue is prior rather than only post censorship.

When prior censorship is involved, we have—in addition to the problems surrounding censorship in general—the additional dilemma of how to balance the dangers of false positive prediction against false negatives.

Courts have, on occasion, employed a simplistic approach that implicitly suggests a formula that seeks to balance false positives against false negatives. Judge Learned Hand proposed, as a First Amendment test, the seriousness of the harm discounted by the unlikelihood of its occurrence. This is how he put it: "Clear and present danger depends on whether the mischief of the repression is greater than the gravity of the evil discounted by its improbability."[7] Though his dual criteria—seriousness and unlikelihood—are extremely vague and not easily subject to quantification; they open the door to formulations that are more specific and amenable to at least rough quantification, such as "better ten" than "even one."

In the Pentagon Papers case, the government asked the Supreme Court to allow prior censorship based on its prediction that certain specified harms to our national security would occur if the Papers were published. The Supreme Court refused, the Papers were published, and no harm occurred.[8] If they had been censored, we should never have known whether the government's prediction was valid. We now know that the government's rejected argument was based on a false positive (a prediction of harm that did not materialize) rather than a false negative (a prediction by the media that no harm would result from publication.)

Today, there are efforts to sensor and deter (a form of prevention) genres of speech that have little to do with national security. These include personal secrets (privileged information) or other traditional bases for prior and post-restraint. They also include deeply offensive and hurtful racist, sexist, homophobic, anti-Muslim, anti-Jewish, and other speech targeting vulnerable groups and individuals (fat-shaming, bullying). This issue is playing out on university campuses throughout the country, where most advocates are demanding free speech for "our side" but not for "theirs." The double standard has become *the* standard on many campuses.

Sometime, the censorship claims are based on predictions of future harms, such as physical attacks. The demand to have safe spaces and to feel safe is based implicitly on a prediction that absent censorship, those who hear the speech may be incited to commit certain future physical harms. Often this alleged fear of future physical harms is combined with allegations of present emotional and psychological harms caused as a result of the "victims" simply hearing the offensive speech.

For the most part, the claimed fear that others who hear the offensive speech will be incited to commit physical harms against the victims of such speech is exaggerated. Consider, for example, the justification offered by at least nine Berkeley Law School groups that banned—subjected to prior restraint—all Zionist speakers (that is all speakers who support the existence of Israel as the nation-state of the Jewish people). They claimed that Palestinian students would feel "unsafe" if Zionists were allowed to speak.[9]

This suggests that allowing Zionists to speak would cause violence against Palestinian students. The evidence does not support this prediction. Their demands for censorship could also mean that Palestinian students are entitled to have their anti-Zionist ideas kept "safe" from criticism by Zionists—to protect their ideas from the marketplace. But this is an illegitimate goal under any theory of free speech, as long as the Palestinian "victims" of Zionist speech have the opportunity to "demonstrate their error" and to correct what they regard as the "erroneous" views of the Zionists—or to offer an alternative perspective.

Put in the context of this book, those who censor Zionists on the basis of false predictions of future physical harm are producing false positives. Those who would censor on the basis of protecting anti-Zionist ideas from Zionist responses are violating the spirit of the First Amendment[10] and the Jeffersonian marketplace of ideas. The same is true of attempts by some pro-Israel advocates to prevent anti-Zionist speech on the ground that it makes them feel unsafe. As long as the same standard is applied to all speech, the marketplace should be open to all speech and closed to all violence.

The offensiveness rationale for censorship (both pre- and post-) has been taken well beyond the above examples. Some universities and other institutions have circulated lists of words that should be censored, sometimes formally, other times by peer pressure. These verboten words and expressions—including "field/field work," "master," "submit," "no can do"[11]—are said to remind certain groups of their history of being oppressed, and thus to cause distress. To the extent that this list of forbidden words are merely suggestions, they do not constitute actual censorship, though peer pressure can serve as a powerful constraint on free speech. Self-censoring also distorts the marketplace.

One common rationale for censorship of some speech grows out of Oliver Wendel Holmes's oft-quoted statement that "the most stringent protection of free speech would not protect a man in falsely shouting fire in a theater, and causing a panic."[12] This analogy has been cited to justify censorship of all manner of speech that should be protected by the First Amendment. But as I have argued, it is a dangerously false analogy.[13]

The case that gave rise to the "Fire!"-in-a-crowded-theater analogy—*Schenck v. United States*—involved the prosecution of Charles Schenck, who was the general secretary of the Socialist Party in Philadelphia, and Elizabeth Baer, who was its recording secretary. In 1917 a jury found Schenck and Baer guilty of attempting to cause insubordination among soldiers who had been drafted to fight in the First World War. They and other party members had circulated leaflets urging draftees not to "submit to intimidation" by fighting in a war being conducted on behalf of "Wall Street's chosen few." Schenck admitted, and the court found, that the intent of the pamphlet's "impassioned language" was to "influence" draftees to resist the draft. Interestingly, however, Justice Holmes noted that nothing in the pamphlet suggested that the draftees should use unlawful or violent means to oppose conscription: "In form at least [the pamphlet] confined itself to peaceful measures, such as a petition for the repeal of the act," and exhortation to exercise "your right to assert your opposition to the draft." Many of its most impassioned words were quoted directly from the Constitution.

Justice Holmes upheld the convictions in the context of a wartime draft, finding that the pamphlet created "a clear and present danger" of hindering the war effort while our soldiers were fighting for their lives and our liberty.

The example of shouting "Fire!" obviously bore little relationship to the facts of the Schenck case. The Schenck pamphlet contained a substantive political message to potential inductees, and then—if they so chose—to act on it in a lawful and nonviolent way. The person who shouts "Fire!" in a crowded theater is neither sending a political message nor inviting his listener to think about what he has said and decide what to do in a rational, calculated manner. On the contrary, the message is designed to force action *without* contemplation. The message "Fire!" is directed not to the mind and the conscience of the listener but, rather, to his adrenaline and his feet. It is not an invitation to discuss, argue, or disagree. It is a stimulus to immediate action, not thoughtful reflection. It is—as Justice Holmes recognized in his follow-up sentence—the functional equivalent of "uttering words that may have all the effect of force."[14]

Indeed, in that respect the shout of "Fire!" is not even speech, in any meaningful sense of that term. It is a *clang* sound—the equivalent of setting off a nonverbal alarm, as a congressman—now a former congressman—recently did.[15] Had Justice Holmes been more honest about his example, he would have said that freedom of speech does not protect a kid—or a congressman—who pulls a fire alarm in the absence of a fire. But that obviously would have been irrelevant to the case at hand. The proposition that pulling an alarm is not protected speech certainly leads to the conclusion that shouting the word "Fire!" is also not protected, but it does not lead to the relevant conclusion that the pamphlet at issue is not protected speech.

The core analogy is the nonverbal alarm, and the derivative example is the verbal shout. By cleverly, but dishonestly, substituting the derivative shout for the core alarm, Holmes made it possible to analogize one set of words to another—as he could not have done it he had begun with the self-evident proposition that setting off an alarm bell is not free speech.

The analogy is thus not only inapt but also insulting. Most Americans do not respond to political rhetoric with the same kind of automatic acceptance expected of schoolchildren responding to a fire drill. Not a single recipient of the Schenck pamphlet is known to have changed his mind after reading it. Indeed, one draftee, who appeared as a prosecution witness, was asked whether reading a pamphlet asserting that the draft law was unjust would make him "immediately decide that you must erase that law." Not surprisingly, he replied, "I do my own thinking." A theatergoer would probably not respond similarly if asked how he or she would react to a shout of "Fire!"

Holmes's false analogy created a dangerous precedent that has caused many false positives—censorships of speech that would have caused no harm.

Another important reason the analogy is inapt is that Holmes emphasizes the factual falsity of the shout "Fire!" The Schenck pamphlet, however, was not factually false. It contained political opinions and ideas about the causes of war and about appropriate and lawful responses to the draft. As the Supreme Court reaffirmed in *Hustler v. Falwell* "the First Amendment recognizes no such thing as a 'false' idea."[16] Nor does it recognize false opinions about the causes of or cures for war.

A closer analogy to the facts of the Schenck case might have been provided by a person's standing outside a theater, offering the patrons a leaflet advising them that in his opinion the theater was unsafe in the event of a fire, or structurally unsound, and urging them not to enter but to complain to the building inspectors. Another would be urging patrons to boycott the immoral movie that was being shown. These analogies, however, would not have served Holmes's argument for punishing Schenck. Holmes needed an analogy that would appear relevant to Schenck's political speech but that would invite the conclusion that censorship was appropriate. So he came up with a deceptively inapt analogy that has endured over time and served as a false justification for restricting much free speech.

Shouting "Fire!" in the theater may well be the only jurisprudential analogy that has assumed the status of a folk argument. A prominent historian has categorized it as "the most brilliantly persuasive expression that ever came from Holmes' pen." He is wrong. It is anything but brilliant. It is dumb and misleading. In spite of its hallowed position in both the jurisprudence of the First Amendment and the arsenal of political discourse, it is and was a deliberately deceptive analogy, especially in the context in which it was originally offered. It has lately become—despite, perhaps even because of, the frequency and promiscuousness of its invocation—little more than a caricature of logical argumentation. But despite its illogic, it has been widely employed by special pleaders to curtail expression of which they disapprove.

All of this suggests that freedom of speech for all is under serious attack today from many sources including government institutions, university administrators, social media, and peers. The case for prior restraint based on predictions that harms will result from certain genres of speech is gaining respectability among some academics and even some traditional civil libertarians.[17] This will result in many false positives—that is, censorship and prior restraint based on false predictions of future harms. There may also be cases—though I doubt there would be many—of false negatives: failures to censor that may result in preventable harm.

The preventive state, taken to its extreme, tends to err on the side of cautious censorship rather than risky speech. The so-called precautionary principle urges governmental intrusion in the face of uncertainty or ambiguous evidence. This may well be sound policy in certain contexts, such as the environment or health. But it is not appropriate when it comes to speech. Freedom of speech entails a degree of risk. So does censorship. We must balance those risks in a manner that favors speech over fear.

History teaches that the appetite of the censor is voracious. Once censorship is authorized to protect the perceived interests of some, it will be demanded for others. Refusing to censor in questionable cases will produce some false negatives—some harms that censorship might have prevented. But censoring in doubtful cases will likely cause many more false positives—denial of speech that would not have caused harm. The First Amendment and the open marketplace of ideas mandates the opposite of the precautionary principle in regard to free expression: in the absence of convincing evidence of significant harm, censorship—especially prior restraint—must not be permitted. As with our criminal justice system, it is better for ten "guilty" speeches to be free than for even one "innocent" speech to be censored. The precise numbers are not written in stone, but the concept—erring on the side of more speech and less censorship—is written in the First Amendment.

The Supreme Court in *Smith v. California*[18] implicitly employed this analysis in striking down a law that permitted the conviction of a bookstore owner for possessing obscene books, even if he did not inspect each book to determine whether it was obscene. In doing so the justices distinguished cases involving food manufacturers who were not aware of toxins in the food. The justices essentially said—without putting it precisely that way—that it is better for some food that is not toxic to be withheld, then for even one toxic food to be sold. But when it comes to books, it is better that many obscene books be sold than that ever one constitutionally protected book be self-censored. The Court thus struck different constitutional balances between false positives and false negatives when it came to food, which is not constitutionally protected, and books, which are.

There are extreme cases in which even prior restraint in the form of injunctions is deemed to be insufficient to prevent the anticipated harm of disclosure.

Throughout history, tyrants have killed enemies who they fear will disclose information. Sometimes the information is merely embarrassing to the tyrant. Sometimes it is thought too dangerous to the state or to certain individuals.[19]

George Bernard Shaw quipped that "the ultimate form of censorship is assassination."[20]

There are also less extreme forms of compelled silence that have been employed by democracies in cases where the disclosure of information is believed to pose great dangers. One such case involved an Israel nuclear technician named Mordechai Vanunu (later known as John Crossman) who disclosed details of Israel's nuclear weapons program and threatened to disclose more. He was convicted and sentenced to be held incommunicado so that he could not disclose any further secret information. After eighteen years, he was released on condition that he not leave the country or disclose nuclear secrets. He violated these orders and was again imprisoned.[21]

Eventually he was freed and continued to violate the restrictions while being denied the ability to leave the country.[22]

With the passage of time, the information he continues to disclose has become less dangerous to Israel. Vanunu is regarded as a whistle-blower and hero by some, and a traitor by others.[23]

His case illustrates the extreme measures—short of assassination but harsher than a prior restraint injunction—that some democracies believe they must take in order to prevent the disclosure of secrets that endanger its national security.

A related issue is the timing of disclosures of information. In the early years of the Holocaust, secret information was received by Jewish leaders disclosing the existence of death camps and mass exterminations. It was uncertain at that time whether the information was accurate, exaggerated, or false. There was a debate among these leaders as to whether to disclose this information publicly. Advocates of nondisclosure feared that disclosing this possibly false information would hurt their credibility, if and when more reliable documentation became available. In other words, they did not want to create false positives. Proponents feared false negatives—failing to disclose truthful information. Tragically, the former prevailed, and the information, which turned out to be understated, was withheld for many months.

A jurisprudential framework governing any form of preventive censorship must strike the appropriate balance even in extraordinary situations like the Vanunu case. But it should consider another famous observation—this one truly brilliant by Oliver Wendell Holmes—that "hard cases make bad law."[24] A jurisprudence, if it is to prove useful in the run of ordinary cases should not be limited to the most difficult, extreme, or rare situations, like Vanunu's, involving nuclear secrets. It should provide guidance on the widest range of conflicting claims to freedom of expression, on the one hand, and prevention of serious harm, on the other. Democracies have been struggling with this conundrum since Socrates was required to drink hemlock to prevent the further corruption of Athenian youths.

CHAPTER 10

RED FLAG LAWS AND GUN VIOLENCE

The answer to the provocative question, "Do guns kill or do people kill"? is obvious: guns kill when they are in hands of violent, unstable, and dangerous people. This reality has led to two rather different approaches to preventing or reducing gun crimes. The first focuses on the guns;[1] the second on the people. Both have predictive and preventive elements that include false positives and negatives. Both are controversial. Both raise constitutional concerns.

There can be little doubt that the widespread and rather easy availability of guns in the United States is a factor that contributes to the extraordinarily high level of gun violence in this country.[2] Regardless of the questionable advocacy and partisan statistics put out by gun advocates and manufacturers, the existence of some relationship between the easy availability of guns and the massive violence cannot be denied. It is the most salient variable that distinguishes our country from other roughly comparable countries with far less gun violence.

Our population does not have more mentally ill, criminally inclined, or inherently evil people than other Western nations—certainly not enough more to explain the great disparities in gun violence. Nor do racial tensions, which exist in many parts of the world. Neither does the pervasive media violence—which doesn't recognize national boundaries. Moreover, we confine more dangerous people—convicted criminals, defendants denied bail, sexual offenders, the mentally ill—than most Western democracies that experience far fewer gun crimes. The only salient difference is the number of guns easily available to be bought or stolen by dangerous people.

This is not to argue that tighter gun control would solve the problem. There are already too many guns out there and too many dangerous people who have access to them to roll back the clock. Absent the kind of massive and expensive buy-back program that succeeded in Australia and the United Kingdom, the reality is that we will continue to have more guns than people in the United States, and some of these guns will fall into the hands of dangerous people who will use them to shoot innocent Americans, including children. Others will be used by ordinary people facing extraordinary pressures or unpredictable circumstances. The easy access to guns will sometimes turn what would otherwise be a fistfight into a shooting, or a depression into impulsive suicide. The Second Amendment, as currently interpreted by the Supreme Court, imposes significant barriers to reducing gun violence by means of controlling the guns themselves, since the vast majority of guns are owned by law-abiding people who have a constitutional right to possess them. That is why much of the focus has shifted away from reducing the number of guns to trying to identify in advance the people who are most likely to misuse them to kill and maim.

This focus takes many forms, including so-called red flag laws.

As the *New York Times* reported, "judges in 19 states and the District of Columbia are issuing orders to keep guns out of the hands of people deemed dangerous."[3] The technical name for such orders is "extreme risk protection orders" or "ERPO's," but the common term for the statutory authority to issue them is "red flag laws." A decade ago, two states had such laws. Now there are twenty-one,[4] with more in the works. Most of them are Democratic majority states. Only two are Republican.[5]

Advocates of such laws claim they save lives. Opponents argue that they violate due process because they produce too many "false positives"—too many people have their guns taken away who would never misuse them. Both may be right, at least to a degree.

So the issue is representative of virtually all intrusive preventive decisions based on uncertain predictions: how many false positives (people predicted to commit violence who would not do so) should we be willing to tolerate, in order to prevent how many false negatives (people not predicted to commit violence who would in fact commit such violence). This depends not only on the accuracy of the predictive decision-making process, but also on the values attached to each type of predictive error. For example, in a criminal trial, we aim for accuracy: convicting the guilty (true positive) while acquitting the innocent (true negative). But we know that the system is imperfect— that it sometimes convicts the innocent, while acquitting the guilty. Although we don't know exactly how often each of these mistakes are made, we do know that we assign a different value to each type: a false positive (convicting the innocent) is worse than a false negative (acquitting the guilty). How much worse is the hard question of degree. The Anglo-American system of justice has decided—perhaps arbitrarily—that it is ten times worse. Hence, we declare (at least in theory) that "it is better that ten guilty go free, than that even one innocent be wrongly convicted."

Is the context of allegedly dangerous free speech, we have not assigned a specific number, but we have decided, as a matter of constitutional law, that it is better that some dangerous speech be allowed than for some non-dangerous speech to be suppressed.[6]

How much may depend on the degree of danger, discounted by the unlikelihood of its actual occurrence.[7] The preference for the freedom of speech over the safety of censorship is mandated by the First Amendment. What then is the preference mandated by the Second Amendment, which guarantees the "right of the people to keep and bear arms," because a "well regulated militia [is] necessary to the security of a free State"?

Is the right to own guns parallel to the right of free speech? Are the stakes in avoiding false positives and negatives similar?

These are some of the questions posed by advocates and opponents of red flag laws, each of whom answers them differently.

If, for argument's sake, one puts aside the constraints of the Second Amendment, it would seem clear that allowing a dangerous person access to a gun is worse than denying a non-dangerous person such access. Making a false negative mistake in this context can cost lives, whereas a false positive mistake only results in depriving a citizen of one right—generally for a limited period of time—not his liberty and not his life. For Second Amendment absolutists, such a deprivation is unacceptable, just as for First Amendment absolutists, any censorship is unacceptable. But there are differences, both in degree and kind. To be sure dangerous speech can occasionally cause death or serious injury, as with direct incitement to violence (which is not protected by the First Amendment). But death and/or serious injury are far more likely from a false negative mistake about a dangerous person having access to a lethal weapon. So even if the value at stake in the deprivations—denying a citizen the right to speech versus the right to keep a gun—are similar, the values at stake with false negatives is almost certainly greater with guns than with speech.

Some gun advocates argue that depriving a qualified person his right to bear arms can be life-threatening because he will be deprived of the right to defend himself, but there is little empirical evidence to support the claims that temporarily depriving non-dangerous people of guns will produce more deaths and injury than permitting dangerous people access to lethal weapons.

Others claim that patriots should not be deprived of their right to overthrow a tyrannical government by armed means because that right is a necessary and continuing means of preserving democracy. But this is more of an abstract defense of the Second Amendment than a prediction of immediate harm to individuals.

Inevitably, there will be many false positives under current red flag laws, because they are civil not criminal, and therefore require a lower burden of proof. They are also generally time-limited and require periodic reconsideration, and so the stakes are somewhat lower for a mistake resulting in a gun deprivation. Accordingly, they do not require the constitutional protections accorded criminal defendants. The criteria are vague and open-ended ("danger to self and others"); the standard of proof is lower than in criminal cases; there is no right to counsel; and doubts are generally resolved against the defendant. Advocates of these laws claim that mass shootings have been prevented, but it is nearly impossible to verify such claims, because the nonoccurrence of such an event does not prove it would have occurred absent the invocation of the law. Anecdotal claims may be true, but they are far from conclusive. As an old Yiddish proverb says: "A for-instance is not an argument"—at least not a compelling one.

According to the *New York Times*, "more than 20,000 petitions for extreme risk protection orders were filed from 1999 to 2021," the vast majority of which—more than 18,600—came after the Parkland shootings. In Florida alone, 8,969 such orders were granted since 2018.[8] It is unlikely that all or even most of these prevented actual shootings (false positives).

We also don't know how many requested orders were denied and if any of the denials resulted in shootings (false negatives).

What we do know is that even in Florida, which is known as a pro-gun state, but which also suffered some of the worst mass shootings, the vast majority of requested orders are apparently granted. No judge wants to be in the headlines as the one who refused the order that resulted in the next mass shooting, whereas improperly granting an order does not generate headlines. So when in doubt, take the gun away. "Better safe than sorry," ("A stitch in time").

The takeaway from red flag laws, for purposes of this book, is not to decide whether they are in fact effective in preventing gun violence. We are unlikely to be able to answer that question with any degree of evidentiary certainty. The takeaway relates to the differences in weighting the costs and benefits of true positives and negatives against those of false positives and negatives in the context of gun possession.

To reiterate, in the context of criminal trials, we have a strong bias against false positives (convicting the innocent) over false negatives (acquitting the guilty.) In the context of censoring allegedly dangerous speech, we also have a bias in favor of allowing possibly dangerous speech over censoring speech that may or may not be dangerous. But in the context of guns—as judged by the actual decisions made by judges under red flag laws—our bias seems to be strongly in favor of avoiding false negatives (not taking guns away from possibly dangerous individuals) even if the result is many false positives (taking guns away from individuals who would probably not use them to kill or maim.)

How many false positives we are willing to tolerate in order to avoid how many false negatives in any particular context is a reflection of, and guide to, our values and priorities. The example of different balances struck for differing risks are building blocks for a more general jurisprudence of preventive intervention, as we shall see in the coming chapters.

CHAPTER 11

THE SURVEILLANCE STATE

Information is power, and information about the future is essential to the power to prevent harms. And so, the preventive state necessarily engages in information gathering on a massive scale through widespread government surveillance of its citizens and others. The ongoing development of artificial intelligence in its many variations increases both the accuracy and intrusiveness of Big Brother and Sister. In this respect the preventive state *is* the surveillance state. Without surveillance, many of the most important aspects of prevention are less viable.

The private sector, too, lives and dies through information or lack thereof. Today, more than ever, profit-driven private companies seek, buy, sell, trade, and create information helpful to their bottom line—and largely without the constraints often (but not always) imposed by law on government information gathering. The Fourth Amendment—which prohibits the government from unreasonably interfering with "the right of the people to be secure in their persons, houses, papers and effects"—applies only to governmental "searches and seizures." It does not constrain private companies, although some legislation and regulations do, at least to a degree.

Even the government is not constrained from conducting all intrusive searches and seizures—only "unreasonable" ones that violate reasonable expectations of privacy. And unreasonableness is always a matter of degree and context. Americans do not have an absolute right of privacy, despite Justice Louis Brandeis's famous statement that "The right to be left alone [is] the most comprehensive of rights."[1] Americans today do not, in practice, have the right to be left alone, either by governments or private companies.[2] A modern-day Thoreau could not live undisturbed at his Walden Pond. Brandeis also said that this fundamental right is the "most valued by a free people."[3] I wish that were true, but too many "free" people are willing to sacrifice or compromise that right in exchange for safety, convenience, material benefits, and other considerations. Few today would seek the splendid isolation of Walden on a long-term basis. To paraphrase Benjamin Franklin, too many Americans are willing to give up fundamental liberties, including privacy, to achieve a small amount of increased security and convenience. Put in the context of current constitutional law, many citizens have reduced expectations of privacy based on the pervasiveness of surveillance in the modern world. And this appears to be more so among the young, which foretells our future.

Moreover, it is in the nature of surveillance that it is generally conducted secretly. So even when citizens want to object to invasions of their privacy, they often don't know enough about it to do anything.

It is this combination of factors—massive and increasing governmental intrusions on the right to "be left alone," coupled with lack of concern and/or information—that gives rise to "the surveillance state" in which we now live. This is exacerbated by the exponential increase of private surveillance and the changing relationships between the public and private sector, which are now working together in many contexts including information gathering.[4]

There has always been surveillance—informers, eavesdroppers, spies, general warrants, rummaging through trash, physical observation, dog sniffing, omnipresent cameras, and other primitive techniques of obtaining information about what the targets are doing, planning, saying, writing, and even thinking.[5]

Today's artificial intelligence, satellite-surveillance capabilities, and nano- and other technologies, makes both the gathering and analyzing of private information easier to conduct and more difficult to detect.

Research is now being done on technologies that can read brain waves and track propensities of which even the subject is unaware.[6] The increasing dangers we now face from criminals, terrorists, enemies, pandemics, and other threats to our safety make this much information gathering more necessary than ever and more acceptable to many citizens.

As with other preventive measures, appropriate balances must be struck among often conflicting values. In a democracy governed by the rule of law, the critical question is who gets to strike these balances in differing contexts.

At the macro level, governments surveil each other's activities through satellites, electronic monitoring, hacking, human spies, drones, and balloons. (I have been told that intelligence agencies seek to obtain the bodily excretions of enemy leaders in order to learn about their health and predict their longevity.) Such information gathering probably helps to prevent miscalculations that sometimes lead to wars or other military actions. History is full of such tragic errors. In the current nuclear age, it is more important than ever to avoid information gaps or errors that could cause false positives, i.e., taking military action when none was justified; as well as false negatives, i.e., failing to take such action when necessary. Some historians have argued that Israel made mistakes both in 1967, when it preemptively attacked Egypt and Syria, and in 1973 when it failed to attack these enemies. Some evidence suggests that President Nasser of Egypt did not intend to attack Israel in 1967, and we know that President Sadat did intend and did attack. These alleged "mistakes" might have resulted from faulty or incomplete intelligence based on surveillance failures.[7] Israel's failure to know about and prevent the massacres of October 7 may go down in history as among the most inexplicable intelligence failures by a nation that spent billions of dollars on information gathering.

Surveillance processes are currently at work in Iran, as Israel and the United States seek to determine the progress and intentions of the mullahs with regard to deliverable nuclear weapons. This includes sophisticated satellite, electronic, and human information-gathering sources. The Iranians try to hide their activities from inspectors and enemies in bunkers and other secret locations. Some such activities are easier to hide than others, but in the end, any decision to try to prevent the development of a nuclear arsenal will be based on incomplete information. The issue will be the relative costs of the inevitable false negatives and false positives. Israel, which would be the intended target of an Iranian bomb, surely will err on the side of avoiding a false negative: an erroneous conclusion that Iran is not preparing to develop a deliverable nuclear bomb capable of destroying the nation-state of the Jewish people. On October 7, 2023, Israeli intelligence apparently concluded that Hamas was not about to attack—a false negative with catastrophic consequences. This devastating false negative error may lead Israeli intelligence to make future false positive errors, since wrongly attacking an enemy is more acceptable politically than wrongly failing to prevent an attack against one's own citizens. More optimistically, it may result in better intelligence gathering, assessment, and coordination.

At the micro level, every government tries to keep tabs on individuals suspected of posing serious threats. Potential terrorists are surveilled though wiretaps, undercover agents, and monitoring social media. Potential mass shooters are reported through neighbors, teachers, social media, and red flag laws. Gang members are informed on by snitches. Potential child molesters are identified through porn sites and scam offers (law enforcement agents posing as children). All of these and other similar tactics produce many false positives but they also identify true positives and succeed in preventing some serious harms. How many there are of each is difficult to determine, since we are more likely to learn about the latter than the former.

Pervasive street cameras, cell phone tracking, DNA testing, social media gathering, and other technological innovations help solve past crimes, and by doing so prevent future ones. When empirically so, they may reduce both false positives and false negatives, thereby increasing the accuracy of the preventive measures with decreased costs in privacy.

I recall my first visit to the Soviet Union in the early 1970s to represent Jewish prisoners of conscience, and being told by a prosecutor that they have less crime because they keep a close eye on "criminal types." I quickly learned that these "types" included dissidents, refuseniks, and other political opponents and critics of the regime. Surveillance was omnipresent, including at our hotel and restaurant. We were followed, our phones tapped, and our rooms bugged.

One of my clients, a young man named Uli, was eventually allowed to emigrate to the United States, and he stayed with my family for a while. On his first day, we showed him around Harvard Square and took him to a local bookstore. He couldn't believe that a citizen could simply pay cash for a book and take it without leaving a record of the purchase. In Moscow, every book sale is recorded and reported to the KGB if the book is at all controversial. Little has changed since the end of the Soviet Union and the tyrannical reign of Vladimir Putin.

Although Americans can still walk into a bookstore and buy any book without creating a record, fewer and fewer do so. Indeed some stores today do not accept cash, and credit cards of course leave a record. Amazon and other online sellers that account for so many transactions not only keep records, but use them to encourage readers to buy more books and other items that fit their reading profile. One of many conveniences with costs in privacy![8]

Not only can these and other purchase records be sold to other private companies, they can be subpoenaed by government agencies, often without the knowledge of the purchaser. The same is true of bank, telephone, social media, school, medical, pharmaceutical, psychological, and other records. It has been estimated that government agencies today have access to hundreds of millions of documents and records of its citizens.[9] It is fair to say that in today's surveillance state, citizens can keep fewer and fewer secrets from the government and from corporate America.[10] We leave trails in nearly everything we do. No one can deny that this intrusive process garners significant benefits in safety, security, and convenience. Nor can it be denied that it incurs considerable costs in privacy and other values. It is impossible to weigh the former against the latter because neither is transparent and subject to the kind of accountability that democratic governance requires. It is in the nature of the surveillance state that both its costs and benefits remain secret. "Trust us to use the data wisely and discretely," is the only assurance we can receive. The question remains: Is that enough? And if not, can we do more to create a better balance between security and privacy?

Constructing a prudential framework for democratic control over the preventive state must include processes, procedures, and substantive rules governing the obtaining, collecting, employing, disseminating, preserving, and destroying private information deemed necessary to prevent future harms. This is part of the larger issue of information gathering for other purposes. But the growth and pervasiveness of the preventive state makes the need to control the growing surveillance state even more urgent.

CHAPTER 12

THE PRIVATE STATE

The concept of a surveillance state fails to tell the full picture, because so much of the surveillance directed at citizens today is conducted by private industry alone, or in combination with governmental agencies. This is part of a more far-ranging development: the delegation of functions that have traditionally been the responsibility of government to private entities. This includes surveillance and retrieval of information that involve data-gathering entities. But the issue of the privatization of government functions—the private state—goes beyond that.

When I was growing up, the mail was delivered by the post office, money was printed by the treasury, votes were counted by election officials, wars were fought by the army, prisons were run by departments of correction, law enforcement was conducted by the police force, space exploration was done by NASA, legal disputes were resolved by judges and juries.

Today, these and other traditional governmental functions are being shared among public, private, and mixed groups. This growing privatization of what used to be deemed the province of the state raises fundamental and rarely discussed questions of constitutional law, political accountability, and the nature of our society.

The motivation behind these changes has generally been efficiency and economic benefit. The private sector often does it better and more cheaply than government bureaucracy. Alternatively, when the private sector competes with government agencies such as the post office, both have incentives to do better. In our free-market economy, even the government must compete and prevail. If a corporation builds a better mousetrap than the government, we buy it. And generally, that is a good idea. But it may come with costs, not easily measurable in dollars or speed.

The Constitution itself was not designed for efficiency. A nonfederal, unicameral, parliamentary system of governance—such as those in many other democracies—is far more likely to get things done more efficiently than our complex federal, bicameral, separation-of-powers, checks-and-balances system. Ours was designed to constrain power, and to balance it against other important values, such as privacy, dignity, due process, the presumption of innocence, freedom of expression, and other constitutional rights. This is different than the private sector, which demands expedited results and profits. We pay a price for our desire to prevent too much centralization of authority in any one person or institution. And sometimes we grow impatient at the slow pace of progress.

We want our mail delivered faster and more frequently; we want to know the outcome of elections tonight, not next week; we want alternatives to paper currency; we want military results more effectively achieved by private operatives than by the hierarchical armed forces; we want to imprison criminals more cheaply and safely; we want our homes and businesses protected by privately paid former FBI agents; we trust entrepreneurs to take space travelers beyond the moon; we want our disputes resolved without months of pretrial discovery. And so, we turn to the classic American solution: private enterprise, free-market competition, capitalism.

This means less intrusion by government but also less protection by our Constitution, which generally constrains state action, not private conduct that is regulated more by private contract than by public law.

The time has come to consider the costs and benefits of this important development. There is no "one size fits all" solution. In some areas, privatization has worked better than in others. Federal Express has proved the virtue of competing with governmentally run post offices. Alternative dispute resolution is often more efficient than court cases, but there are fewer checks on abuse. Privately run prisons, on the other hand, raise serious questions, as do Blackwater-type quasi-military operations. Private space travel has yet to prove its worth. And privately tabulated voting is currently in litigation.[1] As far as crypto currency is concerned, the market used to love it, but recent developments have raised serious questions. Most Americans don't understand it. But many still invest in it.

Then there are new developments that do not fit neatly into the shift from government to private. Social media was never a function of the state, though the Internet probably could not have been constructed without governmental involvement. Now it has become the primary medium of communication—and inevitably of the control and censorship of information. The role of the Constitution is as yet uncertain. Paradoxically, it is the First Amendment that empowers private mega-companies like Facebook (now Meta) and Twitter (now X) to censor and limit access to advocacy and other forms of speech that are protected from governmental control. It is a double-edged sword.

Our history of governmental and private institutions may be somewhat mixed—e.g., fire departments were originally private—but our jurisprudence has been based largely on the assumption that government has a monopoly over certain activities. That monopoly is now being challenged, but our jurisprudence has not kept pace. Constitutional law still operates largely to protect against governmental overreach, on the assumption that the potential for such overreach lies generally with state action. "Big Brother" has generally been feared more than "big corporation." The increasing privatization of traditional governmental functions requires a rethinking of some constitutional assumptions.

The New Deal in the 1930s represented a dramatic shift in many areas from private enterprise to governmental participation. That shift, which some say helped save capitalism, was obvious for all to see. It resulted in a visible change in our constitutional jurisprudence: governmental intrusion that had previously been held unconstitutional became legally acceptable. The current shift, from governmental to private, is more subtle and less visible. It, too, must be accompanied by some adaptation of legal principles.

The relationship between the public and the private is being played out today on university campuses, which are a mix of public, private, and governmentally financed quasi-private institutions. Issues of free speech, race-based affirmative action, combating anti-Semitism and other forms of bigotry are affected by the status of universities.[2] This is very much a work in progress.

Overarching questions include these: Should the state delegate traditional governmental functions to private entities? And if so, should these private entities be as transparent and accountable as the government would have to be if it were performing the governmental function? Relatedly, should a private entity to which governmental functions have been delegated be entitled to claim privileges and immunities generally reserved to governmental entities?

It is not the object of this chapter to resolve these issues or to propose specific jurisprudential shifts that deal with privatization of traditional governmental functions. It is to bring together a number of related changes that have in common the privatization of these activities and to begin a discussion of the legal changes that may be required. It is part, but only part, of the more general subject covered by this book, because a considerable amount of preventive intervention is now done either by private entities alone, or under the supervision, delegation, or control of government. These interventions will result in false positives and negatives that can impact the safety and security of everyone. Because private actions are generally less amenable to constitutional constraints than governmental actions, it is important that any jurisprudence developed to constrain the preventive state include within its parameters the actions of the private sector, or those done in combination with the state.

PART III

CONSTRUCTING A JURISPRUDENTIAL FRAMEWORK

CHAPTER 13

THE "SCIENCE" OF PREDICTION

Any jurisprudential framework for the preventive state requires an understanding of the science of predictions based on probabilities. Since all probabilistic prediction will sometimes be mistaken, it also requires an understanding of different types of errors and the comparative costs of each. With this in mind, let me begin with a story that will resonate with fans of American football. (For those who know noting about this sport, you can skip the next few pages and focus on the research of Paul Meehl beginning on page 150.

I was watching a football game with my children and grandchildren, when one of the teams had to decide whether to try for an extra point kick or go for a two-point conversion. One of my grandkids said that "analytics say go for the two." I said, "Don't you mean statistics?" Another said, "The coach has an instinct for these things." This conversation got me to thinking about the differences and similarities among analytical, statistical, and clinical predictive decision-making. They all involve understanding and assessing accurate data for purposes of making judgments about the future—in this case the comparative likelihood and benefit of succeeding in kicking for a more likely one point or "going for it" for a less likely two points, evaluated against the costs of failing at each.

A simple statistical approach to the extra point(s) decision requires knowledge of how often the one-point kick succeeds in general (around 90 percent) compared to the two-point conversion (about 50 percent). All else being equal, this would suggest a slight preference for the two-point conversion (50 percent of 2 is better than 90 percent of 1). But all things are never equal, and that's where analytics and instinct come in.

The score is a big factor: if two points would turn the existing lead into a two-score rather than a one-score advantage, that would suggest a two-point conversion. A similar analysis would apply to a team that was behind, depending of course by how much. Another factor would be time left on the clock. If the game were close to ending, that might be more of a factor in going for two than if it were early in the game. In several recent games, the clock had run out; the losing team had scored a touchdown that brought them within one point of tying and two points of winning. The decision would determine whether the deciding team would win, lose, or go into overtime. Pure statistics might suggest ever so slightly a 50 percent chance of winning over a 90 percent chance of tying coupled with a 50 percent chance of winning (or losing) in overtime. (The coin toss also has an influence on the likelihood of winning or losing in overtime, depending on the rules.) The coach in both situations opted for two points—and failed. They were accused of being wrong in prospect because it turned out badly in retrospect!

That isn't necessarily a fair assessment. It depends on other factors, some quantifiable, such as home field advantage and the records of his quarterbacks, receiving ends, and kickers in similar past situations. (Brady to Gronkowski or Mahomes to Kelce would raise the odds). Some are less easily quantifiable, such as the exhaustion factor among players facing an overtime and the performance of key players under pressure. All of these factors—the quantifiable and the unquantifiable—must be evaluated in real time and a decision made by the coach. That is called clinical decision-making—or judgment, instinct, or experience. Despite its often-subjective nature, clinical decision-making is also subject to objective statistical validation or invalidation. Some coaches are demonstrably better than others in employing their experience and instinct. Statistics show that!

The kick-conversion decision is relatively simple compared to the decision whether to try for a field goal or the needed yardage for a first down on fourth down. The former decides among only three outcomes: zero, one, or two. It may well determine the result of the game, but the variables are limited. The latter involves multiple possible outcomes beyond the difference between three, seven, or eight points, and no points. It also involves field position for the opposing team, clock management, and time preservation. But most of these factors are statistically quantifiable—at least in theory.

We know what the similarities are among statistical, analytical, and clinical decision-making: they all require knowledge of the relevant data and an ability to combine and prioritize the available information in real time in order to maximize a correct outcome. What then are the differences?

Statistical decision-making merely requires accurate data on relevant past performance and a reliable quantifier. It can be done by a simple computer. Of course the selection of the data—the determination of relevance—is done by humans. This is largely true as well of analytical decision-making. It requires more and better data and perhaps a Bayesian analysis of shifting probabilities as the data changes. But this more sophisticated analysis can also be done—at least in theory—by a computer, with considerable human input. Even some apparently nonquantifiable factors—such as weather, exhaustion, success under pressure, matchups, home field—can be quantified at least to a degree, as they have been in recent years by teams, leagues, and networks that hire specialists to assemble and quickly provide relevant (and sometimes not so relevant) data. (I remember when my beloved Brooklyn Dodgers became the first sports team to hire an accountant named Allen Roth to compile statistics beyond batting averages, won and loss pitching, and errors. This led to the earned run average, on-base percentage, slugging figures, rightylefty numbers, and other now common statistics.[1]) These are some of what go into analytics. In this respect, analytics has no bright line separation from statistics. They are on a continuum, with analytics containing more and better statistics, as well as more nuanced ways of assessing the available data and of obtaining more data. The rapid growth of artificial intelligence promises to improve the accuracy of predictions based on statistics and analytics.

The vice of modern-day sports analytics is that it often contains too much data—such things as the highest on-base plus slugging (OPS) percentage by a left-handed infielder before the age of twenty-five. The additional data may be interesting to fans, but not relevant to real-time decision-making. The virtue is that it can factor in far more relevant variables than the human mind is capable of considering. The goal is to distinguish the more relevant data from the less relevant and to give each its proper weight.

What then of clinical decision-making? It, too, is based on statistics about quantifiable data, but it adds the personal instincts, experiences, hunches, and other less easily quantifiable attributes of the coach and his staff. But these personal qualities are themselves subject to statistical assessment. Some coaches seem to have better instincts or hunches than others, as proved by their records of making more accurate predictions under similar circumstances. So, is clinical judgment also on a continuum with statistical and analytical decision-making? To what extent can it be relied on when its conclusions conflict with statistical and analytical conclusions? Is clinical judgment nothing more than questionable subjective statistical analysis coupled with questionable hunches and instinct? Consider the "genius" of Bill Belichick. We will never know how much of his remarkable win-loss record was attributable, at least in part, to Tom Brady, or conversely, how much of Brady's success was attributed to Belichick. We can garner some insight from their very different records after the partnership ended.

As a general matter no one really knows the comparative accuracy of the different modes of decision-making, although there is some empirical data. Back in 1954, a social scientist named Paul Meehl set out to compare the accuracy of clinical predictions made by psychiatrists and psychologists with statistical decisions based on collected data. In general, he found statistical predictions more accurate.[2] In later studies, Meehl purportedly found that mechanical predictions are more accurate than clinical ones and proposed that clinicians should rarely deviate from mechanically derived conclusions.[3]

Another recent episode from my own life helped me better appreciate the relationship between statistical and clinical predictions. I needed to have my gallbladder removed. There are two methods: open surgery and laparoscopic, which is far less invasive than open but more dangerous if there is inflammation and scarring. The surgeon makes the predictive call regarding which is likely to produce a better outcome under the circumstances—first preliminarily and then after inserting the laparoscope and assessing the degree of inflammation. There are data about how much inflammation warrants open surgery, but the decision must be made in real time by each surgeon with eyes on the inflammation. I selected a surgeon based on his experience and success in making this clinical decision. I didn't want a computer to decide, but I did want my surgeon to make his clinical decision only after reviewing the best statistical data and based on his considerable professional experience with similar cases, and his success rate. I was happy to have a robot do some of the cutting as long as my experienced doctor used his clinical experience and judgment to control the robot. After inserting the laparoscope, he decided not to do open surgery, and all went well. (The same positive result might well have been achieved if the surgeon had opted for open surgery. We will never know!)

So, there are differences among statistical, analytical, and clinical decision-making, but they are often subtle and matters of degree, whether they involve predictions about football, surgery, crime, or war and peace!

Following highly publicized acts of violence—school shootings, domestic terrorism, murder-suicides, and others—there are often conflicting reactions from friends, neighbors, and relatives of the perpetrators. One trope takes the form of: "He was so quiet and nice. We were shocked at what he did. No one could have predicted it from his conduct." The other looks in the opposite direction: "Everyone knew he was capable of this. Why didn't they stop him? They should have known." Together they reflect the difficulty of predicting and preventing most violence based on clinical assessments.

If all people who were "too quiet" were detained, there would be massive over confinement—that is, false positives. There would also be false negatives, because people who aren't quiet commit violence. If only people who expressly threatened violence were detained, there would be a considerable amount of unprevented violence—that is, false negatives. There would also be many false positives, since most people who threaten violence don't actually carry it out.

There are two basic issues involved in the science of prediction. The first is empirical, the second normative.

The empirical question is whether we can improve the accuracy of predictions through science and technology. When Oliver Wendell Holmes predicted that mentally deficient "imbeciles" would eventually be executed "for their crimes" (or "starve"), he was employing junk science (to be generous) or bigotry, generated largely from Harvard "experts"(who were virtually all white, Protestant males), and especially its then racist president A. Lawrence Lowell. He was simply wrong to count alleged "imbecility" as an accurate predictor of capital murder (or starvation). That junk science conclusion was supported by neither statistics nor objective clinical assessments. The "science" has improved since Holmes's day, but not that much. We cannot identify Lombroso's "born criminal or criminaloids" before they have become actual criminals. Nor can we accurately predict adult criminality from the Bible's "stubborn and rebellious son," or from the Glueck's three-year-old pre-delinquent. The "mark of Cain" became visible only after Cain murdered Abel. In retrospect, we can sometimes identify factors that should have led us to foresee what occurred. But retrospective analysis does not always produce accurate prospective conclusions. These factors generally both overpredict and underpredict the harmful results we understandably seek to prevent. Some do more of the former; others more of the latter.

The Glueck studies gathered evidence of numerous factors affecting children and their families. They looked back at adult criminals and identified several factors that were present in many such criminals. These factors managed to identify some future delinquents and criminals, but at a very high cost of also misidentifying as future criminals many who would not and did not commit crimes. The Gluecks, whom I knew in my early days at Harvard, were well-motivated and decent scholars who were right about the childhood influences of home environment factors on adult behavior, but they were not sufficiently knowledgeable about statistical analysis, especially regarding false positives. Their primary focus was reducing false negatives. The cost of false positives varies, of course, with the consequences of being misidentified and mislabeled. If all who were so identified were detained, the cost of the misidentified would be very great. If they were merely surveilled, the cost would be lower. If nothing were done to anyone identified as a future criminal—if they were merely subjects of a study, whose records were discretely observed—the cost would be little or nothing. But there would be a considerable number of false negatives, that is, subjects who were correctly identified as future criminals, but whose crimes were not prevented. That is the dilemma of trying to predict crime and violence and either acting or not acting on the predictions to prevent such harms. If we act, there will be many false positives. If we don't act, there will be many false negatives.

The empirical side of the dilemma is subject to scientific improvement: we can, through science and technology, especially AI, increase the accuracy of predictions. We can, at least in theory, reduce the numbers of both false positives and negatives though not always in equal proportion. And the proportion of errors matters greatly. As I have observed, it is easy to minimize false negatives by being willing to maximize false positives: simply predict that nearly everyone will commit crimes. It is also easy to minimize false positives by being willing to maximize false negatives: simply predict that few, if any, will commit crimes. The difficult task is to strike the appropriate balance, realizing that there will inevitably be mistakes on both sides. Because the accuracy will never approach perfection—the complexity of human behavior is simply too great to allow for the construction of the perfect science-fiction prediction machine described in the introduction—we will always need to make difficult normative judgments: balancing the desirability of increasing the number and percentage of true positives against the undesirability of false positives and false negatives.

The dilemma can be illustrated by the simple four-part box described in the introduction, though the realities will always be more complex.

PREDICTIONS	**OUTCOME**	
	Did commit crimes	Didn't commit crimes
Will commit future crimes	**TP: True Positive**	**FP: False Positive**
Won't commit future crimes	**FN: False Negative**	**TN: True Negative**

The decision analysis represented by this box is applicable to all simple predictive decisions about the future that can be tested by waiting to see whether the prediction turned out to be accurate or inaccurate (as long as both outcomes are equally visible). They require simple yes-no, black-white, on-off decisions—not gray-area matters of degree.

Will it rain or not tomorrow? Will the stock market go up or down this month? Will X become a convicted or self-confessed criminal? Will Germany go to war against France? Will a comet hit the earth? Will the contemplated two-point conversion succeed or fail? Will this marriage endure or end in divorce?

Matters of degree—which most important matters are—will not be as easily subject to my four-part box, but they, too, can be subject to more complex empirical validation or invalidation. Even the accuracy of clinical judgments about matters of degree can be tested and verified.

Now back to my matrix.

Let us return to the predictive decision a judge must make regarding whether a defendant will show up for trial or try to flee.[4]

That is generally a simple yes or no, black or white, on or off issue. Either he will show up for trial or he will flee to avoid justice. (We will ignore, for purposes of analysis, defendants who oversleep or forget their obligation to appear, and focus only on those who actively seek to flee—or who successfully flee.) Here is the box matrix as applied to the decisions and outcome.

PREDICTIONS	OUTCOME	
	Did flee	Didn't flee
Will flee	**TP: True Positive**	**FP: False Positive**
Won't flee	**FN: False Negative**	**TN: True Negative**

It quickly becomes obvious that in real-life situations, no such analysis will be subject to empirical validation, because if the judge erroneously decides that X will flee, X will be detained, and so we will never know that he would not have fled if released. But if the judge erroneously decides that Y will not flee, and he is released and flees, that will be well known. The false positives are invisible, while the false negatives make headlines. So, a calculating judge, anxious that his mistakes not be known, will err on the side of detention. They will operate under the principle of: "When in doubt, don't let him out."

If we wanted to test scientifically the predictive ability of the judge, we would have the judge make his predictions and then release all of the defendants and see which ones fled and which ones didn't (to make the experiment even better, the judge, when he made his predictions, would not know that all the defendants would be released). But it is unlikely that any system of justice would actually release defendants who a judge predicted would flee. This would be even more unlikely if the prediction were about committing crimes pretrial, rather than fleeing.

So, in many real-life situations, false positives are more visible than false negatives, and judges are subject to more criticism for freeing a defendant who flees than for confining one who wouldn't. Accordingly, judges are likely to reverse the rule that it is better for ten guilty to go free than for one innocent to be confined. In the pretrial detention context, the rule would seem to be "better for ten who would not flee to be detained, than for one who would flee to be released."

The problem of the comparative visibility of false predictions plagues many but not all predictive decisions. In some cases, the false negatives may be visible, at least over time. The British decision not to attack Germany in the mid 1930s produced highly visible consequences, though at the time it was made, the false negative mistake—not attacking—was relatively invisible. Had they attacked, killing numerous innocent Germans but succeeding in preventing World War II, it would have been seen as a false positive, though in fact it would have been an invisible true positive.[5] It is these and other conundrums in the science of prediction that make the development of a jurisprudence of preventive intervention so challenging. It is to this challenge that we now turn.

CHAPTER 14

THE NEED FOR A JURISPRUDENTIAL FRAMEWORK FOR THE PREVENTIVE STATE

Constructing a jurisprudential framework for a quickly developing and constantly changing phenomenon is a daunting task. But new threats to liberty must be constrained by law. This is true of all technological, scientific, and political developments, such as social media, artificial intelligence, vaccines, surveillance mechanisms, weapons of mass destruction, globalization, conflicts in space,[1] and other phenomena that were unimaginable to those who built the constitutional structure that has served us for nearly two and a half centuries. We must also try—difficult as it is—to predict the development and growth of even newer phenomena that promise to impact our lives in ways that require jurisprudential intervention.

Some jurists would base any new constitutional jurisprudence on what the Framers of our old Constitution "would have thought," had they been aware of the new developments. For example, in a case involving a GPS device secreted on a car without a search warrant, Justice Antonin Scalia wrote that the Supreme Court must "assure preservation of that degree of privacy against government that existed when the Fourth Amendment was adopted."[2] Fellow conservative justice Samuel Alito disagreed with Scalia's look-to-the-past formulation, observing that "it is almost impossible to think of late-18th-century situations that are analogous"[3] to GPS technology. Alito then quipped: "it is possible to imagine a case in which a constable secreted himself somewhere in a coach and remained there for a period of time in order to monitor the movements of the coach's owner."[4] He then added: "[t]his would have required either a gigantic coach or a very tiny constable or both—not to mention a constable with incredible fortitude and patience."[5]

Other jurists argue that the right to privacy is a "living" right that cannot be constrained by the dead hand of eighteenth-century constitution writers. Technologies that are commonplace today—such as instant global communications subject to instant global hacking, tracking, and AI analysis, as well as weapons of mass destruction and genetic testing—simply do not fit into eighteenth-century formulations.[6]

It is not the function of this book to resolve the enduring debate between "originalists," who, according to Scalia, support a "dead" constitution that can be adapted to changing times only by amendment, and advocates of a "living" constitution who argue that open-ended protections—such as "due process," "equal protection," "cruel and unusual punishments," and "the right of the people to be secure"—were deliberately designed by the framers to "evolve" with changing conditions. In attempting to strike this balance, I have been influenced by the pragmatic jurisprudence of my longtime friend and colleague, retired Supreme Court justice Stephen Breyer.[7] In both his judicial and academic writing, he looks to the past not only to discern the broad intention of the framers, but to learn from our collective mistakes how to encourage the "more perfect union" envisioned by our founders. In his new book, *Reading the Constitution: Why I Chose Pragmatism, Not Textualism*, Breyer emphasizes the judge's "experience," "judicial instinct," and ability to predict the "consequences" of any decisions:

> Without ignoring the text, I normally put more weight on the statute's purposes and the consequences to which a particu-

lar interpretation will likely lead. I will sometimes ask how a (hypothetical) "reasonable legislator" would have interpreted the statute in light of its purposes. And I will sometimes examine the legislative history of a statue in order to answer these questions. I will approach and understand broad statutory or constitutional phrases in light of the values that underlie them—including notions of due process of law.

But by considering purposes, consequences, and values, I place less weight on the so-called plain meaning of a statute or the Constitution then do many of my textualist colleagues. And I do so to arrive at an interpretation that is more faithful to the desire of the Constitution's Framers to establish a workable framework for long-lasting government. The Constitution sets forth a structure and principles that aim to create and hold us together as a single nation for hundreds of years or more. I have approached the interpretive task with that fundamental objective in mind.[8]

Like Justice Breyer, I approach the task of formulating a jurisprudential framework for the preventive state with one eye to past experiences—especially negative ones—and the other eye to creating "a workable framework" for the future that avoids the mistakes of the past.

I look to the past for general principles of governance, such as checks and balances, as well as a presumption in favor of liberty; and to the present and future for guidance as to how to apply these principles to ever-changing circumstances.

It is the purpose of this and the next chapter to outline general jurisprudential principles, not limited to (though influenced by) our own constitution, as currently interpreted, but more broadly applicable to any fair system of justice. It seeks to strike an appropriate balance between the enormous benefits of new preventive technologies and the equally enormous dangers they pose if uncabined by a relevant jurisprudential framework.

As I mentioned in the introduction, I closed my 2008 book *Is There A Right to Remain Silent?* with a challenge to academics, legislators, judges, and citizens to begin a process for "develop[ing] a jurisprudence for the emerging preventive state."[9] To date, this challenge has not been accepted by others. So, it falls to me, and those who agree with my project, to try to meet it. In doing so, I acknowledge the American tradition *against* constructing a priori "juristic theories." As Dean Roscoe Pound put it: "It is true that in Anglo-American law, more than in other systems, juristic theories come *after* lawyer and judge have dealt with concrete case and have in some measure learned how to dispose of them."[10]

This is in part because the Anglo-American legal system is based largely on a common law that relies on cases, with different factual settings, being decided by the courts over time. The Continental system, on the other hand, relies primarily on codification—that is, the enactment of statutes that speak in general terms and must be applied to specific cases as they arise, or even before they come to court.

Lawyers and judges have "dealt" with cases involving preventive intervention largely on an ad hoc basis. Mostly these cases involve the visible failures of the system to prevent harms rather than the largely invisible successes. Accordingly, judges have not always "learned how to dispose" of cases involving such intervention. Thus there has been little occasion to develop overarching juristic theories regarding this important, pervasive, and fast-changing mechanism of social control—this movement toward the preventive state. Case law—through which most American and British lawyers have been educated—deals largely with situations in which the existing law failed to produce a nonlegal resolution to a conflict. The law in practice has more influence on conduct than the cases that end up in courts or in law school classes.

I believe we have now arrived at the "after" phase of legal development, and the time has come to begin constructing a systemic jurisprudential framework for the preventive state. So, I will try to address that challenge—a challenge many of whose components I have been addressing on a subject-by-subject basis for more than sixty years.[11] Now I will try to bring these components together to articulate a holistic framework. It will necessarily be a work in progress, since there are so many quickly moving and changing parts. It is in the nature of any jurisprudence—even more so in constitutions—that they focus on generalities more than particulars. These generalities inform the particulars and can be adapted to suit changing or currently unknown particulars. To be useful and adaptive, a jurisprudence must reflect the enduring values of the society.

So let us first try to identify these enduring values.

The first and foremost principle governing a just society is essential fairness to all based on the ideal that all people have equal value.[12] In order to assure such fairness, the "veil of ignorance"—devised by political philosopher and my longtime colleague John Rawls as part of his "theory of justice"—should be an essential component.

Here is how Rawls described his veil of ignorance. He began his origin story of rights with what he calls "the original position," which he characterized as being one of equality:

> It seems reasonable to suppose that the parties in the original position are equal. That is, all have the same rights in the procedure for choosing principles; each can make proposals, submit reasons for their acceptance, and so on. Obviously the purpose of these conditions is to represent equality between human beings as moral persons, as creatures having a conception of their good and capable of a sense of justice.[13]

He argued that "the idea of this original position is to set up a fair procedure [for decision-making] so that any principle agreed to will be just."[14]

To assure that decisions concerning justice are made fairly and without the bias of status, position, rank, or biology, Rawls imagined a hypothetical "veil of ignorance" placed over every decision-maker:

Somehow we must nullify the effects of specific contingencies which put men at odds and tempt them to exploit social and natural circumstances to their own advantage. Now in order to do this I assume that the parties are situated behind a veil of ignorance. They do not know how the various alternatives will affect their own particular case and they are obliged to evaluate principles solely on the basis of general considerations.

It is assumed, then, that the parties do not know certain kinds of particular facts. First of all, no one knows his place in society, his class position or social status; nor does he know his fortune in the distribution of natural assets and abilities, his intelligence and strength, and the like. Nor, again, does anyone know his conception of the good, the particulars of his rational plan of life, or even the special features of his psychology such as his aversion to risk or liability to optimism or pessimism. More than this, I assume that the parties do not know the particular circumstances of their own society. That is, they do not know its economic or political situation, or the level of civilization and culture it has been able to achieve. The persons in the original position have no information as to which generation they belong. These broader restrictions on knowledge are appropriate in part because questions of social justice arise between generations as well as within them, for example, the question of the appropriate rate of capital saving and of the conservation of natural resources and the environment of nature. There is also, theoretically anyway, the question of a reasonable genetic policy.[15]

Rawls's "veil" does not and could not shield decision-makers from all knowledge:

As far as possible, then, the only particular facts which the par-ties know is that their society is subject to the circumstances of justice and whatever this implies. It is taken for granted, however, that they know the general facts about human society.

They understand political affairs and the principles of economic theory; they know the basis of societal organization and the laws of human psychology. Indeed, the parties are presumed to know whatever general facts affect the choice of the principles of justice. There are no limitations on general information, that is, on general laws and theories, since conceptions of justice must be adjusted to the characteristics of the systems of social operation which they are to regulate, and there is no reason to rule out these facts.[16]

Rawls assumes that such veiled decision-makers will make decisions about justice that are not self-serving or based on what has come to be known as "identity politics," since they will have no knowledge about their identities or those close to them.

In my writing, I have devised a somewhat different theory—or origin story—of rights and justice.[17] Rawls's theory is based on a hypothetical world, and its goal is abstract justice. Mine is based on real-world experiences, and its goal is the broad acceptances of concrete rights and justice. During my early years at Harvard, I was part of a small "study group"—of ten or so—in which both Rawls and I presented our theories. His was in near final form (he was in his late forties, I in my late twenties). Mine was preliminary. We both found our ideas compatible—his more theoretically and mine more experientially based.

Here is how I have described my "secular theory of the origin of rights":

- Rights *do not come from God*, because God does not speak to human beings in a single voice, and rights should exist even if there is no God.
- Rights *do not come from nature*, because nature is value neutral.
- Rights *do not come from logic*, because there is little consensus about the a priori premises from which rights may be deduced.

- Rights *do not come from the law alone*, because if they did, there would be no basis on which to judge a given legal system.
- Rights *come from human experience*, particularly experiences with injustice. We learn from the mistakes of history that a rights-based system and certain fundamental rights—such as freedom of expression, freedom of and from religion, equal protection of the laws, due process, and participatory democracy—are essential to avoid repetition of the grievous injustices of the past. Working from the bottom up, from a dystopian view of our experiences with injustice, rather than from the top down, from a utopian theory of perfect justice, we build rights on a foundation of trial and error and our uniquely human ability to learn from our mistakes in order to avoid replicating them. In a word, *rights* come from *wrongs*.[18]

Mine is a descriptive, empirically based theory that purports to show the historical origin of rights. It may prove to be an accurate, inaccurate, or somewhere in between description of how rights in fact develop over time. Rawls's theory is prescriptive: It teaches us how to think about creating a just society, based on equality. It is not subject to empirical verification; it cannot be shown to be right or wrong (other than by its consequences over time if adopted in real life).

Our very different theories are entirely compatible, especially for purposes of the undertaking of this book: to begin the process of constructing a jurisprudence for the preventive state.

In order to build on the work of Rawls, we should decide which information should be veiled from those who would construct or approve this jurisprudence. The first would be whether the decision-maker would be someone (or part of some group) who would be helped or hurt by particular preventive interventions that might be authorized or prohibited by the proposed jurisprudence. They should not know whether they are or will be terrorists or targets; suspected criminals or victims; sickly or healthful; doctors or patients; Americans or Iranians; Israelis or Palestinians; people of color or white; women or men; residents of areas immediately affected by global warming or workers who may lose jobs if "green" policies are adopted; media and others who engage in free speech or those who are offended or frightened by what is being said; high-tech experts or Luddites; wealthy or poor; religious or secular.

These veils of ignorance are designed to preclude or limit the construction of a self-serving or identity-serving selfish jurisprudence. It would hopefully preclude "free speech for me but not for thee," "NIMBY" (not in my backyard), and "if I am not for myself who will be for me." They are intended to make sure that "if the shoe is on the other foot," it also fits. To quote Rabbi Hillel, "If I am for myself alone, what am I."

My proposed jurisprudential framework for the preventive state will seek to satisfy Rawls's hypothetical criteria for justice based on equality. It is impossible, of course for any actual person, as distinguished from Rawls's hypothetical justice-doer, to take him or herself out of their actual bodies and to ignore their experiences or identities.[19] Both nature and nurture impact ideology. One's philosophy generally depends, at least in part, on one's autobiography, though in different ways—sometimes as a reaction, sometimes more positively, but never without influence.

The Bible recognized an early form of the veil of ignorance. It commanded judges not to "recognize faces" when administering justice.[20] Hence the blindfold on the statue of justice, designed to veil the judges from—to make them ignorant of—any knowledge or recognition of the identity or characteristics of the litigants before them. Justice is supposed to be "blind," that is, veiled from knowing information that should not be relevant to doing equal justice.

It is a tall order to veil oneself from information that may be prejudicial to unbiased justice, but it is as an aspiration worth pursuing. The Bible also commands: "Justice, justice shall you pursue"[21] (*tirdof* in the original Hebrew, which literally means "run after"). The use of that active verb suggests that the Bible understood that perfect justice will never be achieved; that the quest for justice never stays won.[22]

Experience teaches the same caution. We must never rest in the pursuit of justice, because new challenges are always on the horizon. It is this ever-changing experience that forms the basis for my approach to justice and rights. It is our ability—and hopefully our willingness—to learn from past injustices and denials of rights how to construct a jurisprudence that comes closer to justice and a rights-based society.

So which history in particular should inform the quest for a durable jurisprudence of prevention?

The history of interventions by states in an effort to predict and prevent perceived harms is littered with failures based on both false positives and false negatives. Many of these failures are largely invisible to history. Some are visible, as are some successes—true positives and true negatives. But as we have seen with bail decisions, when a judge detains a defendant based on a prediction that he would flee or commit crimes, it becomes impossible to learn whether the detention is based on a true or false positive prediction. Writ larger, it is also impossible to assess the accuracy of the Roosevelt administration's order to preventively detain more than 100,000 Japanese Americans based on a prediction that if allowed to remain free, many would commit espionage or sabotage. The absence of evidence that non-detained Japanese-Americans committed such acts does not prove—though it may suggest—that if those detained had remained free, none would have done so.

Similarly, it is impossible to know how many of thousands of "imbeciles" who were preventively sterilized, would have produced children who committed crimes or starved to death as Justice Holmes predicted. Or how much censorship of speech predicted to do harm would actually have produced that harm if published. There are good reasons for being skeptical.

Writ even larger, how many military decisions to preventively or preemptively attack an enemy who is believed to be preparing to attack turned out to be correct?

Did the murder of the Romanov children actually prevent the restoration of the czarist regime? Did it produce an even worse regime? Did Japan's attack on Pearl Harbor prevent the United States from attacking Japan first? Would an attack against Germany in the early 1930s by Britain and France have prevented World War II? Would an attack against Iran's nuclear weapons program prevent another catastrophe?

As I have said, history is blind to the future and to "what-ifs." But we can learn not to repeat the visible mistakes of the past and to exercise caution about authorizing preventive interventions when the results of mistakes will be invisible.

It is with these guides in mind—veiling us from our biases and learning from our mistakes—that we should approach the challenging task of constructing a jurisprudential framework for the preventive state.

CHAPTER 15

THE PROCEDURAL COMPONENT
OF A JURISPRUDENTIAL
FRAMEWORK FOR
THE PREVENTIVE STATE

It may seem counterintuitive to begin the process of developing a jurisprudence with procedural considerations, rather than substantive ones. After all, procedures must be adaptive to the substance of what is being regulated. But in this case, the absence of appropriate procedural protections has contributed to the absence of substantive rules, because the courts have allowed rules and regulations that are deemed "preventive" rather than "punitive" to be implemented without the need to articulate limiting procedural or substantive safeguards.

As Justice Felix Frankfurter wisely observed: "The history of liberty has largely been the history of the observance of procedural safeguards."[1] This has been especially true in the context of intrusive measures that have been deemed—or labeled—"preventive." This label suggests benign motives and outcomes that do not require the types or degrees of procedural protection required for interventions labeled "punishment."

The courts have distinguished, not always wisely, between criminal punishment and what are deemed "civil" sanctions or regulations, regardless of how punitive the sanction may feel to the one on whom it is imposed. This legal labeling game, as I have called it,[2] purports to derive its rules from the words of the Constitution and from the history of the common law. Whatever its source, it produces results that often make little functional sense. As I have written elsewhere about the civil-criminal labeling game:

> The object of the civil-criminal labeling game is simple: the court must determine whether certain procedural safeguards, required by the Constitution in "all criminal prosecutions," apply to various proceedings. The rules are a bit more complex. The legislature enacts a statute that restricts the liberty of one player—variously called the defendant, patient, juvenile ward, deportee, detainee, et cetera. That player must then convince the court that the formal proceeding through which the state restricts his liberty is really a criminal prosecution. The state, on the other hand, must show that the proceeding is really civil; for support it often claims that the results of the proceeding *help*, rather than *hurt*, its opponent.[3]

In the course of this game's long history, prosecutors have succeeded with the assistance of the court (and all too often, without the opposition of "defense" attorneys) in attaching the civil labels to a wide range of proceedings including the commitment of juveniles, sex offenders, psychopaths, the mentally ill, alcoholics, drug addicts, and security risks. Likewise, sterilization, deportation, and revocation of parole and probation proceedings are regarded as civil. By attaching the civil label the state has successfully denied defendants almost every important safeguard required in criminal trials. Invocation of this talismanic word has erased a veritable bill of rights. As Alice said, "That's a great deal to make one word [do]." To which Humpty Dumpty responded: "When I make a word do a lot of work like that...I always pay it extra."[4] Until quite recently, the word *civil* must have been well paid indeed, for it was doing the work of an army of jurists.

Another labeling game played by the Supreme Court involves the distinction between regulatory and punitive sanctions, as well as between preventive and punitive sanctions. This is what the late chief justice William Rehnquist wrote in the context of ruling that the pretrial preventive detention in a maximum-security jail of a Mafia boss was *not* criminal punishment:

> As an initial matter, the mere fact that a person is detained does not inexorably lead to the conclusion that the government has imposed punishment.... To determine whether a restriction on liberty constitutes permissible punishment or permissible regulation, we first look to legislative intent.... Unless Congress expressly intended to impose punitive restrictions, the punitive/regulatory distinction turns on "whether an alternative purpose to which [the restriction] may rationally be connected is assignable for it, and whether it appears excessive in relation to the alternative purpose assigned [to it]."[5]

Having set out these relatively meaningless criteria, the Court then applied them in a wooden manner that has broad and dangerous applications for other preventive mechanisms. It concluded:

> [T]he detention imposed by the Act falls on the regulatory side of the dichotomy. The legislative history of the Bail Reform Act clearly indicates that Congress did not formulate the pretrial detention provisions as punishment for dangerous individuals.... Congress instead perceived pretrial detention as a potential *solution* to a pressing societal problem.... There is no doubt that preventing danger to the community is a legitimate regulatory goal.... We have repeatedly held that the Government's regulatory interest in community safety can, in appropriate circumstances, outweigh an individual's liberty interest. For example, in times of war or insurrection, when society's interest is at its peak, the Government may detain individuals whom the Government

believes to be dangerous.... Even outside the exigencies of war, we have found that sufficiently compelling government interests can justify detention of dangerous persons.[6]

This absurd dichotomy between *punishment*, on the one hand, and "a potential *solution* to a pressing societal problem," on the other, fails to acknowledge the reality that punishment often *is* the perceived solution to pressing social problems and that such solutions are often punitive in every sense of that word. Anyone who has visited Rikers Island in New York or other similar pretrial detention jails would recognize "punishment" when they see it. Indeed such facilities are often more punitive in practice than many post-conviction prisons. Similarly, the purported dichotomy between "punishment for dangerous individuals" and "preventing danger to the community" fails to recognize the overlapping nature of these related mechanisms of social control. Recall Oliver Wendell Holmes's observations that prevention is the "chief and only universal purpose of punishment" and that "there can be no case in which the lawmaker makes certain conduct criminal without thereby showing a wish and purpose to prevent that conduct."[7]

Taken to its logical conclusion, Rehnquist's meaningless distinction between punishment and "a potential solution" could lead to how Nazi Germany solved its "pressing social problem" of dealing with the mentally and physically infirm. It introduced a "regulatory program" of mandatory "euthanasia"—which literally means "good death"—that resulted in the "nonpunitive" killing of approximately 250,000 disabled children and adults by gas chambers, lethal injections, and starvation. It was not a great leap from this "solution" to the "final solution" to the "pressing social problem" of Jews, Sinti, Roma, and other "social undesirables."

In any event, these labeling games merely lead to the result-oriented negative conclusion that the constitutional jurisprudence governing criminal punishment is *not* applicable to preventive, preemptive, or other "regulatory" mechanisms even when they look, smell, and sound the same as criminal punishment. The cases that rely on these false dichotomies generally fail to articulate an alternative jurisprudence that should govern preventive or preemptive sanctions. If it's not "punishment," almost anything goes.[8]

Since no meaningful jurisprudence of preemption or prevention has been constitutionalized—at least not to the extent that the criminal punishment system has been over the years[9]—there exists more constitutional flexibility to devise and articulate a coherent, consistent, and functional jurisprudence of anticipatory governmental actions. Yet little has been done to fill this important need.

The first step in constructing a jurisprudence of preventive intervention is to require that procedural safeguards reflect the actual degree of intrusion rather than the label it is given. Compelled confinement of any kind—whether in a jail, prison, mental hospital, detention center, or other institution—*is* punishment to the person on whom it is inflicted, regardless of the purported "legislative intent." As such it must be deemed akin to punishment for legal purposes. It constitutes a serious intrusion on liberty requiring a significant degree of procedural protection: a high standard of proof, right to counsel, right to confront witnesses, specific substantive criteria, presumption of "innocence" (or non-dangerousness). The degree of procedural protection should vary with the degree of intrusion: capital and long-term imprisonment crimes warrant greater protections than brief medical detentions or home confinement. Although even the latter require some procedural safeguards, the former require greater ones.

Any reasonable jurisprudence for prevention must calibrate the procedural safeguards and adapt them to the degree and duration of the intrusion on the liberty of the individual.

Here then is my proposed jurisprudential framework for the procedural protections required for preventive state interventions:

Any compelled, involuntary confinement in any institution—penal, medical, administrative, or anything else with bars and locks—should require the following levels of proof, depending on the likely duration. The numbers I have assigned are intended to be suggestive and subject to democratic determination.

- A year or more—proof beyond a reasonable doubt as in criminal cases (say, 90 percent).
- Ninety days to a year—proof by clear and convincing evidence with a substantial burden on the state (say, 75 percent).
- Ten to ninety days—proof by a heavy preponderance, beyond that required in a monetary civil dispute where there is no preference for a mistake on other either side (say, 60 percent).
- One to ten days—proof by a standard akin to more probable than not (probable cause).

These burdens and percentages are intended roughly to mirror the values assigned to false positives and negatives, based on the consequences of either type of mistake. They are mostly suggestive. In a democracy, the specific numbers should be decided by the appropriate government agency subject to checks and balances.

Other procedural protections should also vary with the values placed on different types of mistakes; with regard to confinement for:

- Ninety days or more—right to counsel, discovery, cross-examination, presumption against incarceration, exclusion of hearsay, and scrupulous appellate review.[10]
- Ten to ninety days—right to counsel, cross-examination, limited discovery.
- One to ten days—right to counsel, cross-examination.

Since this purports to be merely a jurisprudential framework, rather than a constitutional amendment or statute, the specifics are not written in stone. These are my suggested numbers, percentages, and list of rights. Others may differ as to these and other specifics. It is the framework for deciding these and other related procedural issues that is important.[11] With that caveat in mind, let us turn to the more substantive content of the proposed framework.

CHAPTER 16

A SUGGESTED JURISPRUDENTIAL FRAMEWORK FOR MISTAKE PREFERENCES

*How Many False Positives
for How Many False Negatives?*

On the border between procedure and substance lies the issue of what I call "mistake preferences." The reality is that any system of intervention—preventive or reactive, civil or criminal, regulatory or punitive—will make mistakes: It will convict some innocent and acquit some guilty; it will confine some who are not dangerous and release some who are; it will shoot some fleeing suspects who are innocent while allowing some guilty to escape. Any jurisprudence must take into account the inevitability of error and decide *which type* of error—false positives (finding against the innocent) or false negatives (finding in favor of the guilty)—is worse. That preference should be reflected in burdens of proof, rules of evidence, and procedural safeguards, as proposed in chapter 15. It should also be reflected in substantive criteria for intervention.

For crimes, we have made the jurisprudential choice—at least in theory and rhetoric—that it is better that ten guilty be wrongly acquitted than even one innocent be wrongly convicted. Whether juries, judges, or the public actually believe and apply this preference for false negatives over false positives is highly questionable.

Its words, however, have become part of our parchment preachment, along with the presumption of innocence. These rhetorical virtue pronouncements may well not govern actual decisions, but they reflect aspirations, if not reality. In any event, the aversion to convicting the innocent has been a backbone of criminal jurisprudence since Abraham argued with God on behalf of the sinners of Sodom, demanding that the multitude of sinners he spared if even a small number are innocent.

We have made no comparable jurisprudential choice with regard to noncriminal preventive interventions. Consider, for example, the mandatory removal and confinement of more than 100,000 Japanese Americans in order to prevent possible acts of sabotage or espionage. The adage there would seem to have been "better one act of sabotage or espionage be prevented even if preventive measures require the confinement of thousands of innocent citizens who would never have committed such acts." No limiting principle was articulated when the Roosevelt Supreme Court upheld this allegedly preventive measure.[1] History has judged this particular episode of preventive detention harshly, primarily because of its racial component.[2] History and science have also judged harshly the Supreme Court's approval of mass sterilization of "the unfit" as a benign measure designed to prevent the mentally "deficient" from starving or being executed for their predicted harm-doing. We must expect from these limited disapprovals that unregulated preventive intrusions do and will go beyond race and mental deficiency, and that legal measures—procedural, burden of proof, and substantive—must be designed to constrain abuses inflicted in the name of prevention.

As previously stated, it is a simple task to eliminate (or substantially reduce) either false positives or false negatives. The former can be accomplished by allowing no (or very few) preventive intrusions, the latter by allowing all (or most) intrusions. The role of a jurisprudence is to strike the proper balance between the number of such unavoidable errors. The recurring question—though it is rarely asked explicitly—is this: How many false positives should we be prepared to accept, in order to avoid how many false negatives? In seeking to answer this question, any jurisprudence must give appropriate weight to the costs and benefits of each such errors in the context in which they will occur. This is a daunting task requiring empirical, moral, legal, and other considerations.[3]

Let us first try to address this undertaking in a relatively simple everyday context:

A judge must decide whether a criminal defendant, who is presumed innocent but may in fact be guilty of armed robbery, should be released or detained pending trial. He is not a flight risk, so the only issue is predicting whether he will or will not commit a serious crime—presumably armed robbery—in the hiatus between now and the end of his trial.

Although the issue seems simple—he either will or won't (see the box on page 155—the decision involves a complex of factors, including the following:

- How long will the hiatus be? Three months, six months? A year or more? Can it be shortened without impacting trial preparation?
- What will the conditions of confinement be like?
- Are there reasonable measures short of confinement that would reduce the likelihood of him robbing?
- How likely is it that he did, in fact, engage in the armed robbery of which he is accused?
- Relatedly, how likely is he to be convicted of that crime at trial? If he is, what is the anticipated sentence?
- Will he seek a plea bargain and plead guilty?
- Will the bail determination impact his decision whether to seek a plea bargain?
- Will it impact his ability to prepare for trial if he decides not to plead?
- Will it impact his marriage, his family, his prospects for employment?

- Is he addicted to a drug, and if so would his addiction be a factor in whether he robs?
- Is he mentally ill or suicidal?
- Are there other factors—such as his age, prior criminal record if any, access to weapons, family situations—that may raise or lower the likelihood that he may rob?

Once the judge decides, or estimates, the likelihood that he will commit a robbery if released—say he puts it at 20 percent—he has to weigh the benefit of reducing that likelihood against the costs to the defendant of remaining confined for that period of time. These costs are difficult to quantify, yet they surely exist, especially if he were to be acquitted at trial. He cannot get back the months during which he was erroneously confined. Indeed, if the judge were to confine him because he erroneously believed he was guilty of the charged armed robbery and would recidivate, that would be a *double* false positive: erroneously *predicting* he would commit a future crime based on erroneously *post-dicting* that he had committed the past crime, (or predicting that he will be convicted, whether guilty or innocent).

If, on the other hand, the judge were to correctly predict that he committed the armed robbery and that he would recidivate, the first prediction would be validated by the subsequent conviction, while the second prediction—that he would have recidivated—could not be validated, because he remained confined and unable to recidivate during that time.

Other costs to the confined defendant would be his ability to prepare for trial, the pressure placed on him by the confinement to plead (even if innocent), and the dangers to which he would be exposed in pretrial detention facilities such as Rikers Island.

Now comes the hard part: weighing the benefit of reducing from 20 percent to zero the risk of defendant committing an armed robbery before trial if he were released against the unquantifiable costs to him if he would not have committed a robbery if released.

The costs though unquantifiable could be substantial in terms of liberty. A high number must be assigned to such costs in any system that values liberty. Perhaps not the ten to one assigned to false negatives in the context of convicting or acquitting at trial, because the cost of a false conviction carrying a long prison sentence is higher than the relatively short confinement pretrial. And that cost may be discounted by the likelihood of conviction and sentence that would count as time served in pretrial confinement.

So what would a proper answer be to the question of how many false positives, i.e., defendants falsely confined, should the justice system be willing to accept in order to prevent a single false negative, namely, an armed robbery committed by the falsely released defendant pending trial?

In implicitly answering this question every day in routine bail decisions, judges are inevitably influenced by the reality that if they make false positive mistakes, no one will find out that they were wrong, but if they make false negative mistakes, they will become headline news, endangering their career.[4] They may also cost the lives of innocent victims of the freed defendant's crimes.

One important question is whether a jurisprudence that assigned a higher negative score to false positives than to false negatives would pressure trial judges to release more people. This is unlikely in the present atmosphere where judges are being publicly excoriated for letting too many people remain free pending trial. But it might have an impact on appellate review of bail decisions. In any event, it is important for the jurisprudence to get it right, even if its impact on actual current decision-making is questionable. After all, how many judges and jurors actually believe that it is better for numerous serious criminals to go free than for even one innocent accused to be falsely convicted? In my experience few and far between, as manifested by their actual decisions. But it's still important to maintain the jurisprudential aspiration, even if it turns out to be largely ignored in practice. Today, however, even that aspirational fiction is not part of any jurisprudential framework for making or evaluating predictive decisions.

So let me turn to the question of what number—comparable to the number ten that has been assigned to the jurisprudence of true versus false convictions—should be assigned in the context of preventive confinement. First, a preliminary word about the "better ten" ratio for criminal convictions. It would have been far more just if that number were part of a sliding scale that depended on multiple factors, such as the length of the sentence that would be imposed on the one innocent defendant, and the seriousness of the crimes of the ten released guilty defendants. For example, if both groups involved accused murderers and sentences of life imprisonment, that might be different than if the groups involved accused fraudsters facing single-digit sentences. Although the ten-to-one ratio originated with death penalty cases—most felonies were capital in our early history—it has been mechanistically applied to all crimes, at least in theory.

In constructing a new jurisprudence for preventive intervention, we need not start with a general number, akin to the ten-to-one conviction ratio, because there are simply too many variables—moving parts—to warrant a single number in that context. Preventive confinement, for example, is different than preventive censorship, preventive vaccination, preventive war, and the numerous other preventative measures that are employed by governments. Even the singular mechanism of preventive confinement is too varied for a single number. A sliding-scale ratio based on a multifactor analysis would seem more appropriate. Some generalities however, may be helpful. No involuntary confinement, regardless of duration or location, should be authorized without considering the costs of false positives. Even momentary stops and arrests must be based on "reasonable" or "probable" cause, which implicitly suggests ratios, though relatively permissive ones, especially as contrasted with "proof beyond a reasonable doubt," which is required for conviction.

Any state-authorized involuntary confinement—whether denominated "civil," "criminal," "punitive" or "regulatory," whether lengthy or brief—should be based on ratios that give more negative weight to false positives than to false negatives. In other words, it is *not* better that one future crime be prevented than that one non-dangerous individual be wrongly confined. So the general rule for confinement should be: "it is better for more than one future crime to be committed than for one erroneously predicted crime-doer to be wrongfully confined." The precise ratio should depend of course on the seriousness of the predicted crime and the likelihood that it may be committed. The ratio should reflect the higher value we generally place on liberty than on safety. Reasonable people may disagree with this preference, but it derives from the ten-to-one ratio for convictions, the presumption of innocence, the requirement of proof beyond a reasonable doubt, and other procedural safeguards designed to make it difficult to convict the guilty (true positives), even if that means acquitting some guilty (false negatives). There is no persuasive reason why this general preference should not also apply to confinements that are preventive, civil, or regulatory.

With that in mind, let us now seek to apply this general preference for liberty to various types and durations of preventive confinement.

Here are some suggested ratios:

- A year or more—better ten
- Ninety days to a year—better six
- Ten days to ninety days—better four
- One to ten days—better two

These rough numbers, which are presented as illustrative, could be stated verbally rather than numerically (beyond a reasonable doubt, clear and convincing, heavy preponderance, probable cause) and are also not written in stone. They purport to represent a degree of preference for liberty over security in different contexts. The ratios should also assign numbers to the seriousness of the predicted crime and the likelihood it will occur. Comparable numbers can be assigned to other preventive intrusions, such as shooting of fleeing suspects, government mandated censorship, vaccination, extreme interrogation measures, and red flag laws. It would be more vexing to try to come up with numbers for steps taken to prevent climate change, preventive military actions, or other macro measures.

Some suggested ratios for other micro measures might be as follows:

The application of lethal force to a fleeing or resisting suspect involves several variables including immediate danger to the officers, longer-term danger to the public, and the seriousness of the suspected crime. In the *Garner* situation—an unarmed suspect in a nonviolent crime who is likely to escape unless shot—the Supreme Court has ruled that no number of false negatives (suspects who might escape) would justify even one shooting.[5]

As the costs of false negatives increase—the fleeing subject is more dangerous either to the arresting officers or the public—the permissible number of false positives might also increase. But because the cost of any positive—the shooting and possible killing of a fleeing subject—is so high, the acceptable ratio between false and true positives, must be at least as high as for criminal conviction. Hence, it is better that ten dangerous suspects go free than that even one suspect be shot. This does not apply, of course, to situations in which a policeman has the right to defend himself or others under traditional principles of self-defense. In the context of legitimate self-defense, the ratio favors the innocent victim over the guilty assailant: better ten (or some other number) of likely guilty assailants be killed than even one innocent victim be killed. Hence, a reasonable mistake of fact by the victim, even if turns out to be mistaken, is generally a defense in the cases of self-defense.

As to government mandated censorship, the permissible ratio is governed by the First Amendment under which freedom is the rule ("shall make no law") and censorship, especially prior censorship, the rare exception. So, it is better that ten (or another multiple thereof) potentially dangerous instances of speech be permitted than that even one instance of prior censorship be authorized. The number might be somewhat lower for post-speech punishment (or civil liability) than for prior censorship.

For mandatory vaccination, the number of dangerous side effects to the individual as compared to the danger to the public of not requiring vaccination must be extremely low. Compelling the injection of a vaccine is so intrusive that it must carry a near zero (absolute zero is impossible) risk.

Extreme interrogation measures—including torture, physical pain, waterboarding, electrodes—are generally illegal. If they are ever to be justified, the costs of a false negative must be extremely high, both in terms of immediate likelihood and potential mass victims. A nuclear device in the area, or 9/11- or October 7–type attacks, might satisfy these criteria, but the threat of a smaller terrorist attack would not. So in general it is better that ten acts of terrorism be tolerated than that even one act of torture be authorized, but the ratio should be different when a false negative is likely to produce mass casualties.

Recall again that these numbers are intended to be illustrative of how the ratios of false to true positives could be explicitly quantified or implicitly articulated in nonquantified terms that reflect the comparative values ascribed to different kinds of inevitable errors. As with any jurisprudential framework, the numbers themselves can vary, and reasonable people can assign different values to errors. The key point is to try to create a rational framework for making and evaluating these kinds of detailed decisions. Even the ten-to-one ratio for false convictions is merely heuristic, and the numbers are subject to challenge.[6] But it provides a jurisprudential framework for deciding how many false positives (convictions of the innocent) we should be willing to accept in order to avoid how many false negatives (acquittals of the guilty).

A similar analytic framework is appropriate for preventive decisions in which false positives can have a considerable impact on liberty, while false negative decisions can have a considerable impact on security. The most essential role of any jurisprudence is to strike an appropriate balance between the two types of inevitable errors. In a democracy governed by the rule of law, the precise values given to false positives and negatives in different contexts must be decided by elected officials, subject to the checks and balances of judicial review.

Academics can, however, assist in this process by suggesting analytical frameworks. Proposing numeric ratios for mistake preferences is an essential first step in constructing a substantive jurisprudence. The next steps must be taken by others. The goal of this book is to help rationalize and make transparent this critical and ongoing decision-making process.

CONCLUSION

PREDICTING THE FUTURE OF THE PREVENTIVE STATE

As the baseball sage Yogi Berra once put it: "It's tough to make predictions, especially about the future." He also said: "I really didn't say everything I said,"[1] so I'm not sure of the attribution, but the substance is correct, regardless of who said it. And so, it is difficult to predict the future of the preventive state, though certain trends seem relatively certain, despite the wide pendulum swings of history.

The preventive state is here to stay because the dual phenomena, described below, that give rise to it are only becoming more evident. The dire threats we face—nuclear and environmental disasters, rampant crime and terrorism, pandemics and other medical dangers, racial, religious, and ethnic divisions—are not diminishing. And our technological capacity to predict and prevent them is dramatically increasing and will continue to increase, because the rule is that new technology always generates even newer and more powerful technologies. Another rule is that it is impossible to predict precisely what new technologies will be developed and when. A related rule is that if we develop a useful technology, we will use it, despite its cost to other values.

So, the elements that give rise to the preventive state persist and promise to increase in urgency. Both the need for mechanisms to prevent disasters and the availability of such mechanisms have increased and will continue to increase exponentially. This means that absent significant changes, the preventive state will only become more intrusive and pervasive.

There are several significant changes that could impose some constraints on the increasing deployment of intrusive measures that inhere in the preventive state. Primary among them is a change in the legal landscape that would be brought about by the development of a calibrated jurisprudence that cabins the permissible use of preventive measures and balances them against the liberties that are inevitably compromised by their pervasive deployment.

Another change would be technological: the development of protective technologies to limit the negative effects of technological improvements. The problem is that every technology begets a counter-technology that begets a counter-counter-technology, generally without immediately enforceable legal constraints. Technology alone cannot be relied on to protect liberty. We need laws that constrain, control, and detect technological intrusions on privacy, liberty, and other important values that are currently endangered in the legitimate interest of preventing serious harms. But here is the paradox: laws may constrain law-abiding states and individuals; they are less likely to prevent their misuse by rogue states and lawless actors. And it is inevitable that any technology that is deemed useful to law violators will find its way into their dirty hands. This is true of low-tech instruments such as guns, primitive surveillance tools, communication devices, and other everyday mechanisms. It is equally true of the most sophisticated technologies such as Israel's spyware Pegasus and satellite communications. The goal is to minimize misuse without giving the bad guys an advantage—not an easy tightrope to walk, especially in democracies governed by the rule of law. As the former president of Israel's Supreme Court, Aharon Barak, put it in the context of a decision banning the use of torture as a means of obtaining real-time intelligence about terrorist plans: "Although a democracy must often fight with one hand tied behind its back, it nonetheless has the upper hand [because] the rule of law and liberties constitute an important aspect of her security stance."[2]

But law and science alone will not be sufficient to protect us from ourselves. Some of the most dangerous developments that we are currently experiencing are not amenable to either legal or scientific constraints. The divisions among us, and the hatreds these divisions sow, make it difficult to subject these irrationalities to intelligent discourse and fair compromise resolutions—in other words, to demo-cratic compromise. These divisions and their negative consequences will continue to get worse, because they are most extreme among our future leaders—young, educated, often well-intentioned zealots who believe that they and they alone know The Truth, and that there is no need to tolerate untruthful dissenting views. Many also undervalue privacy and liberty in their zeal to achieve their utopian goals without regard to dangerous means. As with past revolutionaries, their self-proclaimed noble ends are claimed to justify many ignoble means.

The great justice Louis Brandeis warned us a century ago that: "The greatest dangers to liberty lurk in insidious encroachment by men [and women] of zeal, well-meaning but without understanding."[3]

An equally great judge, Learned Hand, took this warning to the next step during the horrors of World War II: "Liberty lies in the hearts of men and women; when it dies there, no constitution, no law, no court, can even do much to help it."[4]

I disagree that no law can help, but I agree that no law alone can prevent tyranny.

So am I a pessimist or an optimist about the uncertain future of the preventive state? An old joke defines a pessimist as one who says, "Things are so bad, they can't possibly get worse." The optimist responds enthusiastically, "Yes they can!"

I am an optimist. I believe things could get worse but I also think we have the ability to stem this dangerous tide, to turn things around, and to make them better. That is why I have been thinking and writing about the benefits and costs of prevention in general and the preventive state in particular during my entire career. Preventing harms before they occur is indeed a noble goal. But it must be pursued justly, with noble means tested by experience. For the past sixty-five years, I have been trying to suggest—in articles, classes, and books—appropriate ways to strike this balance. In this book, I have put my ideas into a more systematic and comprehensive format. My goal is to contribute to the promotion of liberty in the hearts and minds of our citizens, to try to influence our future leaders to use their zeal in the service of liberty, and to try to prevent the preventive state from striking the balance too much on the side of security and too little in favor of liberty. It is still a work in progress, as are all efforts to follow the biblical command: "Justice, justice shall you pursue."[5]

APPENDIX

THE ANCIENT RABBINIC APPROACH TO PREVENTION

Every society that aspires to govern within the rule of law finds it necessary to create (or discover) exceptions to the formal rules for what its leaders deem to be emergencies, extraordinary situations, or the "needs of the time."[1] This is because codified rules of law cannot anticipate all contingencies and threats, and because formal rules often make it difficult to incapacitate all dangerous people. We see this phenomenon operating in post-9/11 America where Guantanamo has filled gaps left by the criminal law, and in Israel where administrative detention serves to confine dangerous terrorists who cannot be convicted of past crimes.

Rabbinic authorities anticipated this issue and provided what they believed were proper responses within the Jewish traditions. Their questions have endured the test of time. Their answers, for the most part, have not.

Classical Jewish law, which is among the most ambitious attempts to function within the constraint of formal rules set out in the Torah and its authoritative interpretations, is also among the most innovative in creating (or discovering) ways around these constraints. (Maybe that's why there are so many Jewish lawyers!)

During different periods of Jewish history, rabbinical authorities have authorized practices—some of which appear to be in direct contradiction to the clear words of the Torah—empowering the authorities to do what needs to be done to prevent grave harms to the community.

These practices invariably accomplish several things: they weaken the protections afforded those suspected of criminal or deviant behavior; they strengthen the power of authorities; they pander to the ever-present popular fear of disorder; and they do so in the benign name of "prevention."

These preventive actions—ad hoc practices devised to go beyond what is authorized by the formal code of laws in order to prevent grave harms—have a long and troubling history within the Jewish tradition (as they do among Western traditions in general). Western parlance distinguishes between what it considers "punishment" (which is backward looking) and "coercion" (which is forward looking). The distinction is, however, at best imprecise, because punishment coerces (and looks forward as well, to deter) and coercion punishes (and looks backward, for evidence of danger). A more apt distinction is between formal laws that err on the side of protecting the accused, and informal practices, that err on the side of empowering the authorities in the name of protecting the community.

For example, the Torah explicitly requires the testimony of two witnesses before a defendant can be convicted of a capital crime and executed. This daunting procedural protection makes it difficult to convict the guilty, in order to assure a high level of protection for the innocent. What then should be done with an obviously guilty and dangerous murderer whose crime was witnessed by only one highly credible witness? Should he simply be acquitted and allowed to return to the community, and perhaps kill again, taking care not to be seen by a second witness? The literal words of the Torah would suggest that unacceptable result. So the rabbis devised a series of informal, preventive measures designed to satisfy the needs of the time without purporting to violate the letter of biblical law.

These measures, which include the accordion-like concept of the *rodef*—traditionally defined as one who is pursuing another to do harm—are so broad and open-ended that they threaten to swallow up the very concept of the rule of law and to substitute vigilante justice (an oxymoron if there ever was one) for thoughtfully calibrated codes that strike the balance between community safety and due process in favor of the latter.

The expansive use of emergency measures also demonstrates the dangers of making it too difficult to convict the guilty, thereby necessitating informal "safety nets." It suggests the need for the kind of balance reflected in Abraham's argument with God over the sinners of Sodom. The "world's first Jewish lawyer" persuaded God to spare the city of Sodom if He found ten righteous people therein. By stopping at ten and not insisting that all the guilty be spared if there were as few as one or two innocent townsfolk, Abraham (and God) recognized the need for proportionality in any just legal system, while at the same time expressing a preference that some guilty go free rather than some innocents be wrongly condemned. But proportionality and nuance are often the first causalities of perceived emergencies.

Jewish law may have been among the first to acknowledge the conflict between formal laws that offer extraordinary protections to the accused, and the danger to the community posed by such heightened protections, but other rule-oriented systems have also addressed this problem, and experience provides some generalizations.

The rabbis failed to address these issues in a sufficiently nuanced and systemic way, or to develop modes of analysis for answering them, beyond clichés extolling the virtues of building fences, satisfying needs, and protecting the community. We must come to understand and acknowledge the harms that could be caused by ounces of preventive coercion or by stitches of preventive confinement.

The relationship between the formal criminal procedures set out in the Torah and the less formal mechanisms for dealing with the needs of the day presents a fascinating area for study, since it is an ongoing area of conflict in all contemporary nations governed by the rule of law.

The formal rules that make it difficult to convict not only the innocent but also the guilty are often used as an example of the "liberal" value reflected in the Torah. But there is a dark side of this moon, often hidden from view by apologists for Jewish law or preventive law in general. This dark side is the broad, discretionary power arrogated by the rabbis to themselves in the name of protecting the community from danger. Invoking such talismanic phrases as "the needs of the hour," a "fence around the Torah," and "emergency measures," the rabbis essentially created a supplement to the Torah that has virtually erased the safeguards contained in the Five Books themselves. The "fence" has become a black hole; the needs of the hour have become the convenience of every hour; discretion has substituted for procedure; and prevention has trumped the presumption of innocence. This is not a system of which liberals should be proud.

Consider the case of Rabbi Kahana who "tore out [the] windpipe" of a man who threatened to inform against a fellow Jew's property. How can such an act of disproportionate vigilante injustice be justi-fied by the principles of the Torah? Rabbi Eliezer ben Yakov wrote: "I have received by tradition that a court may impose flagellation and [other] punishments not [warranted] by the Torah; not to transgress against the words of the Torah, but rather to erect a fence around the Torah." But what about fences around those parts of the Torah that demand protection of the accused? Why not three witnesses? Why do the fences make it easier, not more difficult to punish or coerce? Why do the needs of the time never seem to require greater protection of the accused from the likes of Rabbi Kahana or the biblical vigilante Pinchas? Because the concept of fences is largely a ploy to give the rabbis more power. (Some current Haredi rabbis have ruled that "the fence" prohibits smartphones, because such technology may give its owner "outside" information with which to challenge the authority of the rabbis.) In this regard, the fence is reminiscent of the oven of Akhnai story that elevates the power of the rabbis over God's voice.[2] The fence concept elevates the power of the rabbis over the clear words of the Torah.

The power-grabs reflected by fences, needs, and the Akhnai story have been repeated throughout history. The United States Supreme Court demanded the authority to interpret the words of the Constitution in the famous case of *Marbury v. Madison.* It too has built fences and created exceptions for emergencies. The British courts authorized extralegal measures during the world wars. The Israeli courts—without a written constitution or Torah to constrain them—have allowed exceptions during periods of emergency.

What is needed is a thoughtful jurisprudence of prevention and emergencies. (The Israeli Supreme Court, more than any other, has at least begun to develop such a jurisprudence.) We currently live in an age of continuing, perhaps permanent, emergencies. The needs of the time are daunting. We are experiencing the emergence of "the preventive state" that requires a jurisprudence to cabin the enormous power of such a Leviathan.

This jurisprudence should contain both substantive and procedural rules governing all actions—formal and informal, punitive and preventive—taken by officials to prevent harmful conduct, such as terrorism. Black holes in the law—whether they are dug by rabbis, judges, or other functionaries—are anathema to democracy, accountability, human rights, and the rule of law.

The rabbis, as usual, pose the right questions, but their answers were less than satisfactory. Experience—mostly bad experience—has given us the wisdom to do better. We must do better, if the values explicit and implicit in the Torah are to be served, along with those of democracy and the rule of law.

ACKNOWLEDGMENTS

The roots of this book go deep into my past. Many research assistants helped to develop my ideas. Most recently, Aaron Voloj provided suggestions and research. My late colleague Dr. Alan Stone taught seminars with me on this subject. My assistants Annie Hoyos and Maura Kelly helped produce the manuscript. As usual, my loving wife Carolyn Cohen and my children and grandchildren inspire me to continue to think and write as I grow older.

ENDNOTES

NOTES TO INTRODUCTION

1 Steven Pinker, *The Better Angels of Our Nature: Why Violence Has Declined* (New York: Viking, 2011).

2 Charles Dickens, *A Tale of Two Cities* (1859): "It was the best of times; it was the worst of times."

3 This assumes the existence of a God who punishes people who don't believe in him—an assumption that Jefferson and others have challenged.

4 See my student note, "Why Do Criminal Attempts Fail: A New Defense," *Yale Law Journal* 70, no. 1 (November 1960): 160–69; see also, Alan M. Dershowitz, "On 'Preventive Detention,'" *New York Review of Books*, March 13, 1969.

5 A similar cost-benefit calculus is at work when governments take lesser preventive measures—such as surveillance or detention—against individuals or small groups suspected of planning terrorist acts. In both macro and micro contexts, the cost of what scientists call a type 1 error must be weighed against the cost of a type 2 error.

6 See Alan M. Dershowitz, "Terrorism and Preventive Detention: The Case of Israel," *Commentary* (December 1970): 67–73.

7 See generally, Alexander Volokh, "N Guilty Men," *University of Pennsylvania Law Review* 146, no.2 (November 1997): 173–216.

8 See Alan M. Dershowitz, *The Genesis of Justice*, chapter 4 (New York: Warner, 2000).

9 See, e.g., Jason Burke, "Yahya Sinwar: The Man Who May Hold Key to Release of Gaza Hostages," *Guardian*, November 21, 2023.

10 Tamir Pileggi, "Palestinians Freed in Shalit Deal Killed 6 Israelis Since 2015: Arrest of Hamas Operatives behind Deadly West Bank Terror Last Month Highlights the Cost of Prisoner Exchange," *Times of Israel*, July 20, 2015.

11 Jewish tradition identifies values that cannot be counted, such as rendering kindness and studying Torah. Mishna Peah 1:1.

12 See film *Don't Look Up* (Netflix 2021).

13 Alan M. Dershowitz, "Preventive Confinement: A Suggested Framework for Constitutional Analysis," *Texas Law Review* 51, no. 7 (November 1973): 1277–1324, quoting Robert Sheckley, "The Academy," in his *Pilgrimage to Earth* (New York: Bantam, 1957).

14 See generally, Nita Farahany, *The Battle For Your Brain: Defending The Right to Think Freely in the Age of Neurotechnology* (New York: St. Martin's, 2023).

15 Benjamin Franklin, "Pennsylvania Assembly: Reply to the Governor, November 11, 1755."

16 Exod. 21:15, 17; Deut. 21:20; cf. also Lev. 20:9 (requiring children who curse or strike their parents to be put do death).

17 Num. 5:1–4; see also Num. 12:10–15.

18 Quoted in Paul Johnson, *Modern Times: The World from The Twenties to the Eighties* (New York: HarperCollins, 1983), 341. Germany, of course, started the war by invading Poland in 1939.

19 See generally, Alan M. Dershowitz, *Preemption: A Knife That Cuts Both Ways* (New York: W. W. Norton, 2007), 64–69.

20 Ibid., chapters 5–6.

21 Ibid., 108–14.

22 Alan M. Dershowitz, *Is There a Right to Remain Silent? Coercive Interrogation and The Fifth Amendment after 9/11* (New York: Oxford, 2008), 176.

23 Roscoe Pound, *Justice According to Law* (New Haven: Yale University Press, 1951), 2.

24 Stephen Breyer, *Reading the Constitution: Why I Chose Pragmatism, Not Textualism* (New York: Simon and Schuster, 2024), xxv.

25 Ibid., xxiii (discussing Montaigne).

26 Ibid., xxiv (discussing Montaigne).

27 Roscoe Pound, introduction to Raymond Saleilles, *The Individualization of Punishment* (1911), trans. Rachel Szold Jastrow (Montclair, NJ: Patterson Smith, 1968), xi (emphasis added).

28 "Why Do Criminal Attempts Fail? A New Defense." As a law student, I worked on two additional student articles, each of which dealt with the need for articulated criteria and public accountability. I wrote a comment on corporate crime in which I proposed a new system of sanctions for corporations, suggesting criteria that were more explicit and more targeted at those who made policy for the corporations. "Comment, Increasing Community Control Over Corporate Crime—A Problem in the Law of Sanctions," *Yale Law Journal* 71, no. 2 (December 1961): 280–305. I then edited a comprehensive draft of a penal code in which Professor George Dession attempted to find, as I stated it, "the proper role of a law of crimes in a society which postulates maximum toleration of nonconforming behavior while seeking to preserve its preferred form of public order." "Comment, Professor George H. Dession's Final Draft of the Code of Correction for Puerto Rico," *Yale Law Journal* 71, no. 6 (May 1962): 1050–1160.

29 Early writings include Alan M. Dershowitz, "Psychiatry in the Legal Process: 'A Knife That Cuts Both Ways,'" *Judicature* 51, 370 (1968); Alan M. Dershowitz, On "Preventive Detention,"(1969, cited above); Alan Dershowitz, "Preventive Detention of Citizens During a National Emergency—A Comparison between Israel and the United States," *Israel Yearbook on Human Rights* 1 (1971): 295–321; Alan M. Dershowitz, "Imprisonment by Judicial Hunch," *American Bar Association Journal* 57, no. 6 (June 1971): 560–64; Alan Dershowitz, "'Stretch Points' of Liberty," *The Nation*, March 15, 1971; Alan M. Dershowitz, "Preventive Disbarment: The Numbers Are Against It," *American Bar Association Journal* 58, no. 8 (August 1972): 815–19; Alan M. Dershowitz, "Wiretaps and National Security,"

Commentary, January 1972; Dershowitz, "Preventive Confinement: A Suggested Framework for Constitutional Analysis" (1973, cited above); Alan Dershowitz, "The Origins of Preventive Confinement in Anglo-American Law—Part I: The English Experience," *University of Cincinnati Law Review* 43, no. 1 (1974): 1–60 (hereafter "Preventive Confinement, Part I"); Alan Dershowitz, "The Origins of Preventive Confinement in Anglo-American Law—Part II: The American Experience," *University of Cincinnati Law Review* 43, no. 4 (1974): 781–846.

30   Dershowitz, *Preemption,* 1–2.

31   In a decision by the Supreme Court of Israel forbidding the use of "physical pressure" to secure information deemed necessary to prevent future terrorist attacks, former chief justice Aharon Barak put it this way, "A democracy must sometimes fight with one hand tied behind its back. Even so, democracy has the upper hand." Public Committee against Torture v. Government (December 14, 2006); an English translation from the Hebrew original is accessible at https://versa.cardozo.yu.edu/opinions/public-committee-against-torture-v-government).

32   See, e.g., Alan M. Dershowitz, "The Torture Warrant: A Response to Professor Strauss," *New York Law School Law Review* 48, no.1 (January 2004): 275–94. As I wrote in Why Terrorism Works: "In my debates with two prominent civil libertarians, Floyd Abrams and Harvey Silverglate, both have acknowledged that they would want nonlethal torture to be used if it could prevent thousands of deaths, but they did not want torture to be officially recognized by our legal system." As Abrams put it: "In a democracy sometimes it is necessary to do things off the books and below the radar screen." Alan M. Dershowitz, *Why Terrorism Works: Understanding the Threat, Responding to the Challenge* (New Haven: Yale University Press, 2002), 151.

33   Quoted in Dershowitz, *Preemption,* 3.

34   Ibid.

35   See Alan M. Dershowitz, *War Against the Jews: How to End Hamas Barbarism* (New York: Skyhorse Publishing, 2023).

36   Korematsu v. United States, 323 U.S. 214 (1944).

37   Buck v. Bell, 274 U.S. 200 (1927).

38   Jacobson v. Massachusetts, 197 U.S. 11 (1905).

39   John Rawls, *A Theory of Justice* (Cambridge, MA: Harvard University Press, 1971).

40   Siddharta Mukherjee, "Will We All Soon Live in Cancerland?," *Wall Street Journal,* December 17, 2021.

41   Ibid.

42   Ibid.

43   Ibid.

44   Ibid.

45   See Alan M. Dershowitz, *The Case Against the New Censorship: Protecting Free Speech from Big Tech, Progressives and Universities* (New York: Skyhorse Publishing, 2021); see also chapter 9, below.

46 Alan M. Dershowitz, *Rights from Wrongs: A Secular Theory of the Origins of Rights* (New York: Basic Books, 2004).

NOTES TO CHAPTER 1

1 Gen. 41:29–32.

2 Joshua 10:12.

3 David Sedley, "'Joshua Stopped the Sun' 3,224 Years Ago Today, Scientists Say," *Times of Israel*, October 30, 2017.

4 Num. 13:2.

5 Esther 1:13.

6 Deut. 21:18.

7 Cesare Lombroso, *The Criminal Man* (1876).

8 Eleanor T. Glueck, "Identifcation of Potential Delinquents at 2–3 Years of Age," *International Journal of Social Psychiatry* 12, no. 1 (1966).

9 Gen. 4:11–16.

10 See "Abbott Lawrence Lowell and Discrimination in Admissions and Housing," chapter 5 in *Harvard and the Legacy of Slavery*, available at https://legacyofslavery.harvard.edu/report/abbott-lawrence-lowell-and-discrimination-in-admissions-and-housing.

11 Buck v. Bell, 274 U.S. 200, 207 (1927).

12 Olmstead v. U.S., 277 U.S. 438, 537 (1928).

13 Alan Dershowitz, "Karyotype, Predictability and Culpability," in *Genetics and the Law*, edited by A. Milunsky and G. Annas (New York: Plenum Press, 1976).

14 Korematsu v. United States, 323 U.S. 214 (1944).

15 Alan Dershowitz, *The Case for Vaccine Mandates* (New York: Skyhorse Publishing, 2021).

16 Lewis Carroll, *The Annotated Alice* (New York: Norton, 2000), 196–98.

17 Everett v. Ribbands [1952], 2 QB 198, 206 (C.A.). The Lord Justice made this generalization in deciding that the English provision for sureties of peace required proof of "something actually done" in the past by the person to be confined, rather than a bare prediction of future harm.

18 Oliver Wendell Holmes Jr., *The Common Law* (1881), 43, 46.

19 Ibid., 46.

20 William Blackstone, *Commentaries on the Laws of England* (1769), book 4, 252–53.

21 Francis Wharton, *Treatise on Criminal Law*, § 2 (12th ed., 1932).

22 Beccaria, *An Essay on Crimes and Punishments* (Philadelphia: Nicklin, 1819), 148.

23 Immanuel Kant, *Metaphysical Elements of Justice* (1797), trans. John Ladd (Indianapolis: Hackett 1999), 138.

24 Immanuel Kant, *The Science of Right* (1790), trans. W. Hastie, available online.

25 Blackstone, *Commentaries*, book 4, 252–53.

26 Dershowitz, *Preemption*, 32.

27 The confinement of defendants acquitted by reason of insanity is also a way of holding past criminals who cannot be convicted. (In the modern context, it is

clear that sexual psychopathy and defective delinquency statues are often used against "known" criminals who cannot be convicted because of evidentiary inadequacies or the like.)

28 "Preventive Confinement, Part I."

29 Blackstone, *Commentaries*, book 4, 208.

NOTES TO CHAPTER 2

1   For a list, see Statista.

2   Robert J. Donovan, *The Assassins* (New York: Harper, 1955), 63–79.

3   F. Cas. 886 (nos. 15,576 and 15,577) (C.C.D.C 1835).

4   Donovan, *The Assassins*, 76, n58.

5   Ibid.

6   "Every free person who shall be convicted . . . of an attempt to commit any one of the crimes or offenses hereinbefore [d]escribed [murder was one the crimes described] shall . . . be confined at hard labor or in solitude, not exceeding five years, and fine[d] not exceeding one thousand dollars." An Act for the Punishment of Certain Crimes and Offenses, Within the District of Columbia, Code of Laws for the District of Columbia, Prepared Under the Authority of the Act of Congress of 29th of April, 1816. (Washington, D.C., 1819), 236 (in Harvard Law School Treasure Room).

7   John W. Curran, "Criminal and Non-Criminal Attempts," *Georgetown Law Journal* 19 (1930–31): 185, 321–22. At this point in time, there was an intimate connection—indeed significant confusion—between attempted murder and assault with intent to kill.

8   United States v. Hudson, 11 U.S. (7 Cranch) 32 (1812).

9   26 F. Cas. at 888.

10 Id.

11 Id.

12 Id.

13 Id., at 889.

14 British Newspaper Archive, *Chester Chronicle*, June 27, 1800.

15 The question, "Should he be confined?," if answered affirmatively, leads to the questions, "Where and for how long?" The question, "Should he be released?," if answered affirmatively, leads to the questions, "Conditionally?" and if so, "Under what kinds of conditions?" or "Subject to what kinds of forfeitures?"

16 He could, of course, be acquitted outright or the charges dropped, but the assumption here is that the defendant did, in fact, attempt to commit a serious crime.

17 It was not at this time completely settled—at least as a matter of formal law— that a person found incompetent to stand trial must necessarily be confined rather than released on bail pending the restoration of his competency. Compare Commonwealth v. Bradley, 1 Mass. 103 (1804), with Zembrod v. State, 25 Tex. 519 (1860). It is clear, however, that the practice was to confine defendants found incompetent to stand trial who were regarded as dangerous.

18 An exaggerated version of the common, but erroneous, view was taken by Dr. Donald W. Hastings. See Hastings, "The Psychiatry of Presidential Assassination," *Journal-Lancet* 85 (1965): 93, 95: "Lawrence pleaded insanity, which was the only defense that was possible. Francis Scott Key undoubtedly could have arranged a quick trial and execution as he desired, thereby winning a victory as a prosecutor; the public was seething and wanted Lawrence to die. To Key's everlasting credit, he did not hang this sick man" (emphasis added). Dr. Hastings cites the Donovan book as the source of this information, but Donovan himself points out that Lawrence's crime was "only a misdemeanor, punishable by fine and imprisonment." Dr. Hastings seems to have invented the fiction that "Key undoubtedly could have arranged a quick trial and execution," just as he apparently made up the fact that the public "wanted Lawrence to die." It is also not true, as indicated above, that insanity was the "only defense that was possible." The validity of federal courts' employing a common law crime could also have been challenged.

19 The words "offspring of the disease" which were used in Lawrence are not very distant from the "product" concept of Durham.

20 Donovan, *The Assassins*, 78 n58.

21 26 F. Cas. at 891.

22 For a description of the breakdown, see Cambill Robertson, "Police Commander Provides More Details on Trump Rally Shooting," *New York Times*, July 23, 2024.

23 Vice President Nixon took a goodwill tour of Venezuela in 1958 over the objection of the Secret Service and was nearly killed.

NOTES TO CHAPTER 3

1 Blackstone, *Commentaries*, book 4, 252–53.

2 Inchoate crimes are also used by prosecutors in plea bargaining. Even in cases in which harms are in fact caused, prosecutors frequently offer to reduce the charge to an inchoate crime in exchange for a plea of guilty and/or cooperation.

3 The reality that most charged defendants are in fact guilty may not be true of tyrannical regimes that charge innocent civilians. They also convict innocent defendants, thus hiding the number of false arrests.

4 The first Congress also included in the Judiciary Act of 1789 a provision establishing that for "all arrests in criminal cases, bail shall be admitted, except where the punishment may be death." An Act to Establish the Judicial Courts of the United States, 1 Stat. 73, § 33 (1789).

5 Holmes, *The Common Law*.

6 Dershowitz, "On 'Preventive Detention.'"

7 Judges tend to be accurate in predicting which defendants will be convicted for the simple reason that the vast majority—more than 90 percent—will be. That is because in democracies like the U.S.—as contrasted with tyrannies like Iran and Russia—the vast majority of prosecuted defendants are in fact guilty. But a much smaller percentage would flee or commit crimes, so judicial predictions about flight and crime are likely to include more false positives.

8 Some researchers hope that AI tools will correct biases and subjective elements that judges may have in setting bail. See Sam Corbett-Davies, Sharad Goel, and Sandra Gonzalez-Bailon, "Even Imperfect Algorithms Can Improve the Criminal Justice System," *New York Times*, December 20, 2017. Others worry that AI programs operate in a black box and are not subject to the same standards used for evaluating expert testimony. Judge Jed Rakoff wrote powerfully about COMPAS, a software program designed to predict recidivism rates. He notes that "no one knows if judges who don't use such programs are any better at predicting recidivism (though one study…finds that even a random sample of laypeople is as good as the most frequently used algorithm). But the use of such programs supplies a scientific façade to these assessments that the large error rate belies." Jed Rakoff, "Sentenced by Algorithm," *New York Review of Books*, June 10, 2021.

9 One of the reasons I have always devoted half my practice to pro-bono representation of defendants who can't afford to pay for a lawyer, is to do my small part in helping to promote equal justice, but this doesn't address the larger societal problem.

10 The current common formulation includes "justice to the victim."

11 I was not his lawyer; I sought commutation as an opponent of capital punishment.

12 The case of Dr. James Grigson, who was known as Dr. Death for his perpetual findings of future dangerousness for capital defendants is discussed in Estelle v. Smith, 451 U.S. 454 (1981).

13 Sentencing guidelines employ various factors that purport to predict violence and recidivism. For instance, Virginia's sentencing guidelines use age and gender as aggravating factors in sentencing decisions. If one is a young offender—age twenty or younger—that offender is given more "points" than an offender above the age of twenty. Likewise, male offenders get more points than female ones, on the theory that men are more likely to recidivate than women. As one scholar put it, "The…question is whether youth should be included in any prediction instrument meant to be used, or that might be used, in deciding whom to imprison or for how long. The trade-off is between predictive accuracy and punishing people because they are young. If the trade-off concerned eye color, race, or religion, few people would consider it. Even if any of them predicted reoffending, basic requirements of justice forbid their use." Michael Tonry, "Predictions of Dangerousness in Sentencing: Déjà Vu All Over Again," *Crime and Justice* 48 (2019): 455.

14 In Kansas v. Hendricks, the U.S. Supreme Court held that a civil commitment law allowing the indefinite detention of a sex offender immediately upon conclusion of his prison sentence was civil in nature and therefore the detention was not punishment. I wrote about " the legal labeling game" in which states call laws "civil" rather than "criminal" to make it easier to detain individuals and for courts to evade responsibility. Dershowitz, "Preventive Confinement: A Suggested Framework for Constitutional Analysis," 1295–1301.

15 Jessica Mitford, *Kind and Usual Punishment* (New York: Vintage, 1974).

16 Some states use an actuarial risk assessment instrument called Static-99, which

has been subject to mounting criticism, including unclear statistical methods and dubious risk scores. See Alexander J. Blenkinsopp, "Dangerousness and the Civil-Criminal Distinction: Another Reason to Rethink the Indefinite Detention of Sex Offenders," *Connecticut Law Review* 45 (November 2012).

17 See Andrew Manuel Crespo, "No Justice, No Pleas: Subverting Mass Incarceration through Defendant Collective Action," *Fordham Law Review* 90, no. 5 (April 2022).

18 Alan M. Dershowitz, "Most Plea Bargains Are Unconstitutional," *Wall Street Journal*, November 5, 2019.

19 In the civil context, conditional release exists in some jurisdictions for persons with mental illness and sex offenders who face mandatory outpatient treatment. In the criminal context, conditional release can take the form of probation and parole. For a discussion, see Naomi Weinstein, "The Legal Aspects of Conditional Release in the Criminal and Civil Court System," *Behavioral Sciences & the Law* 32 (September 2014): 666.

20 L. F. Javik, V. Klodin, and S. Matsuyama, "Human Aggression and the Extra Chromosome—Facts or Fantasy?," *American Psychologist* 28 (August 1973) (discussing studies that indicate that "some of society's most notorious murderers...had the extra y chromosome.") The problem with this approach is as follows: even if 90 percent of certain types of criminals have a particular marker, it may also be true that only 1 percent of people with that marker will become criminals. See Dershowitz, "Karyotype, Predictability and Culpability."

21 Aldous Huxley, *Brave New World* (1931).

22 *Minority Report*, DreamWorks Pictures (2002).

23 Williamson v. United States, 1950 WL 42366, at *2 (U.S. Sept. 25, 1950).

24 Id.

25 In Hawaii, martial law was declared, rather than mass detention of the large Japanese ethnic population. The general in charge had wide discretion to detain individuals of Japanese background on the basis of individual predictions. See Dershowitz, Preemption, 111 (comparing the treatment of Japanese Americans with that of U.S. citizens of Italian and German descent).

26 Alan M. Dershowitz, "The Law of Dangerousness: Some Fictions about Predictions," *Journal of Legal Education* 23, no. 1 (January 1971): 24.

NOTES TO CHAPTER 4

1 Tennessee v. Garner, 471 U.S. 1 (1985).

2 Id. at 8, quoting United States v. Place, 462 U.S. 696, 703 (1983). Justice Byron White described the balancing process as follows: "notwithstanding probable cause to seize a suspect, an officer may not always do so by killing him. The intrusiveness of a seizure by means of deadly force is unmatched. The suspects fundamental interest in his own life need not be elaborated upon. The use of deadly force also frustrates the interest of the individual, and of society, in judicial determination of guilt and punishment. Against these interests are ranged governmental interests in effective law enforcement." Id. at 9.

3 Id. at 11.

4 Id.

5 Id. at 11–12.

6 Terry v. Ohio, 392 U.S. 1, 26 (1968).

7 California v. Ciraolo, 476 U.S. 207 (1986); Dow Chemical Co. v. United States, 476 U.S. 227 (1986); Florida v. Riley, 488 U.S. 445 (1989).

8 California v. Greenwood, 486 U.S. 35 (1988).

9 United States v. Jones, 565 U.S. 400 (2012).

10 Kyllo v. United States, 533 U.S. 27 (2001).

NOTES TO CHAPTER 5

1 Edward Gibbon, *The Decline and Fall of the Roman Empire* (1776) (New York: Modern Library, 2005), 587–88.

2 Niccolo Machiavelli, *The Prince* (1532), trans. David Wootton (Indianapolis/ Cambridge: Hacket Publishing Co., 1995), 11.

3 See Babylonian Talmud, Tractate Sanhedrin, portion 72, verse 1.

4 Esther 9:5.

5 See Alan Dershowitz, *The Case Against the Iran Deal: How Can We Stop Iran Getting Nukes?* (New York: Rosetta Books, 2015).

6 Dershowitz, *The Case Against the Iran Deal*.

7 See Dershowitz, *Preemption*, 67.

8 Ibid., 76–89.

9 Quoted in ibid., 96.

10 Dershowitz, *War Against the Jews*.

11 Summer Said and Rory Jones, "Gaza Chief's Brutal Calculation: Civilian Bloodshed Will Help," *Wall Street Journal*, June 10, 2024.

12 As early as October 2023, the New York Times famously (or infamously) fell for Hamas' false claim that innocent civilians were killed by an alleged Israeli attack on al-Ahli Hospital in Gaza City. It turned out that the "attack" almost certainly came from a misfire by a Palestinian Islamic Jihad projectile. "NY Times Admits Its Coverage of Gaza Hospital Blast Relied Too Heavily on Hamas Claims," *Times of Israel*, October 23, 2023.

13 On May 16, 2024, the Israeli government said that the ratio of terrorists to Palestinian noncombatants killed is approximately one to one, claiming it killed roughly 14,000 combatants and 16,000 noncombatants. "Israel Releases New Gaza Death Toll, Claims Historically Low Civilian Deaths," *Jewish News Syndicate*, May 16, 2024, JNS.org. These numbers have changed over time, and there are no absolutely reliable figures.

14 Ibid.

15 John Spencer, "Israel Has Created New Standard for Urban Warfare. Why Will No One Admit It?," *Newsweek*, March 26, 2024. The author is the chair of urban warfare at the Modern War Institute at West Point.

16 Ibid.

NOTES TO CHAPTER 6

1   The Supreme Court had ruled that the "cruel and unusual punishment" prohibition is applicable only to past conviction punishment, not to interrogation methods. See Dershowitz, *Is There A Right to Remain Silent?*, discussing Chavez v. Martinez, 538 U.S. 760 (2003).

2   In the past, torturing enemies of the state was justified as an added deterrent to mere execution. That justification is rarely offered today.

3   Dershowitz, *Why Terrorism Works* (2002). See also Alan M. Dershowitz, "Reply: Torture without Visibility and Accountability Is Worse Than with It," *University of Pennsylvania Journal of Constitutional Law* 6, (2003): 326; Dershowitz, "The Torture Warrant: A Response to Professor Strauss," 277; and Alan Dershowitz, "Tortured Reasoning," in *Torture: A Collection*, ed. Sanford Levinson (New York: Oxford, 2004).

4   Dershowitz, *Why Terrorism Works*, 137. In Germany, a kidnapper disclosed the location of his child victim after being merely threatened with torture. This well-publicized case sparked a debate about the use of torture in the case of emergencies. Richard Bernstein, "Kidnapping Has German Debating Police Torture," *New York Times*, April 10, 2003. I wrote about this case in an op-ed piece for the *Los Angeles Times*, "German Issue Is One for U.S. Too: Can Torture, or Threat of It, Be Right?," April 17, 2023.

5   Leon v. Wainwright, 734 F.2d 770 (11th Cir. 1984).

6   Marcy Strauss, "Torture," *New York Law School Law Review* 48, no. 1 (January 2004): 269–70.

7   Ibid., 275–76.

8   Fyodor Dostoevsky, *The Brothers Karamazov* (1880).

9   Jeremy Bentham, "Value of a Lot of Pleasure or Pain, How to Be Measured," in *An Introduction to the Principles of Morals and Legislation* (Oxford: Clarendon Press, 1902), available at https://www.econlib.org/library/Bentham/bnthPML.html.

10 Jeb Babbin, "The Silence of the Lambs: Torture Is Not Appropriate Treatment for Terrorists," *Washignton Times*, March 21, 2002, A19.

11 Dershowitz, "The Torture Warrant: A Response to Professor Strauss."

12 Carol Rosenberg, "C.I.A. Violently Cut Off 9/11 Suspect When He Tried to Talk about Attacks," *New York Times*, February 29, 2024.

13 David Cole, "An Executive Power to Kill?," *New York Review of Books*, March 6, 2012.

14 Unlike in the U.S., where the president alone makes the decision to employ this tactic, in Israel, the Supreme Court closely regulates the practice of targeted killings. See Alan Dershowitz, "Targeted Killing Vindicated," *HuffPost*, March 2, 2011.

15 See Alan M. Dershowitz, *On Killing: How the Law Decides Who Shall Live and Who Shall Die* (New York: Skyhorse Publishing, 2023).

NOTES TO CHAPTER 7

1   See e.g., State v. Perricone, 37 N.J. 463, 181 A.2d 751 (1962).

2   See also Hart v. Brown, 29 Conn. Supp. 368, 289 A.2d 386 (1972).

3 See generally, Dershowitz, *The Case for Vaccine Mandates*.

4 John Stuart Mill, *On Liberty* (1859), chapter 1 (emphasis added).

5 Elizabeth Weise, "Omicron Could Be More Contagious, Less Dangerous," *USA Today*, December 7, 2021.

6 "5 Things You Should Know about COVID-19 Vaccines," CDC, October 13, 2023, available at https://www.cdc.gov/ncird/whats-new/5-things-you-should-know.html.

7 Florida's surgeon general told parents of unvaccinated children that they have a choice whether to send their children to school thereby defying federal guidelines. AP story, "Florida Refuses to Bar Unvaccinated Students from School Suffering a Measles Outbreak," *US News*, February 23, 2024.

8 Letter to Dr. William Shippen, January 6, 1777, in George Washington Papers at the Library of Congress, 1741–1799: Series 4. General Correspondence, 1697–1777, available at https://www.nlm.nih.gov/exhibition/georgewashington/education/materials/Transcript-Shippen.pdf. I own another letter from George Washington to his generals reiterating this compulsion.

9 Jacobson v. Commonwealth of Massachusetts, 197 U.S. 11, 13 (1905).

10 Id. at 25.

11 Id.

12 Id. at 26.

13 Id. at 30.

14 Id. at 38–39.

15 Id. at 28.

16 Id. at 29.

17 Buck v. Bell, 274 U.S. 200, 207 (1927).

18 Skinner v. Oklahoma 316 U.S. 535 (1942).

19 See generally, James Q. Whitman, *Hitler's American Model: The United States and the Making of Nazi Race Law* (Princeton, NJ: Princeton University Press, 2017).

20 For an interesting intellectual history, see Adam Cohen, *Imbeciles: The Supreme Court, American Eugenics, and the Sterilization of Carrie Buck* (New York: Penguin Random House, 2016).

21 See Dershowitz, *Rights from Wrongs*.

NOTES TO CHAPTER 8

1 *Don't Look Up* (Netflix 2021).

2 D. Kriebel, J. Tickner, P. Epstein et al., "The Precautionary Principle in Environmental Science," *Environmental Health Perspectives* 109, no. 9 (September 2001): 871–76; see also Cass R. Sunstein, *The Law of Fear: Beyond the Precautionary Principle* (Cambridge University Press, 2005).

3 Kriebel et al., "The Precautionary Principle in Environmental Science," 873.

NOTES TO CHAPTER 9

1 This sentence—often attributed to Voltaire—is probably from Evelyn Beatrice Hall, who wrote it in *The Friends of Voltaire* (1906) to describe Voltaire's attitude.

2 First Amendment of the U.S. Constitution.

3 Alien and Sedition Acts (1798).

4 Letter to Elijah Boardman dated July 3, 1801. See Alan M. Dershowitz, *Finding Jefferson: A Lost Letter, a Remarkable Discovery, and the First Amendment in an Age of Terrorism* (Hoboken, NJ: Wiley, 2017).

5 Ibid.

6 See Alan Dershowitz, *Taking the Stand*, "Part II: The Changing Sound of Freedom of Speech" (New York: Broadway Books, 2013).

7 United States v. Dennis, 183 F.2d 201, 212 (2d Cir. 1950), affirmed, 341 U.S. 494 (1951).

8 New York Times Co. v. United States, 403 U.S. 713 (1971).

9 Arsen Ostrovsky and Gabriel Groisman, "Why We Filed a Civil Rights Claim against Berkeley Law School," *Newsweek*, November 23, 2022.

10 Whether they are violating the First Amendment itself is a more complex issue, beyond the scope of this book. See Alan Dershowitz, "For Universities Facing Lawsuits Over Antisemitism, First Amendment Offers Uncertain Defense," December 5, 2023, available at https://dersh.substack.com/p/for-universities-facing-lawsuits.

11 Susan D'Agostina, "Amid Backlash, Stanford Pulls 'Harmful Language' List," *Inside Higher Education*, January 10, 2023.

12 Schenck v. United States, 249 U.S. 47, 52 (1919).

13 See Alan M. Dershowitz, "Shouting 'Fire!'," *Atlantic* (January 1989).

14 Schenck v. United States, 249 U.S. 47, 52 (1919).

15 In fact, the House censured Rep. Jamaal Bowman for pulling the fire alarm on September 30, 2023, on his way to vote on a stopgap spending bill. No one argued that his pulling the fire alarm should be protected under the Speech or Debate clause of the First Amendment, which gives members of Congress absolute immunity for legislative acts taken in the course of their official responsibilities, including, but not limited to, speech and debate.

16 Hustler Mag., Inc. v. Falwell, 485 U.S. 46, 51 (1988) quoting Gertz v. Robert Welch, Inc., 418 U.S. 323, 339 (1974).

17 See Alan Dershowitz, *Cancel Culture: The Latest Attack on Free Speech and Due Process* (New York: Skyhorse Publishing, 2020).

18 Smith v. California, 361 U.S. 147 (1959).

19 See the murder and disappearance of journalists and dissidents in Russia, North Korea, and China.

20 Alternately he said: "Assassination is the extreme form of censorship." Bernard Shaw, *The Shewing-up of Blanco Posnet* (1913).

21 "Israeli Nuclear Whistle-Blower Back in Jail," CNN, May 23, 2010.

22 Mark Weiss, "Nuclear Whislteblower Vanuu Denied Permission to Leave Israel," *Irish Times*, December 16, 2019.

23 Dan Baron, "Vanunu: Hero or Traitor?," *Jewish Journal*, April 22, 2004.

24 Northern Securities Co. v. United States, 193 U.S. 197 (1904) (Holmes dissenting).

NOTES TO CHAPTER 10

1 Including restrictions on ammunition.

2 After the school shooting in Uvalde, Texas, I wrote the following op-ed: "The NRA's anti-American Narrative: No Excuse for Gun Violence Like the Uvalde School Shooting," *The Hill*, May 31, 2022.

3 Sheryl Gay Stolberg, "A Florida School Received a Threat. Did a Red Flag Law Prevent a Shooting?," *New York Times*, January 16, 2023.

4 At the time of this writing, in February 2024, Michigan became the twenty-first state to adopt red flag laws.

5 Stolberg, "A Florida School Received a Threat."

6 See chapter 8.

7 See Judge Learned Hand's formulation, quoted on page 119.

8 Stolberg, "A Florida School Received a Threat."

NOTES TO CHAPTER 11

1 Olmstead v. United States, 277 U.S. 438, 479 (1928).

2 See generally, Danielle Citron, *The Fight for Privacy; Protecting Dignity, Identity, and Love in the Digital Age* (New York: W. W. Norton, 2022).

3 Olmstead v. United States, 277 U.S. 438, 478 (1928).

4 See, e.g., Citron, *The Fight for Privacy.*

5 Louis Brandeis co-wrote his famous Right to Privacy article in 1890 out of a frustration over journalists' increasing ability to intrude upon private lives of citizens due to new technology (in his days, the advent of photography). Louis Brandeis and Samuel D. Warren, "The Right to Privacy," *Harvard Law Review* 4, no. 5 (1890).

6 Farahany, *The Battle for Your Brain*. As of this writing, Elon Musk's Neuralink is working to develop brain implants that will let people control computers and other devices using their thoughts. Christina Jewett, "Despite Setback, Neuralink's First Brain-Implant Patient Stays Upbeat," *New York Times*, May 22, 2024. While this use of brain implants carries potential benefits, the same technology can be used for more sinister purposes. For example, China is reportedly using headphones and earbuds to spy on its citizens' thoughts. As Professor Farahany said, "China has very clearly said that they believe that the sixth domain of warfare is the human brain. . . . They are investing tremendous dollars into developing brain computer interface, but also figuring out ways to disable brain or to spy on brains." Stefano Kotsonis and Meghna Chakrabarti, "'Battle for Your Brain': What the Rise of Brain-Computer Interface Technology Means for You," WBUR.org, March 17, 2023,

7 See Dershowitz, *Preemption*, 76–89.

8 In my own life, I benefited enormously from pervasive documentation. When I was falsely accused of sexual misconduct by someone I never even met, I was able to prove conclusively that I was not in the places she claimed she had met me. See Alan M. Dershowitz, *Guilt by Accusation: The Challenge of Proving Innocence in the Age of #MeToo* (New York: Skyhorse Publishing, 2019). She

then admitted that she may have mistaken me for someone else.

9 The government also buys personal data from data brokers without requiring a warrant or complying with other constitutional constraints. See Byron Tau, "U.S. Spy Agencies Know Your Secrets. They Bought Them," *Wall Street Journal*, March 8, 2024. Currently, Congress is considering legislation to close the data broker loophole by requiring a warrant. Emile Ayoub and Elizabeth Grotein, "Closing the Data Broker Loophole," Brennan Center, February 13, 2024, available at https://www.brennancenter.org/our-work/research-reports/closing-data-broker-loophole.

10 See Byron Tau, *Means of Control: How the Hidden Alliance of Tech and Government Is Creating a New American Surveillance State* (New York: Penguin Random House, 2024).

NOTES TO CHAPTER 12

1 I have consulted on the issues of transparency of the workings of voting machines.

2 While public universities need to adhere to the First Amendment, private universities do not need to (though in practice some adhere to the spirit of the First Amendment. Yet universities receiving federal financial assistances, which also includes private universities receiving federal grants, must comply with Title VI of the Civil Rights Act.

NOTES TO CHAPTER 13

1 See Michael Lewis, *Moneyball: The Art of Winning an Unfair Game* (New York: W. W. Norton, 2003).

2 Paul E. Meehl, *Clinical versus Statistical Prediction: A Theoretical Analysis and Review of the Evidence* (University of Minnesota Press, 1954).

3 Paul E. Meehl, "When Shall We Use Our Heads Instead of the Formula?" *Journal of Counseling Psychology* 4, no. 4 (1957): 268–73.

4 For purposes of this analysis assume that monetary bail has been replaced by a system in which the judge decides whether to release or detain pretrial.

5 Dershowitz, *Preemption*, 66–69.(To be sure, we also make invisible mistakes in our post-dictive criminal justice system. We confine some innocent defendants who can never prove their innocence, but the number and percentage of invisible false positives in the predictive preventive context is almost certainly greater.)

NOTES TO CHAPTER 14

1 At the time of this writing, Russia is reported to have developed space weapons. See Bill Chappell, "What to Know about the 'Space Weapon' the U.S. Says Russia Recently Launched," NPR, May 30, 2024.

2 U.S. v Jones, 565 U.S. 400, 407 (2012), quoting Kyllo v. United States, 533 U.S. 27, 34 (2001).

3 Id. at 420.

4 Id.

5 Id. n.3.

6 Even the most zealous advocates of a living constitution acknowledge that some of its provisions are "dead" and not subject to adaptive interpretations. These include the age qualifications, the requirement of a 2/3 supermajority for treaties (though what constitutes a "treaty" is subject to interpretation—see Iran nuclear "non-treaty"), the number of senators from each state, and other highly specific provisions. And even the most zealous advocates of a dead constitution have interpreted open-ended provisions without regard to what the Framers may have intended. For a critique of the current modes of constitutional interpretation, see Dershowitz, *Is There A Right to Remain Silent?*, chapters 3 and 4.

7 Both of us were also influenced by the late Justice Arthur Goldberg, for whom we both clerked.

8 Breyer, *Reading the Constitution*, xvi–xvii.

9 176.

10 Pound, introduction to *The Individualization of Punishment*, xi.

11 As cited above, see my "Why Do Criminal Attempts Fail: A New Defense," *Yale Law Journal* 70, no. 1 (November 1960): 160–69; "Psychiatry in the Legal Process: 'A Knife That Cuts Both Ways,'" *Judicature* 51, 370 (1968); "On 'Preventive Detention,'" *New York Review of Books*, March 13, 1969; "Preventive Detention of Citizens During a National Emergency—A Comparison between Israel and the United States," *Israel Yearbook on Human Rights* 1 (1971): 295–321; "Imprisonment by Judicial Hunch," *American Bar Association Journal* 57, no. 6 (June 1971): 560–64; "'Stretch Points' of Liberty," *The Nation*, March 15, 1971; "Preventive Disbarment: The Numbers Are Against It," *American Bar Association Journal* 58, no. 8 (August 1972): 815–19; "Wiretaps and National Security," *Commentary*, January 1972; "Preventive Confinement: A Suggested Framework for Constitutional Analysis," *Texas Law Review* 51, no. 7 (November 1973): 1277–1324; "The Origins of Preventive Confinement in Anglo-American Law—Part I: The English Experience," *University of Cincinnati Law Review* 43, no. 1 (1974): 1–60; "The Origins of Preventive Confinement in Anglo-American Law—Part II: The American Experience," *University of Cincinnati Law Review* 43, no. 4 (1974): 781–846. My 2006 book, *Preemption: A Knife That Cuts Both Ways*, was my first monograph on the subject.

12 For purposes of this discussion, I regard "people" as already born. Different concepts of equality may be applicable to adults and children (however defined), as well as to the mentally deficient (however defined).

13 Rawls, *A Theory of Justice*, 136.

14 Ibid.

15 Ibid.

16 Ibid. It is possible to imagine people in the "original position" projecting that they are of a different race, gender, or economic situation. It is far more difficult to believe that an intelligent person could realistically imagine himself as seriously mentally challenged or just plain dumb.

17 Dershowitz, *Rights from Wrongs*.

18 Ibid.

19 As Michael Sandel put it in his critique of Rawls, there is "always a distinction between the values I have and the person I am." Michael Sandel, "The Procedural Republic and the Unencumbered Self," *Political Theory* 12, no. 1 (February 1984): 86.

20 Deut. 16:18.

21 Deut. 16:20.

22 See also Dershowitz, *Cancel Culture*, chapter 8: "Cancelling the Bible, Which Demands Personal Justice, Not the Double Standard of 'Identity Justice.'"

NOTES TO CHAPTER 15

1 McNabb v. United States, 318 U.S. 332, 347 (1943).

2 Dershowitz, "Preventive Confinement."

3 Ibid., 1295–96 (emphasis added).

4 Lewis Carroll, *Through the Looking Glass* (New York: Random House, 1965), 95.

5 United States v. Salerno, 481 U.S. 739, 747 (1987) (internal citations omitted)

6 Id. at 748 (emphasis added).

7 Holmes, *The Common Law*, 43, 46.

8 In addition to the labeling game's distinctions of criminal, civil, regulatory, and punitive are some intermedial labels such as "quasi-criminal." For instance, the Supreme Court has called the imposition of punitive damages quasi-criminal. Cooper Industries, Inc. v. Leatherman Tool Group, Inc., 532 U.S. 424, 432 (2001).

9 There are some constitutional constraints on regulatory, nonpunitive sanctions: clear and convincing burden. There has been an increase in the imposition of overlapping civil, administrative, and criminal sanctions for the same conduct, as well as an increase in the severity of sanctions, which led to a series of litigations arguing that legislatively authorized sanctions in civil cases are unconstitutional when they violate the double jeopardy, due process, excessive fines, and cruel and unusual punishments clauses in the Bill of Rights. See Nancy J. King, "Portioning Punishment: Constitutional Limits on Successive and Excessive Penalties," *University of Pennsylvania Law Review* 144, no. 1 (November 1995): 101–96.

10 The privilege against self-incrimination and exclusion of illegally seized evidence are not primarily part of the truth-seeking process. They are designed to protect privacy, autonomy, and other values. Trial by jury has multiple rationales. Reasonable people can disagree whether they should be factored into a jurisprudence for the preventive state.

11 Intermediate forms of confinement—such as home detention—may require different numbers.

NOTES TO CHAPTER 16

1 Korematsu v. United States, 323 U.S.214 (1944).

2 In Trump v. Hawaii, Chief Justice Roberts offered the most powerful rebuke of Korematsu since Justice Jackson. Roberts wrote that "[t]he forcible relocation

of U.S. citizens to concentration camps, solely and explicitly on the basis of race, is objectively unlawful and outside the scope of Presidential authority." Trump v. Hawaii, 585 U.S. 667, 710 (2018).

3 An example of a governmental agency demanding no false negatives even at the cost of multiple false positives is NASA's criteria for selecting astronauts. A relative of mine was a prime candidate but was disqualified on the ground that he had been born with only one kidney. The likelihood that the absence of a second kidney would actually cause a problem in space is near zero. But the claim that it may be more than zero was enough to have him become a false positive.

4 The *New York Post*, for instance, ran a story under the headline "How a Lenient NYC Judge Left a Reputed Gangbanger Free to Allegedly Kill an Innocent Dad" (June 9, 2021), which recounts how a judge released a teenager who committed a violent crime while awaiting trial. In 1999, the same judge let a homeless person live in a shelter and attend therapy sessions who then committed a spree of sexual assaults while awaiting sentencing. After the *New York Post* editorial wrote "Judge Denis Boyle's Leniency May Have Cost New Yorkers' Lives" (November 15, 2021), the judge stopped handling youth cases, which the *New York Post* also reported widely: "Controversial NYC Judge Denis Boyle No Longer Handling Youth Cases," February 2, 2022.

5 Tennessee v. Garner, 471 U.S. 1 (1985).

6 Daniel Epps, "The Consequences of Errors in Criminal Justice," *Harvard Law Review* 128, no. 4 (February 2015): 1065–1151.

NOTES TO CONCLUSION

1 Yogi Berra, *The Yogi Book* (New York: Workman, 2010).

2 Public Committee Against Torture v. Government (December 14, 2006),

3 Olmstead v. United States, 277 U.S. 438, 479 (1928).

4 Learned Hand, "The Spirit of Liberty" (1944).

5 Deut. 16:20.

NOTES TO APPENDIX

1 I wrote this article several years ago for a symposium on Jewish law.

2 "On that day R. Eliezer made all the arguments in the world, but they didn't accept them. He said, if I am right let the carob tree prove it. . . ." The tree flies through the air. The majority says, we don't accept halakhic—legal—rulings from trees. Then he makes the stream flow backwards. Same result. Then he orders the walls of the synagogue to collapse. They begin to fall inward, but Rabbi Yehoshua rebuked them, saying "If Talmudic Sages argue with one another about Halakhah, what business do you have interfering?" So they don't collapse, but out of respect for R. Eliezer, they remain leaning. Finally, logic and miracles having failed, R. Eliezer appeals directly to Heaven. And the Bat Kol—a voice from Heaven, the still small voice that spoke in the wilderness—went forth, saying: "Why are you disputing with R. Eliezer, for the Halakhah is accordance with him everywhere." Rabbi Yehoshua rose to his feet and said, "It is not in Heaven" (Deut. 30:12). The Torah was already given

on Mt. Sinai, and it says in it, "Follow the majority's ruling" (Exod. 23:2). God, he is told, smiled and said "My children have defeated me, my children have defeated me." From Daniel J. H. Greenwood, "The Oven of Akhnai," online at https://sites.hofstra.edu/daniel-greenwood/the-oven-of-akhnai/. A longer version, "Akhnai: Legal Responsibility in the World of the Silent God," was published in *Utah Law Review* (1997): 309–58.

INDEX

Abraham, 8, 176, 191
absolutism, 72, 93, 117, 132
Adams, John, 116
addiction, 60, 62, 170, 178
aerial photography, 79
Afghanistan, 91
Al Qaeda, 91
Algeria, 93
Alien and Sedition Laws, 116, 117–18
Alito, Samuel, 157–58
Allen, Woody, 50
Alphabet (Google), 24
Alzheimer's, 23
anti-Communist statutes, 117
anti-Semitism, 18, 144
anti-vaxxers, 100–101
armed robbery, 67, 70, 177–78, 179
artificial intelligence (AI), 4, 10, 18, 24, 136, 153, 157
Ashcroft, John, 19
Assange, Julian, 118
assassinations, 7–8, 93, 126, 127; presidential, 27, 41–55; targeted, 17, 19, 82, 97–98
"attempts", law of, 16, 36, 43, 57
Attlee, Clement, 13
Australia, 72, 130

Baer, Elizabeth, 122
Baghdad, Iraq, 85
bail, 7, 33, 43–45, 46, 47, 49, 57, 60–66, 68, 166, 177, 179; denial of, 73, 130
Bail Reform Act, 171
Barak, Aharon, 186
Bayesian analysis, 149
Bazelon, David, 16
Beccaria, Marchese di, 31
Begin, Menachem, 85
Belichick, Bill, 150
Ben Yakov, Eliezer, 192
Bentham, Jeremy, 93, 95
Bernard, Brandon, 67
Bernard Shaw, George, 23, 126
Berra, Yogi, 185
Bible, the, 11, 25, 26, 82, 152, 165, 166

big tech, 23–24
Bin Laden, Osama, 91
biological attacks, 9, 14, 17
Black, Hugo, 29
Blackstone, William, 30–31, 32–33, 37, 59
Bolsheviks, 12
Booth, John Wilkes, 49
border control, 19, 20
Brady, Tom, 148, 150
Brandeis, Louis, 28, 105, 107, 136, 187
Brave New World, 71
Breyer, Stephen, 15, 16, 158, 159
bribery, 70
Buck, Carrie, 27, 106
Buck v. Bell, 27–28, 106, 107
Bundy, Ted, 27
Bush, George W., 13

Cain, mark of, 26, 152
calculus, moral, 34
Cambridge, Massachusetts, 103, 105
Canada, 72
cancer, 21–22, 23, 101
Carroll, Lewis, 29
Castro, Fidel, 28
censorship, 7, 9, 18, 121–22, 124, 125–6, 132, 134, 143, 166; before-the-fact, 17, 34, 113, 115–16, 117, 118, 119, 120, 127, 180; government mandated, 181, 182; of "forbidden words", 121; self-censorship, 121; "unsafe", speech censored as, 120–21, 131
Chauvin, Derek, 76
Churchill, Winston, 13
CIA, 92, 93, 97, 118
"civilianality", 86, 88–89
climate change, 9, 73, 109–10, 111, 181
coercion, 70, 190, 191, 192
Columbia, District of, 43, 44, 46, 130
combatants, 86, 88–89
common law, 30, 31, 35, 42, 43, 46–47, 160, 170
confidentiality, 117
confinement, 47, 48, 69, 71, 152, 173, 174,

176, 177, 178; civil, 180, 181; criminal, 180; erroneous, 63; home, 65, 173; post-sentence, 58; pretrial, 61, 64, 179; preventive, 29, 35–37, 46, 49, 180, 181, 191; punitive, 180; regulatory, 180, 181
conspiracies, 44, 57, 60
Constitution, US, 11, 44, 61, 71, 104, 122, 142, 143, 157, 158–59, 170; Eighth Amendment, 61; First Amendment, 115, 116, 117, 118–19, 121, 122, 124, 125–26, 131, 132, 143, 182; Fourth Amendment, 77, 135, 157; Second Amendment, 130, 131–32
coronary illness, 21
cost-benefit ratio, 7, 9, 10–11, 13, 22, 23, 29, 33, 76, 78, 83, 98, 107, 110–11, 113, 133, 140, 177, 178, 187
counterfeiting, 42, 51, 76
COVID-19, 7, 20, 29, 33, 100, 102, 107
crime; elements of, 58–59; inchoate, 16, 43, 47, 52, 57, 59; predictive of future harms, 58–60; preventive, 57, 60
criminality, 26, 35, 152; future, 58, 68, 69
criminology, 26, 31
Crooks, Thomas, 50, 52, 53
crypto currency, 143
Cuban Missile Crisis, 13
Czolgosz, Leon, 50

Dallas, Texas, 50–51
Darwinism, social, 107
death penalty, 8, 12, 27, 32, 67–68, 106, 152, 176, 180, 190
democracy, 9, 11, 15, 22, 23, 37, 73, 83, 97, 108, 110, 111, 132, 137, 164, 174, 183, 186, 193
democratic values, 34, 37, 117
Democrats, 109, 130
Denning, Tom, 30
deportation, 20, 170
detention, preventive, 17, 19, 62, 68, 69, 70, 71, 72, 73, 171, 176; post-sentence, 68–71
deterrence, 7, 33, 41, 59, 67, 85, 116
Dickens, Charles, 4
Diplomatic Services, State Department, 51
discretion, judicial, 46, 64, 79
Donovan, Robert, 48
Dostoyevsky, Fyodor, 95
Doxing, 18
driving, dangerous, 58–59, 60
drones, 84, 137
Durham rule, 49

Egypt, 13, 84, 85, 137
emergencies, 16, 72, 189, 191, 192, 193

environmental catastrophe, global, 109–13
eugenics, 27, 107, 108
euthanasia, 172
executions. See death penalty
exile, 11

Fall River rape case, 87
false negatives, 5, 6, 9, 13, 14, 18, 22, 27, 28, 34, 52, 53, 54, 55, 61, 62, 64, 66, 77, 78, 80, 83, 84, 85, 86, 95, 106, 108, 111, 112, 113, 119, 120, 125, 126, 127, 129, 131, 132, 133, 134, 137, 138, 144, 152, 153–54, 155, 156, 166, 174, 175, 176, 177, 179, 180, 181, 182, 183
false positives, 4, 5, 6, 8, 9, 10, 11, 14, 18, 22, 27, 28, 34, 52, 53, 54, 55, 61, 62, 64, 66, 77, 78, 80, 85, 86, 106, 108, 111, 112, 113, 119, 120, 125, 126, 127, 129, 131, 132, 133, 134, 137, 138, 144, 152, 153–54, 155, 156, 166, 174, 175, 176, 179, 180, 182, 183
FBI, 92, 142
First World War, 12, 122
flight, predicted, 61, 62, 76–77, 78, 156, 175, 181–82
Florida, 51, 102, 133
Floyd, George, 76
football, American, 147, 167
force, lethal, 76, 77, 182
Ford, Gerald, 41, 55
Framers, the, 61, 157, 158, 159
France, 12, 13, 83, 85, 116, 154, 167
Frankfurter, Felix, 169
Franklin, Benjamin, 11, 136
fraud, 58, 180
French Resistance, 93
Freud, Sigmund, 119
Fromme, Squeaky, 55

gag orders, 117, 118
Garfield, James, 27, 41, 42, 49
Gaza, 85, 86, 87, 89, 91
genetic engineering, 3, 21
genetic testing, 10, 23, 28, 71, 158, 162
George III, king of Great Britain, 46
Germany, 12, 27, 83, 84, 154, 156, 167, 172
Gibbon, Edward, 81
globalization, 157
Glueck, Shelton and Eleanor, 26, 152–53
Goebbels, Joseph, 12, 83
Goldberg, Arthur, 16
Gonzales, Alberto, 19
GPS, 79, 157–58
Guantanamo Bay, 189
Guiteau, Charles, 27

gun crimes, 9, 110, 113, 129–34, 186. *See also* shootings

Haman, 82
Hamas, 7, 9, 19, 85, 87, 88, 89, 91, 138
Hamilton, Alexander, 116
Hand, Learned, 119, 187
Harlan, John Marshall, 104
harms, 5, 10, 11, 12, 15, 16, 18, 20, 24, 28, 29, 32, 33, 34, 37, 52, 58, 59, 60, 71, 73, 110, 125, 135, 138, 140, 153, 160, 166, 186, 187, 190, 191; medical, 108; psychological, 120; short-term, 62, 63; types of, 9
Harvard University, 27, 28, 107, 139, 152, 153, 163
hate speech, 3, 7
Hatfield, James, 46–47
Hawaii, 72
health care, 3, 65
Hezbollah, 85, 91
Hillel, Rabbi, 165
HIPPA, 24
Hitler, Adolf, 12–13, 25–26, 28, 83
Holmes, Oliver Wendell, 27–28, 30, 32, 33, 62, 93, 105, 107, 122, 123–24, 127, 152, 166, 172
Holocaust, the, 28, 127
Homeland Security, Department of, 42
homicide. *See* murder
house arrest, 64, 65–66
Houthis, 7, 85
human shields, 87, 89, 90
Hussein, Saddam, 14
Hustler v. Falwell, 124

ideas, marketplace of, 18–19, 118, 119, 121, 125
identification documents, 20
identity politics, 20–21, 163
IDF (Israel Defense Forces), 87, 89–90
Independence, Declaration of, 118
inequality, 65
imprisonment. *See* confinement
incitement, 7, 18, 33, 120, 132
insanity. *See* mental illness
intelligence, 17, 18, 19, 51, 54, 75, 84, 85, 92, 93, 97, 137, 138, 186
intent, legislative, 171, 173
international law, 83, 88
intervention, preventive, 12, 15, 18, 30, 32, 36, 112, 113, 134, 144, 156, 167, 180; environmental, 111; judicial, 160, 176; medical, 21–24, 99–100; police, 75–80; state, 173
Iran, 4, 14, 18, 82–83, 84, 85, 137–38, 165, 167

Iraq, 82, 83
Iraq War, 13, 14, 85
ISIS, 7
Israel, 7, 8–9, 18, 19, 24, 72, 82–83, 84–86, 87, 88, 89, 91, 97, 119, 121, 126, 127, 137, 138, 165, 186, 189, 193

Jacobson, Henning, 103–104
Jacobson v. Massachusetts, 105–106
Jackson, Andrew, 42–43, 49
Jackson, Robert, 71
Japan, 14, 72, 84, 167
Japanese Americans, detention of, 4, 19, 28, 72, 166, 176
Jefferson, Thomas, 116, 118
Jehovah's Witnesses, 99
Jewish law, 30, 189–93
Jews, 82, 119, 172
Joseph, 25
Justice Department, US, 19

Kahana, Rabbi, 192
Kant, Immanuel, 31–32, 33, 67, 93
Kennedy, John F., 41, 50
Kennedy, Robert, 41, 50
Key, Francis Scott, 43, 48–49
Khrushchev, Nikita, 13

"labeling game", legal, 169–71, 172
law, rule of, 3, 11, 15, 32, 37, 61, 71, 73, 103, 108, 137, 183, 186–87, 189, 191, 193
Lawrence, Richard, 42–43, 45, 47–49
Lebanon, 85
libertarianism, 29, 30, 98, 101, 106, 117, 125
liberties, 3, 4, 11, 34, 136, 186, 187; civil, 69, 73, 117
Lincoln, Abraham, 41, 42, 49
Lincoln, Robert Todd, 49–50
Lombroso, Cesare, 26, 152
Lowell, A. Lawrence, 27, 152

McKinley, William, 41, 42, 49, 50
Machiavelli, Niccolo, 81
magical thinking, 30
Mao Zedong, 28
Marbury v. Madison, 193
Marshal Service, US, 51
martial law, 72
mask mandates, 20
mass destruction, weapons of, 33, 84, 157, 158
Massachusetts, 103, 104
maximal restraint technique (MRT), 76
measles, 100, 102

medicine, preventive intervention in, 21–24, 99–108
Meehl, Paul, 147, 150–51
mental illness, 16, 35, 36, 45, 46, 47, 48, 49, 52, 53, 72, 129–30, 170, 178
Meta (Facebook), 23–24, 143
Middle East, the, 18
military action, 12, 13–14, 19, 81–90, 91, 137, 181
Mill, John Stuart, 101, 102
Minority Report (film), 26, 71
mistake preferences, 174, 175–84
Mohammed, Khalid Sheikh, 97
monitoring, electronic, 64–65, 66, 137
Mordechai, 26
Moscow, Russia, 139
Moses, 26
Mossad, 92
Mukherjee, Siddhartha, 21–22, 100
murder, 9, 11, 32, 42, 49, 63, 67, 76, 88, 152, 167, 180, 190; attempted, 47, 58; murder-suicides, 151

NASA, 141
Nasser, Abdel, 137
natural disasters, 9
Nazis, 12–13, 28, 93, 106, 119, 172
New Deal, 143–44
New York City, New York, 70, 94
nuclear war, 3, 4, 13, 14, 18, 82–83,
nuclear weapons, 9, 13, 18, 82–83, 84, 85, 93, 94, 95, 97, 118, 126, 137, 138, 167, 183, 185
Nuremberg trials, 106

obscenity laws, 59, 117, 126
October 7 massacres and kidnappings, 9, 19, 85, 88, 93, 137, 138, 183
Oswald, Lee Harvey, 50

pandemics, 3, 4, 9, 18, 102, 137, 185
paramilitaries, 88
Parkland shootings, 133
parole, 68, 69, 170
partisanship, 20–21, 101, 109, 111, 118, 129
Pascal, Blaise, 5
Pascal's Wager, 5
Pearl Harbor, attack on, 4, 14, 19, 72, 84, 167
Pennsylvania, 51
Pentagon Papers case (1971), 116–18, 120
PET scans, 10
Philippines, the, 93
Pinker, Steven, 4
Poland, 13, 84

pollution, 9
pornography, 59–60, 119
Pound, Roscoe, 15, 160
precautionary principle, 111–12, 125
prediction, 4–6, 11, 14, 16, 20, 21, 22, 23, 24, 53, 58, 61, 62, 68, 69, 71, 72–73, 83, 84, 90, 112, 119–20, 121, 125, 131, 132, 166, 178, 185; history of, 25–37; "science" of, 147–56
preemption, 7, 17, 19, 28, 82, 172–73; warfare, 16, 57, 83, 84, 85, 90, 137, 166
prevention, jurisprudence of 14–19, 20–21, 24, 36, 108, 127, 166, 173, 193
"previvors", 21, 24
privacy, 78, 135–36, 138, 139, 140, 157–58, 186, 187
private sector, 135, 136, 141–42, 144
privatization, 141, 143, 144
probability, 13, 59, 85, 90, 112, 147, 149
probable cause, 55, 78, 79, 174, 180, 181
profiling, 19, 28
pronouncements, judicial, 45, 71–73
prophecy, 25, 26
punishment, 15, 19, 30–31, 32, 33, 37, 42, 45, 47, 49, 59, 60, 68, 69–70, 169, 171–73, 182, 190, 192; collective, 86, 88; "cruel and unusual", 158
Putin, Vladimir, 28, 115, 139

Rabbinic tradition, 30, 189–93
racism, 4, 18, 120, 152
rape, 9, 33, 58, 59–60, 87
Rawls, John, 21, 161, 162–64, 165
Reagan, Ronald, 41
recidivism, 8, 67, 69, 70, 75, 178
reckless conduct, 57, 58, 60
"red flag" laws, 113, 130, 132, 133, 134, 138, 181
regulation, 24, 29, 97, 104, 105, 107, 135, 142, 169, 171, 172, 175, 180, 181
rehabilitation, 67
Rehnquist, William, 171–72
Republicans, 70, 109, 130
restitution, 67
retail crime, 73
retaliation, 7
retribution, 32, 67
review, judicial, 183
rights, origin of, 163–64
Rikers Island, 172, 178
risk tolerance, 23
rodef, 190–91
Romanovs, 12, 167
rocket attacks, 84, 86, 88, 89
Roosevelt, Franklin, 28, 41, 50, 166, 176

Roosevelt, Theodore, 41, 50
Roth, Allen, 149
Routh, Ryan Wesley, 51, 52
Russia, 115

Sadat, Anwar El, 137
Scalia, Antonin, 157, 158
Schenck, Charles, 122, 123–24
Schenck v. United States, 122
science fiction, 9–10
search warrants, 157
Second World War, 12, 156, 167, 187
secrecy, 98, 118
Secret Service, 7, 41–42, 50–51, 52–55; powers of, 54
security, 73, 78, 79, 117–18, 120, 127, 131, 136, 139, 140, 144, 170, 181, 183, 187, 188
sentencing, 58, 66–68, 69, 70
September 11 attacks (9/11), 4, 16–17, 19–21, 91, 93, 97, 183, 189
serial killers, 27
sex offenders, 69, 71, 170
sexism, 4, 18, 120
sexual assaults, 9, 59
Shin Bet, 92
Shippen, William, 102
shootings, 50, 51, 53, 54, 55, 77, 130; of fleeing suspects, 181–82; mass, 3, 133; preventive, 8; school, 9, 151
Sinwar, Yahya, 9, 87
Six-Day War, 84, 137
Smallpox, 17, 20, 33, 100, 102, 103, 104
Smith v. California, 126
social media, 18, 24, 125, 138, 139, 143, 157
Socrates, 127
Sodom, 8, 176, 191
Soviet Union, 13, 139
speech, dangerous, 18, 119, 131, 132, 134, 182; "Fire!" in a crowded theater (analogy), 122–24
speech, freedom of, 113, 115–17, 120, 121, 131, 144, 165
speech, offensive, 115, 120, 121
spying, 26, 98
spyware, 186
Stalin, Joseph, 28
statistics, 112, 129, 147–48, 149–51, 152, 153
sterilization, mass, 19–20, 27–28, 32, 73, 105, 106, 108
Stone, Harlan, 28
"stop and frisks", 75, 78
Strauss, Marcy, 94–95
subpoenas, 139

surety bonds, 11
surveillance, 19, 23, 26, 66, 157, 186; genetic, 21–22
surveillance state, 135–40, 141
"swatting", 79–80
Syria, 82, 84, 137

Taft, William Howard, 28
Talmud, 26
technology, 4, 10, 21, 65, 79, 152, 153, 158, 185, 186, 192
Teheran, Iran, 85
Tel Aviv, Israel, 18, 85
Tennessee v. Garner, 76–77
terrorism, 3, 4, 6, 7, 8, 9, 15, 16, 17–20, 21, 33, 34, 71, 72, 80, 86–88, 89, 90, 91–98, 137, 138, 151, 164, 185, 189, 193
Texas, 68
Thoreau, Henry David, 136
Torah, 30, 189–90, 191–93
Torquemada, Tommaso de, 96
torture, 18, 92–97, 183, 186; warrants for, 96–97, 98
transplants, organ, 99–100
treason, 43, 47
trial, right to, 69–70
true negatives, 4, 5, 6, 7, 8, 11, 34, 155, 181, 182, 183
true positives, 4, 6, 7, 34, 155, 182, 183
Truman, Harry, 41, 50, 55
Trump, Donald, 7, 8, 41, 50–51, 53–54, 55, 118
trust, 9, 142
tyranny, 4, 28, 50, 115, 132, 139, 187

Ukraine, 18
utilitarianism, 93, 95, 97

Vanunu, Mordechai (John Crossman), 126–27
"veil of ignorance", 21, 161–62, 165
Versailles, Treaty of, 12, 83
vigilantism, 191, 192
violence, 4, 28, 52, 62–63, 65, 66, 69, 79, 95, 111, 118, 121, 151–52, 153; gun violence. *See* gun crime
Voltaire, 115

war, preventive. *See* military action
Warren, Earl, 28
Warren Commission, 50
Washington, George, 102–103, 116
Waterboarding, 91, 92, 97, 183
weather, 5, 6, 41, 109, 149

Wharton, Francis, 31, 32
whistleblowers, 127
"White House Cases", 52–53

X (Twitter), 24, 143

Yang, Bong Bol, 52–53
Yom Kippur War, 84, 137

Zionism, 119, 121